SPORT AND SOCIETY IN THE GLOBAL AGE

Sport and Society in the Global Age

Timothy Marjoribanks
and
Karen Farquharson

palgrave
macmillan

First published 2012 by
PALGRAVE MACMILLAN

Palgrave Macmillan in the UK is an imprint of Macmillan Publishers Limited, registered in England, company number 785998, of Houndmills, Basingstoke, Hampshire RG21 6XS.

Palgrave Macmillan in the US is a division of St Martin's Press LLC, 175 Fifth Avenue, New York, NY 10010.

Palgrave Macmillan is the global academic imprint of the above companies and has companies and representatives throughout the world.

Palgrave® and Macmillan® are registered trademarks in the United States, the United Kingdom, Europe and other countries

ISBN 978–0–230–58468–6 hardback
ISBN 978–0–230–58469–3 paperback

This book is printed on paper suitable for recycling and made from fully managed and sustained forest sources. Logging, pulping and manufacturing processes are expected to conform to the environmental regulations of the country of origin.

A catalogue record for this book is available from the British Library.

A catalog record for this book is available from the Library of Congress.

10 9 8 7 6 5 4 3 2 1
21 20 19 18 17 16 15 14 13 12

Printed and bound in Great Britain by
CPI Antony Rowe, Chippenham and Eastbourne

For Rebecca and Megan

Contents

PART II SPORT AND SOCIETAL PROCESSES

List of Tables and Figures

TABLE

FIGURE

Acknowledgements

In writing this book, we have had wonderful support, advice, encouragement and assistance. In particular, we thank our colleagues at Palgrave Macmillan, the publishers of this book. Anna Marie Reeve was an exemplary Commissioning Editor, working closely and professionally with us through all stages of the book. Similarly, Esther Croom was a very constructive and supportive Editorial Assistant. We also thank Emily Salz for her role in the initial stages of the book proposal and text development, Cecily Wilson, the Division Administrator, and Steven Kennedy, Publisher and Director at Palgrave Macmillan for his initial and ongoing support for the overall project. Finally, we thank Keith Povey and his team for their excellent copy-editing and preparation of the index.

Tim thanks his colleagues in the Graduate School of Management at La Trobe University for their support. Tim also thanks his colleagues in the School of Social and Political Sciences at the University of Melbourne, where he worked prior to moving to La Trobe. He is grateful to the Faculty of Arts at The University of Melbourne for their SSP(Long) program. Some research discussed in this book emerged from an Australian Research Council Discovery Project (DP0343731). Tim thanks Ann Capling, his co-chief investigator on that project, and the ARC.

Karen is grateful to her colleagues at the Faculty of Life and Social Sciences at Swinburne University of Technology for their support. We also thank the academic reviewers for their feedback on the initial proposal and on the complete manuscript.

Finally, we thank Rebecca and Megan, our two daughters, who have lived through all stages of this book.

TIM MARJORIBANKS
KAREN FARQUHARSON

The authors and publishers wish to thank the following publishers, organizations and authors for granting permission to reproduce copyright material: the Australian Bureau of Statistics (ABS) for Table 5.1, originally from ABS (2007) *Participation in Sports and Physical Recreation, Australia 2005–06*, cat. No. 4177.0, Australian Bureau of Statistics, reproduced under Creative Commons Attribution 2.5 Australia licence; Department of Sport and Recreation, South Africa (SRSA), also for Table 5.1, originally from Department of Sport and Recreation (2005) 'Participation Patterns in Sport and Recreation Activities in South Africa: 2005 Survey', Pretoria, Republic of South Africa Department of Sport and Recreation.

About the Authors

Timothy Marjoribanks is Professor of Management in the Graduate School of Management at La Trobe University in Melbourne, Australia. He has a PhD and an MA in Sociology from Harvard University, and completed his undergraduate degrees with Honours in Law and Arts (with a major in Politics) at The University of Adelaide, Australia. Prior to taking up a position at La Trobe, he researched and taught in Sociology in the School of Social and Political Sciences at The University of Melbourne, Australia. His research explores the role of power in organizational practice, with a particular focus on the sport, media and health industries. He has taught a wide range of subjects at undergraduate and masters levels, including organizational behaviour, management, media, health, and work, as well as social research methods and sociological theory.

Karen Farquharson is Associate Professor of Sociology and Head of the Humanities, Arts and Social Sciences group at Swinburne University of Technology in Melbourne, Australia, where she also teaches Sociology. She has MA and PhD degrees in Sociology from Harvard University and a BA in Social Science from the University of California at Berkeley. She was a Fulbright Fellow to South Africa. Karen's research focuses on race and ethnic relations, sports and health policy. She has taught a variety of sociology subjects in areas such as race, ethnicity and migration; research methods; the Internet and society; and introductory sociology.

Chapter 1

Introduction: Sport and Society in the Global Age

INTRODUCTION

In 1995 the Rugby World Cup was held in South Africa. The first major international sporting competition held in South Africa since the end of its racially separatist apartheid policies, the World Cup symbolized South Africa's re-entry to the global sporting community from which it had long been ostracized due to its apartheid practices. Rugby union, particularly as represented by the national Springbok Rugby team, was at that time a contentious sport in South Africa, associated with the Afrikaner community and widely hated by African groups who had been excluded from playing. Through hosting the World Cup, and under the political leadership of then President Nelson Mandela and Archbishop Desmond Tutu, rugby union was reframed in South Africa as a South African sport that was for all South Africans (see *Invictus*, 2009; Farquharson and Marjoribanks, 2006). This historically racially exclusive sport came to symbolize hope for a racially united South Africa, and for all South Africans.

As this example shows, contemporary sport is an important site of social, political, cultural and economic engagement, action and struggle in the global age. As such, sport is an important topic for sociologists, social scientists who are concerned with understanding how society is structured and operates. Millions of people around the world participate in sport in a range of ways on a daily basis. People of all ages and from all walks of life play, coach, participate in and support all types of sport. They discuss it with family, friends and co-workers. It is an important, perhaps integral, part of the lives of many, who invest many resources into sport, both personally and at broader societal levels.

During the late 20th and early 21st centuries, sport has been characterized by a number of trends. First, sport at all levels is becoming increasingly professionalized. This means that where sporting clubs and organizations have typically been run by volunteers, they are increasingly relying on paid professionals to coach and to manage day-to-day operations. Related to this, sports are becoming increasingly commercialized, with corporate sponsorship present at all levels, from community-based children's sport through to professional sport. In addition, globalization has led to sports spreading to new countries, and markets. And there are increasing connections between sports and media companies, with the sale of media rights, for example, a key source of revenue for professional sporting leagues, and media and sport companies often sharing the same owner. Sport is also promoted as a source of social inclusion, a vehicle for the disadvantaged and excluded to enter the middle classes. All of these trends have brought sport increasingly to the attention of political and policy regulators and other state, corporate and non-government organizations. These processes of transformation are significant not only for sport, but also for broader social relations locally, nationally and globally. In particular, these trends raise questions around current sporting practices and future directions for the relationship between sport and society in the global age (Rowe, 2003).

This book explores the interactions between sport and society, focusing on the social, political, policy and organizational dimensions of these relationships. It critically analyses three dimensions of the relationship between sport and society, as reflected in Parts II, III and IV of the book:

■ Sport and Societal Processes
■ Regulating Sport
■ The Global Cultures of Sport

It also discusses theoretical debates, methodological issues and up-to-date research, showing the importance of undertaking theoretically informed and empirically grounded research as a means to describe and understand sport in society.

The central argument of *Sport and Society in the Global Age* is that sport and society are in a constant and ongoing process of interaction. Sport does not exist independently of society, but is fundamentally influenced by its social context. At the same time, the practice and organization of sport has an influence on the societal context in which it operates. That is, sport does not merely reflect its societal context. It is a site of social action in its own right, providing insights into the interactions and relations between organizations central to the contemporary world, including the state, corporations, non-government organizations and social movements. The 1995 South African Rugby World Cup exemplifies this. South Africa had been largely excluded from the global sporting community due to its racist policies. Global pressures, including from sports organizations which prevented South Africa from competing in sporting competitions, contributed to the social changes that brought about the end of apartheid. The end of apartheid by itself did not change local feelings about rugby. Work needed to be, and was, done at the local level to change the Springbok Rugby team from symbolizing division to symbolizing unity.

In the current global age, the interactions, practices and organizations around sport are undergoing profound changes at the local, national and global levels, which themselves require analysis. Analysing sport from a sociological perspective reveals the ways that these transformations involve the exercise of various forms of power, ranging from overt (as in the case of one organization buying another) through to hegemonic (as in the everyday acceptance of sport as a symbol of nationhood). A central goal of this book will be to uncover the power dynamics of the interactions between sport and society, in particular analysing the societal relations that both sustain power dynamics in sporting contexts, and challenge them. The engagement with questions of power, while central to sociology as a discipline, also means that our discussion will engage with debates and issues in a range of other disciplines that have considered power in sport, including political science and policy studies, organizational and management studies, cultural and media studies, anthropology and history.

What holds these various ideas together in the context of the sociology of sport is that they provide a means for thinking about the sociological imagination, a concept developed by the American sociologist C. Wright Mills (1959) as a means of capturing a central contribution of sociology. Thinking sociologically, or mobilizing the sociological imagination, involves a process through which we aim to problematize the familiar by critically examining it, and to not take for granted the social arrangements we encounter. Perhaps most importantly, the sociological imagination requires that we consider people in their social contexts. This means considering how historical, cultural and structural factors relate to and connect with each other (Bauman and May, 2001; Germov, 2005; Germov and Poole, 2011b; Willis, 2004).

Although it is important to explore sport at a global, national or organizational level, sport gains much of its significance because of its important place in the lives of individual people. Sport is a set of social practices that is experienced by the individual who plays a particular sport, or who supports or works for a club or an athlete, or who consumes sport in a variety of ways, including through media. In this regard, it is important not to forget that participation in sport, and consumption of sport, are crucial forms of enjoyment and passion for people in their everyday lives. As such, analysis of sport from a sociological perspective recognizes that the actors in the world of sport are individuals. At the same time, individuals do not live in isolation, but exist as members of a range of groups or collectives, and much of the meaning of our lives comes from our membership of, or exclusion from, particular groups. Individuals also operate within social structures or patterns of relationships such as the economy, family, ethnicity and gender, which are influenced by power relations. So, sociological analysis of sport looks at individuals, groups and social structures, and their interactions (Giulianotti, 2004, 2005).

DEFINING SPORT

Defining sport is more difficult than it might seem at first glance, as sport has multiple meanings – some of which try to capture the activities that are understood to constitute sport and others that refer to the processes of sport.

Sport as an activity

Sport can be thought of as an activity that involves exerting your body and is competitive. This very broad definition would include very informal sports, such as a social game of beach volleyball, and more formal ones that require special equipment, such as ice or field hockey or rowing, also known as crew in the US. A more precise definition limits sports to activities that occur in formal structures (Nixon and Frey, 1996). This definition would include officially organized running races, but not casually racing a friend. An even more precise definition introduces an element of skill, saying that sports are not only 'institutionalised competitive activities', they also 'involve rigorous physical exertion or the use of relatively complex physical skills' (Coakley and Pike, 2009, p. 5; see also Nixon and Frey, 1996). While these definitions of sport as an activity vary somewhat, combined they emphasize that sport: (1) is institutionalized or organized; (2) involves competition and reward; (3) and involves physical exertion and skill. These definitions exclude certain activities, such as individual exercise. A key element distinguishing sport from exercise is the element of competition. For example, running does not become a sport until it is competitive and organized. Yoga, while being organized and requiring physical exertion and skill, is not generally considered a sport because it is not competitive. A casual game of pickup basketball involves the institutionalized structure of rules and is competitive, so it may be sport, even if it is not formally organized. However, when children engage in a spontaneous form of unorganized play, such as playing chase, this may not be considered sport as there are no accepted rules, and the game is not commonly considered to be sport.

Sport as a process

Sport can also be thought of as a process. While certain activities may be defined as sport at a particular moment, they may not always be so defined. Social understandings of what constitutes sport may change over time, or by place, and the elements that make up a particular activity that has been defined as sport may themselves be transformed (Giulianotti, 2005). For example, while football (soccer) is now a global phenomenon and played as a sport all over the world, from an historical perspective, it was not always accepted as a sport. Indeed, at certain points in English history, for example, its status as a form of activity was questioned by those in positions of authority (Goldblatt, 2006). Similarly, as new activities emerge and stake a claim to being sport, those involved in already existing sports may contest the claims. The rise of extreme games and online gaming and the struggles over whether they are real sports are examples of these contests. For example, is skateboarding a real sport? Certainly, the impassioned debates around whether skateboarding should be included in the Olympics, both from within and from outside the skateboard community, suggest this is not a settled question. And what about e-gaming? While elite e-gamers spend hours every day practising, and they compete in competitions with sizeable prize money, does working a computer console connect with everyday understandings of professional sport? While the status of e-gaming is highly contested, in Chapter 13 a range of arguments for considering it as a sport will be considered, providing insight into the contested domain of what constitutes sport.

What these examples suggest is that, while it is possible to develop an understanding of what activities are considered to be sports at particular moments, it is important not to assume that those activities have always been, or always will be, counted as sport. Rather, sport is a social and political construction. That is, how sport is constituted and what is defined as sport are the outcomes of struggles, contests and decisions that occur within particular societies at particular moments. This is well captured by the idea that for an activity to be defined as sport, it needs to be 'generally accepted as being a sport' (Australian Sports Commission, 2010). In short, what is and is not considered sport emerges out of societal processes. Sport is not static or independent of society, but is inextricably linked to society and to social practices at particular moments (Coakley and Pike, 2009). The idea of sport being a social construction is a vital one for the sociology of sport, and is a theme that recurs throughout this book.

SPORT AS DEFINED IN THIS BOOK

The focus in this book is on activities that are organized or institutionalized, involve physical activity and skill, and involve competition and reward. The starting point is that sport in the early twenty-first century involves at least these dimensions. At the same time, sport does not exist separately from or independently of society and politics. The types of sports that nations choose to support financially, for example, are not neutrally selected. Rather, sport has deep connections with other social and political practices, so it is important to consider both how sport is influenced by its societal and political context, and how sport influences that context. Finally, it is vital to consider how sport changes over time and location; in other words, there is a need to consider the process dimensions of sport, which suggests in turn that sport is a social construction. Based on these arguments, sport is defined in this book as being constituted by activities that:

- are organized or institutionalized;
- involve physical activity and skill;
- involve competition and reward;
- are inextricably linked to their social, political and economic context, and will both be influenced by that context and will influence that contest; and
- are the outcome of social processes, such that they can be transformed over time and will vary by location.

(For further discussion of definitions of sport which also inform our discussion, see Coakley and Pike, 2009; Giulianotti, 2005; Nixon and Frey, 1996.)

OVERVIEW OF *SPORT AND SOCIETY IN THE GLOBAL AGE*

Sport and Society in the Global Age engages with theoretical debates and empirical examples in the context of the sociology of sport, with a particular emphasis on the processes through which sport is socially, politically and organizationally constructed. The next two chapters (Part I) engage with these issues by considering the main theoretical and methodological approaches in sociology to understanding sport. In particular, the next chapter further investigates the process dimensions of sport, arguing that there is a need to understand sport as a relational process involving questions of power. As mentioned above, the book then has three further parts (Parts II, III and IV), each focusing on a set of debates and tensions in sport. These three parts are:

- Sport and Societal Processes
- Regulating Sport
- The Global Cultures of Sport

Examples throughout the text are drawn from an international body of research and from a range of academic disciplines. Taking a multidisciplinary approach, requiring consideration of a range of ways of thinking about and engaging with sport, enriches and complements sociological analysis (Allison, 1998; Hill, 2003; Slack, 2004). While sociology is a significant and influential discipline in its own right, there is much that sociologists can learn by engaging with other disciplines. For example, engaging with anthropology reminds sociologists of the importance of culture, while engaging with political science and policy studies reminds sociologists of the need to engage with the political dimensions of society. Through the book, examples are drawn from both professional and amateur sports, the difference broadly being that participants are paid in professional sports. The examples are also from a diverse range of international contexts, thereby exploring the interactions of the global, national and local in the constitution of sport. Consideration of such examples provides evidence in support of one of the arguments of the book, which is that, while the global and international dimensions of sport are increasingly important, local experience remains vital (Maguire, 2005). Further to this, while the definition of sport used in the book recognises the importance of history and of change over time, and some historical examples are presented through the book, the primary focus is on contemporary sport: that is, sport in the global age of the twenty-first century.

CONCLUSION

The central objective of this book is to provide a theoretically informed and empirically grounded sociological understanding of sport, emphasizing the need to consider the interactions between sport and society. In moving towards this objective, this chapter has provided a preliminary foundation for the development of an analytic framework which enables a critical engagement with existing and emerging issues in sports, based in an argument that sport is the outcome of human action located within particular social, political and economic contexts – in other words, that sport is a social construction.

CHAPTER SUMMARY

This chapter has shown:

- Sociology can provide an important contribution to understandings of sport, in particular by engaging with the social, political, cultural and economic dimensions of sport.
- In proposing definitions for sport, and for related social and political processes, it is important to remember that all definitions are contested.
- While it is important to consider sport as a particular form of socially located and organized activity, it is also vital to recognize that sport, and what is understood to be sport, is constantly changing. In this regard, sociology recognizes that sport is a social construction.

DISCUSSION QUESTIONS

1 What do you think a sociological approach to the study of sport can contribute to understandings of sport? Does this seem worthwhile to you? Why or why not?
2 How would you define sport? What factors have influenced your decision to define it in this way?
3 Think of an example where sport and politics have mixed. What are the key features of your example? What do they suggest about the relationship between sport and politics?
4 When people think of culture, they often think of activities such as going to a movie, a play or a concert, or reading a book. Does it make sense to think of sport as a cultural activity?

FURTHER READING

Allison, Lincoln (1998) 'Sport and Civil Society', *Political Studies*, XLVI, pp. 709–26.

Bourdieu, Pierre (1990) 'Program for a Sociology of Sport', in Pierre Bourdieu, *In Other Words: Essays Towards a Reflexive Sociology*, translated by Matthew Adamson, Stanford, CA, Stanford University Press, pp. 156–67.

Giulianotti, Richard (2005) *Sport: A Critical Sociology*, Cambridge, Polity.

Stewart, Bob and Smith, Aaron (2000) 'Australian Sport in a Postmodern Age', *International Journal of the History of Sport*, 17(2 and 3), pp. 278–304.

Part I

Understanding Sport and Society

The goal of Part I of the book is to:

- Engage with sociologically based theoretical and research approaches to studying the relationship between sport and society.
- Show how this relationship between sport and society is both constructed and contested theoretically and empirically among researchers in the field.
- Establish the analytic framework for this book.

Chapter 2 discusses theoretical debates in the sociology of sport, and sets up the theoretical framework for this book. Chapter 3 explores a range of research approaches used by sociologists who have studied sport.

Chapter 2

Theorizing Sport and Society

INTRODUCTION: WHY THEORY?

Even before discussing theories around the sociology of sport, the question arises as to why there is a need for a theoretical framework or frameworks to analyse sport. For many people, sport exists primarily as a form of leisure and entertainment, albeit a form of activity that can inspire fierce commitment and passions. From this view, the idea that it is important to engage with sport through a theoretical lens may well appear odd.

The answer to the question of why we need theory lies both in how we understand the sporting activities that take place in the world around us, and how we seek to engage in practice as sociologists. One role of sociologists is not only to describe what is going on in society, but also to try to understand and explain why events are occurring in particular ways. While describing what is going on in any particular social context is important, for sociologists it is usually not enough. They want to get to the meaning of activities occurring within society. Theory provides sociologists with the tools for the tasks of understanding and explaining, as well as describing, social practices. For example, if a sociologist investigated how much elite men and women athletes are paid for competing in sporting competitions, she or he would observe that in most cases men are paid more highly than women competing at the same level. Once this has been observed, the sociologist would want to think about why this is the case. This is where theory can provide a means of going beyond description to explaining and understanding (Burawoy, 2005; Germov and Poole, 2011a).

Sociological theory involves 'trained reflection on ways of knowing social life' (Harrington, 2005a, p. 6). Sociologists are interested in theory because it helps to explain why things are the way they are. Two of the aims of this book are to:

1 Show how sociology provides a theoretically, empirically and critically grounded means of engaging with sport.
2 Provide tools to engage in a theoretically informed and empirically grounded manner with sport.

This chapter introduces key theoretical debates in sociology around how society is structured and operates, and relates them to sporting contexts. It also outlines the theoretical underpinning of this book, that sport is a contested set of relational processes that involve issues of power and occur in particular social contexts and at particular times.

A challenge for sociology as a discipline is to question what we take for granted in our everyday lives. This does not mean engaging in criticism just for the sake of it, or out of a sense of cynicism. Rather, it is a questioning based in an argument that everyday practices and social structures are embedded in power relations, and that it is only by questioning that we can engage with power and propose alternative societal arrangements. For example, during the American civil rights movement of the 1950s and 1960s, discrimination against African-Americans was protested against in a variety of ways. One significant protest occurred at the 1968 Olympic Games, when 200 metre gold medallist Tommie Smith and bronze medallist John Carlos, both Americans, with the support of Australian silver medallist Peter Norman, gave the Black Power salute while on the podium receiving their medals. The media reporting at the time criticized the athletes, and the International Olympic Committee (IOC) Executive Committee banned Smith and Carlos from the Olympics for their actions. Instead of condemning the athletes, as was done by the IOC and in the media, a sociological analysis of their protest might instead argue that their actions were important manifestations of the civil rights movement, linking individual experience to a national and international social movement (Zirin, 2008).

In the context of sport, then, theory is important in a number of ways. Not only does it provide a means of explaining why things occur in the way they do in sport, it also shapes the questions that we ask about sport, and the research that we undertake to answer those questions (also see Giulianotti, 1999, 2004).

SOCIOLOGICAL THEORY AND SPORT

Sociologists examine social relations at a variety of levels, from micro to macro. Since its inception, sociology has engaged in a range of theoretical debates that provide different explanations for how society operates (see Elliott, 2009; Seidman, 2008; Harrington, 2005b, for a discussion). These include debates about how society is generally organized, usually characterized as the debate between consensus and conflict; debates about the relationship between individuals and society, usually characterized as the debate between human agency and social structures; and more general debates about social transformation and social relations, including issues of gender, race, ethnicity and other social categories (see Elliott, 2009, for this framework, and for an analysis of how sociological theorising has developed around these themes). Sociological theorising around sport has been framed within these broader debates.

Consensus and conflict

The debate between consensus and conflict is probably the key theoretical debate in sociology. Those on the consensus side of the debate, for example, Durkheim (1984) and Parsons (1970), argue that society is organized so that it has all the parts required for its smooth functioning. Also known as functionalism, consensus approaches argue that social institutions such as the family, the education system and sport, contribute to the smooth operation of society by socializing people into appropriate and socially functional ways of behaving. These institutions teach the rules that enable everyday social interactions. Conflicts or problems in society emerge when these institutions are challenged or break down. As such, conflict is problematic for society.

In this view, sport is potentially functional, or good, for society in a number of ways. For example, when they participate in sports, people improve their health. This enables them to better participate in other important activities such as paid employment and raising families. For children, sport teaches important lessons such as how to cooperate, how to follow instructions and rules, and how to participate in groups. A more critical view would also note that, as sport mirrors broader social inequalities, it also teaches children that these inequalities are both normal and acceptable and therefore it further entrenches them. As is discussed in later chapters, for example, men are more likely to occupy decision-making roles in sports such as coaching, and women are more likely to take supporting roles. Consensus theorists may argue that inequalities such as gender inequality are actually necessary for the smooth functioning of society, and are therefore not necessarily a bad thing.

Conflict approaches take a different view, arguing that as society is organized around inequality, conflicts over the resulting inequities are central to social organization. Conflict theorists, including Marx (1976) and Gramsci (1971), argue that the conflict is a key source of social change. In the context of sport, conflict theory might suggest that sport is problematic in that when people are engaging in sport, whether playing or watching, they are not engaging in more important political or social struggles. Sport has also been viewed by conflict theorists as a means through which the ruling classes in society further their domination. For example, some conflict theorists would argue that sport is organized so that men maintain their dominance in sport, and therefore in society. This is evident in the pay disparities between men and women mentioned earlier. A gender-based theoretical analysis from a conflict perspective enables us to understand that differences in pay are related to the fact that most societies in today's world are patriarchal, whereby men are privileged over women in many regards, including pay rates (Walby, 1990). In this way, gendered norms in sport help to maintain gender discrimination.

Conflict theorists also argue that social change can come about through conflicts over unequal arrangements, so from this perspective sport can also be a vehicle for social struggle and transformation. In terms of gender inequalities, a crucial insight that this theoretical orientation provides is that gender-based differences in pay are not innate or justified by some supposed state of nature, but are the outcome of social practices and social structures. These in turn are the outcome of human action, which means that change to an alternative set of arrangements is possible. In professional tennis, for example, while inequalities in pay continue to exist along gender lines, women and men competitors now receive the same prize money in the grand slam competitions, at least for the competition winners (BBC Sport, 2007). Such equality of pay only came about through political and social struggle, including on the part of competitors. As this example indicates, by undertaking a theoretical analysis of gender and pay rate differences in sport, it is possible to go beyond describing gender differences in pay rates to explaining them, and then to providing a basis for arguing for an alternative and more equitable set of arrangements.

There are a number of sociological approaches that focus on social relations. These generally emerge from conflict theory approaches and tend to focus on particular social relations such as gender, race, ethnicity, sexuality, disability and class, on the inequalities that exist around such relations, and on ways of challenging and transforming such inequalities. Theorists working on these topics argue that everyday human experiences need to be understood in terms of how they are influenced by social relations. Feminist scholars of sport, for example, argue that sport needs to be understood through a gendered lens (Hargreaves, 1994). From this perspective, to understand why men dominate the upper reaches of sporting administration, there is a need to analyse the gendered contexts that shape contemporary society, because those same contexts shape sport. This analysis would show that the gendered social organization of society privileges men, so that men are enabled to achieve positions of power and influence in sport, while women are constrained from reaching similar positions. While women can and do achieve success in moving through the levels of sporting administration, social and organizational structures make it more difficult for women than for men, which is why there are fewer women leaders in sport. Similarly, a theorist engaging with issues of disability would argue that the means through which society defines disability, and uses that concept as a means of promoting forms of inclusion and exclusion, have a profound effect on the organization and practice of sport (DePauw and Gavron, 2005). For example, while the Paralympic Games, organized as a means to enable athletes with disabilities to compete against each other at the highest level, provide an important mark of recognition for athletes with disabilities, athletes in the Paralympic Games do not receive the same financial awards, celebrity status or media exposure as athletes in the Olympic Games. That this is the case is an outcome of social organization and social attitudes that situate athletes with disabilities as not as highly regarded as other athletes. There is nothing natural or necessary about this situation. It is the outcome of social practices.

Consensus and conflict theories provide very different explanations for how societies work, and how sport fits into society. What they have in common is their focus on the macro, or society-wide, level of analysis. A key difference is that conflict theory approaches usually have a social justice aim, an aim of lessening societal inequalities. Consensus approaches argue that change should come about through existing social institutions, maintaining the status quo.

Structure and agency

Another set of debates within sociology relates to the question of how, or indeed whether, people can act in particular contexts. Many sociological theorists engage with the question of whether people are free to act of their own volition as autonomous individuals, or whether they are controlled by their social context with little or no scope for individual action (Elliott, 2009). In other words, theorists in this area are concerned with the question of how to analyse and understand the relationship between structure and agency. A social structure is a patterned form of social behaviour, and it can be as small as a norm of behaviour, as large as the class system, or at numerous levels in between. Some approaches, such as symbolic interactionism, focus on the importance of human action and interaction at the micro or everyday level, without focusing necessarily on broader social structures (Goffman, 1966). By contrast, structuralist approaches emphasize the need to understand the ways in which societal structures constrain or enable human behaviour (Althusser, 1969).

Research concerned with the debate between structure and agency has focused on different aspects of the world of sport. Symbolic interactionists focus their attention on how individuals interact with each other. In the context of sport this may involve researching the interaction of players on the field of play or the interactions of injured players with other members of a sporting organization as they seek to return the player to the field. Away from players, the focus of symbolic interactionism may be on supporters, in terms of how they relate to each other in the grandstands or how they use sport as a means to negotiate their every day lives. From this perspective, the social world is constituted by these everyday interactions between individuals.

By contrast, structuralist approaches emphasize factors such as class, gender and race as means to explain why certain people succeed in sport, or are able to afford to pay to attend games, and why others are unable to do so. For example, from a structuralist perspective, the reason why certain nations perform better than others at the Olympic Games in particular events is linked to the financial and other structural resources that nations put into developing sport. So countries that put many resources into their Olympic campaigns are likely to outperform those that do not. Similarly, the success of individuals in sport is not so much a factor of their individual ability but of their position in a social hierarchy that has given them access to resources that enable them to compete in the first instance and then potentially to succeed. These resources do not necessarily need to be monetary. The US documentary *Hoop Dreams* (1994) followed the stories of two disadvantaged African-American young men as they pursued their dreams of playing professional basketball. The portrayal shows a culture that values playing basketball, including providing spaces for the play to occur and community approval and support for time spent playing, even to the detriment of other activities. Although the young men had few financial resources for their early play, their success was enabled by the cultural resources they did have. Once they were identified as potential talents by recruiters, financial resources eventuated. Had they not had access to these cultural resources, their likelihood of playing basketball at all would have been very small. The point here in terms of theory is that, from a structuralist perspective, we need to engage with the social structures of society if we are to understand sporting outcomes, even at the level of individual performance.

While both agency and structuralist approaches provide important insights into the possibilities for human action, an ongoing critique is that they tend to overemphasize the importance of either structure or agency, without considering more fully how the two interact. Within this context, theorists such as Giddens (1984) and Bourdieu (1990) have argued that, rather than considering structure and agency as separate from each other, it is crucial to consider the ways in which structure and agency intersect or connect with each other. Indeed, it is important to consider the ways in which individual people act within a set of socially constructed structures which either enable or constrain forms of action (Seidman, 2008). French sociologist Pierre Bourdieu (1990) emphasized the importance of adopting a relational approach to the study of the social world. What this means is that, rather than considering individuals, organizations, nation-states, or other social entities, as independent or isolated from the world around them, they need to be considered and analysed in the context of their relationships with other actors, always considering the constraints that social structures may place on the relationship. Indeed, it is only by considering relationships that social beings can be understood, be they human or organizational actors. In the context of sport, this means that it is important to analyse both the individuals participating in sport and the organizations that constitute sport in terms of their relationships with others. For example, competition in a league can only survive if there is more than one team existing in a relationship with other teams. Similarly, at the level of the individual competitor, their play generally makes sense only in the context of their interactions and relations with other competitors.

Bourdieu's approach also suggests that social relations around race, gender and so on, can only be understood in the context of their interaction and relationship with other social relations. Some theorists who focus on social relations argue that the particular issue, for example, gender or sexuality, should be the primary or even sole point of focus, while others argue that it is important to analyse the interactions of social relations with each other. The intersectionality approach of theorists such as Patricia Hill Collins (2000) is a good example of this latter approach. Collins argues that while particular social relations are important in themselves, in everyday life, people occupy multiple social positions – for example, around class, gender and race – and that human experience can be understood only by analysing how these particular relations intersect with each other. From a research perspective, this means that the sociologist of sport needs to be attuned to the ways in which a range of social relations interconnect with each other, and influence both the organization of sport and what is possible for individuals within sport.

Whether or not those structures enable or constrain action is an empirical question, requiring analysis of specific social contexts, and is one that will be considered through this book. The crucial point here for the sociology of sport is that there is a need to move away from overemphasizing either the freedom of individuals to act as they wish or the constraining features of social structures, to consider instead how structure and agency interact in specific contexts.

Social transformations

In addition to theoretical debates around conflict versus consensus and structure versus agency, many sociological theorists are also concerned with the way that societies are organized and transform over time (Elliott, 2009; Harrington, 2005b). Theories of society as organized around network structures become relevant here. The concept of the network society has been developed over a number of years by theorists such as Castells (2000, 2009) and Wellman (2002). These theorists note that societies are no longer organized primarily around physical places, such as neighbourhoods or workplace organizations, where most of one's relationships were shared with others who were in the same proximity. They are organized around networks, where social networks are groups of individuals linked through their social relationships. This form of social organization is now possible beyond local shared contexts because advances in communications technologies have enabled people to genuinely connect with others who are far away. So, people can maintain relationships with family and friends who live elsewhere, can work from home in real time and can watch sports taking place on the other side of the world. If e-gaming is considered as a sport, then people can even compete in real time with others all over the world.

Looking at social relations as interconnected networks enables us to consider points of connection and disconnection, as well as how connections work more generally. This helps us to better understand the global aspects of sport. For instance, the global movement of athletes can be analysed by looking at the networks that can facilitate such movement. How a young African football (soccer) player is identified as a promising prospect, how that player is developed, trained and recruited to an elite European team can be understood as a mobilization of a global football network. Further, the money he sends home to his family, and in this context the financial rewards of sport are clearly gendered, and the personal relationships he maintains at home and in Europe are also organized around interconnected networks of relations.

This argument indicates that it is important to analyse the networks of relations that exist between organizations, and between individuals, how those networks come together at particular moments and then are redeveloped or fall apart at later moments. By tracing these processes, it is possible to understand where power is located within society, who is included in decision-making processes at the global, national and local levels, and who is excluded. The relevance of this analysis is that, as sport becomes increasingly integrated into these global processes, so it becomes part of the dynamic of the network society.

All of the theoretical approaches discussed here are united in recognizing that sport and society need to be analysed by engaging with social organization, social relations and social practices. These concerns then connect to more specific discussions around sport, and constitute an important contribution that sociology makes to understandings of sport. In particular, a sociological approach reveals that the social cannot be considered as simply a peripheral element of sport, but it is central to the constitution of sport. A sociological approach also argues, and provides evidence for the argument, that sporting practices, organizations and relations are not natural or pregiven, but are the outcome of human action. This in turn suggests that, while change can be difficult, it is possible to achieve through the struggle of people in their social contexts.

The question of power

The question of power, and how power is produced, reproduced and challenged in sport is crucial to understanding the role of sport in society. The importance of power is embedded in all of the theoretical perspectives discussed above. Who is able to exercise power and why they (and not others) can do so is important in understanding how societies are structured, and how they change (Castells, 2009; Elliott, 2009; Foucault, 1995; Gramsci, 1971; Henslin, 2008).

Power is the ability or capacity to get others to do what you want. At the same time, as identified by Lukes (2005), power operates in different dimensions. It can be exercised overtly, with one person compelling another to do something (Lukes, 2005). For example, a coach may instruct a player to play in a particular way. Power can also be exercised covertly, for example, when particular groups are excluded from the decision-making process (Lukes, 2005). This type of power is exercised when decisions are made without input from potential stakeholders. For example, a decision by a government to invest in a bid to host a major international sport event may be taken without consulting all members of the community who may be affected by the decision.

A third type of power is that which people do not even recognize is being exercised (Lukes, 2005). This type of power is closely linked to the idea of hegemony (Gramsci, 1971), or subordination by consent. With this type of power, the social arrangements are often such that decision-making arrangements are so normal that they are unquestioned. This type of power is embedded in everyday social structures and interactions (Foucault, 1995). For example, at various times in history and in particular national contexts, it was accepted as common sense that only people of certain races could be selected for national sporting teams or could participate in particular competitions. That such ideas are now considered abhorrent is an example of the need to study power, ideas and practices within historical contexts.

Power relations are essential to sport, and are considered throughout the book. For example, contests around overt expressions of power occur when a media owner uses their financial resources to buy a sporting team. Here, the exercise of overt financial and political power is clear and can be readily identified as such. Rules around how playing fields are allocated by the local city council can be an example of everyday hidden power structures. For example, when boys' sports teams always have priority over fields because historically their teams have always played on those fields, relegating girls' sports to sub-standard fields simply because the girls' teams are newer (Messner, 2002), the arrangements are rarely questioned. Yet, such allocations clearly involve forms of power.

DISCUSSION POINT

One of your friends argues that theory is irrelevant to an understanding of sport. After all, they argue, sport is just something we do for fun, there is no need to make it more complicated than it is. How would you respond to this argument?

ANALYTIC FRAMEWORK OF THIS BOOK

As the discussion above shows, there is an ongoing range of theoretical debates in sociology, both in general and around sport. What this suggests is that there is not one best way to study sport as a social phenomenon. But the choice of theoretical position is crucial, not only in terms of its influence on how particular social issues are studied, but also because theoretical frameworks have an important influence on the very questions that are asked. For example, a theorist of sport interested in processes of globalization may ask different questions than a theorist interested in micro-level interactions between players on the field, or between spectators in the grandstand. To the extent that this is the case, research in the area of sport, as in other areas, is not value free or neutral. It is shaped by the questions that are asked which in turn emerge from what are thought to be the important issues to engage with in the first instance.

This books proposes that to understand the connections between sport and society from a sociological perspective, it is beneficial to adopt a multi-dimensional approach that recognizes the importance of:

- the societal context of sport;
- the relationships that constitute sport;
- the dynamics of power that underpin sport; and
- the processes that unfold over time within sport.

In other words, the analytic framework in this book is based on the argument that:

> **Sport can be understood as a contested set of relational processes that involve critical issues of power and which occur within particular societal contexts at particular times.**

This framework emerges from broader conflict theory approaches that argue that, in order to understand society, questions about power must be considered.

It builds on the idea that the ways that society is organized at specific times and places benefits particular groups who aim to maintain their positions of power. Social transformation occurs through struggle between those who have power and those who want it. The capacity for change is constrained by the social structures within which individuals operate.

This book adopts a relational approach to the study of sport. This means analysing the relations within and between the following three levels (see Cottle, 2003, for this typology in a different context, adapted here):

- **Micro-level:** This dimension of sport includes the range of activities that occur in the context of relations between individuals. This includes the performance of individuals on the field of play, the health of individual athletes and relations at an individual level between participants in sport, including athletes, fans and administrators. The importance of analysing relations at the micro-level is that it provides insight into the everyday practice of sport as it is constituted by individuals.

- **Meso-level:** This dimension engages in particular with organizational relations in sport. Such relations include those between clubs, between clubs and regulatory bodies, and between sport organizations and policy organizations. The importance of analysing relations at this level is that professional sport is constituted in fundamental ways by its organizational processes. That is, sport involves particular forms of organizations, and relations between organizations.

- **Macro-level:** This dimension includes the social and political relations which constitute the context within which sport exists. In addition to the political and economic context, the macro-level also includes social relations organized around race, gender, ethnicity, disability, sexuality and so on. These relations provide the societal context within which the micro- and macro- dimensions of sport occur. For example, whether analysing the micro-level performance of players on the field, or the ways in which sport organizations are constituted, it is important to consider how social relations around race and gender, to take two examples, influence those micro- and meso-level activities.

It is also important to analyse sport as a social process, and to be aware of the historical groundings of sport, and of the importance of time in analysing sport. While sociologists may focus on particular sport practices at particular times, there is a need to locate them within a longer time frame. For example, it is difficult to understand the 2010 FIFA World Cup (football/ soccer) without taking into account factors such as historical relations within FIFA, the organization responsible for the Cup, as well as relations between nations over time, and previous World Cup events. In other words, considering sport as a social process means that a full understanding of contemporary events cannot be developed by focusing on those events alone. Contemporary events do not emerge out of nowhere, but rather are the outcome of a range of social and historical processes.

CONCLUSION

This chapter has emphasized the importance of theory for the sociology of sport, both because it provides a means of understanding sport and because it can provide a basis for arguing for and seeking to bring about change. However, theory by itself can only take us so far. It is also crucial to consider how sociologists engage with the social world through research. The task of the next chapter is to consider the varying approaches to social research that sociologists have taken and, in that way, to consider the relationship between theory and research. This then provides a foundation for the argument that there is a need to conduct theoretically informed and empirically grounded research if we are to understand sport in its social contexts.

CHAPTER SUMMARY

This chapter has shown:

■ The importance of theory in engaging with sport and society in the global age.
■ A range of theories have been developed in sociology which emphasize different aspects of sport.
■ The analytic model adopted in this book proposes that sport can be understood as a contested set of relational processes that involve critical issues of power and which occur within particular societal contexts.

DISCUSSION QUESTIONS

1 Studying the social is central to sociology. Why is an understanding of the social important for our understanding of sport? How does this differ, or does it, from the approaches of other disciplines?

2   Why is power such an important concept for sociologists concerned to study sport? Do you think the distinctions that Lukes draws between different dimensions of power (overt, covert, hegemonic) are helpful in the context of sport? Can you think of examples of each of the three dimensions of power in the world of sport?

3   How does Castells' model of the network society contribute to our understanding of sport?

4   Go to a website or your daily newspaper, and find any story about sport. How can the various theoretical issues discussed in this chapter help to critically read that story? What do the theoretical issues discussed in this chapter add to your understanding of the particular story you have chosen?

FURTHER READING

Castells, Manuel (2000) 'Materials for an Exploratory Theory of the Network Society', *British Journal of Sociology*, 51(1), pp. 5–24.

Elliott, Anthony (2009) *Contemporary Social Theory: An Introduction*, London, Routledge.

Giulianotti, Richard (ed.) (2004) *Sport and Modern Social Theorists*, Basingstoke, Palgrave Macmillan.

Seidman, Steven (2008) *Contested Knowledge: Social Theory Today*, 4th edn, Malden, MA, Blackwell.

Chapter 3

Researching Sport and Society

INTRODUCTION

One contribution that sociological researchers make to our understanding and analysis of sport is to mobilize a range of research methods that can provide systematic and rigorous evidence about sport. This evidence can then be used both to understand sporting processes, and as a basis for suggesting change in particular contexts. Sociologists aim to investigate patterns in social life (Walter, 2006a). For example, the American ritual of singing the national anthem at the start of a sporting event is a social pattern, as is the norm in many nations of the British Commonwealth that girls play netball while boys play cricket. These norms and patterns have emerged over time.

This chapter examines the variety of ways in which social scientists, including sociologists, study sport. In particular, it discusses quantitative and qualitative research approaches as they have been used in research on sport. Research starts with a research question. Research, and related research questions, in sociology will typically have one or both of the following broad objectives, namely, 'understanding the complexity of social life and generating knowledge with the potential to transform society' (Ragin and Amoroso, 2011, p. 34).

There are two main approaches to sociological research: qualitative research methods and quantitative research methods. Researchers in sociology typically use one or both of the two dominant types of research method, based on the research question they want to answer. Qualitative research can be understood as an interpretative approach to knowledge, in which 'the main research questions are "what meaning" questions' (Ezzy, 2006, p. 35) or 'why' questions. Typically, researchers employing a qualitative approach will use methods such as interviews, observations in the field and document analysis. Interviews in which the researcher talks with a range of participants about the research topic, using a more or less structured set of questions, are used because they are considered an important means through which people can verbalize their experiences and understandings of situations. As such, they can provide a researcher with a means of accessing how people make meaning of particular events. Observations allow the researcher to see what people actually do in their everyday lives. Document analysis allows the researcher to see how events have been recorded and discussed.

In contrast, quantitative research is an approach to knowledge that focuses on 'how many' questions (Ezzy, 2006, p. 35). In quantitative social research, the major tool used is the survey, although in some disciplines – for example, psychology – experiments are also used. Surveys involve the development of a set of structured questions, typically with a range of predefined options for answers provided (for example, strongly agree, agree, neither agree or disagree, disagree, strongly disagree; or yes or no). Surveys are an important means for collecting data that can be represented in numerical form.

A third approach, comparative research, seeks to advance knowledge by comparing situations, often with a view to uncovering and seeking to explain similarities and differences. A common comparative approach is to compare countries around a particular issue, for example, participation levels in sport, but comparisons may also be conducted between organizations, or between particular sorts of groups. Researchers adopting a comparative approach will use either quantitative or qualitative methods to collect their data (Walter, 2006b).

Research methods are closely connected to theory. That is, empirical, or evidence-based, research does not exist independent of theoretical frameworks, but rather is informed by those frameworks, and contributes to their further development.

APPROACHES TO KNOWLEDGE

For sociologists engaging in empirical work on sport, questions arise around what methods are appropriate to use. The research approach, the research methods chosen, should be guided by the research question we are trying to answer. Research questions emerge from a variety of contexts, depending on our own understandings of the world, on who the stakeholders are, and on what tools and other resources we have at our disposal. That is, our knowledge of the world does not simply descend from the sky above, or exist independently of us. Our knowledge is deeply embedded within our social context and is influenced by our social location and the context for our research (Ragin and Amoroso, 2011). If we are doing research on behalf of our local sporting club, for example, the club's interests will be reflected in the questions asked (and not asked) and the research methods used to answer them. Given this, it is important to recognize that when sociologists and other social researchers conduct research, they mobilize a particular way of understanding society and the social world, or particular paradigms, as a means of framing and developing their research project (McGee, 2007, p.72). While a number of paradigms for understanding the social world exist, two of the most common within sociology are positivism and interpretivism.

Positivism vs interpretivism

Historically, sociologists have been divided between those who believe that there is an objective reality that can be measured with precision in ways that are free of bias (positivists), and those who believe that knowledge is situated in particular contexts and must be studied from the viewpoint of relevant actors (interpretivists). This debate between positivism and interpretivism has tended to follow methodological lines, with positivists tending to employ more quantitative approaches, and interpretivists tending to use more qualitative approaches. More recently, though, the divide has lessened, and many sociologists use both methods, depending on the research questions they seek to answer (Walter, 2006b).

While agreeing with positivists that research must be rigorous, well justified and based on empirical observation, interpretivist researchers also recognize the importance of seeking the subjective meaning of social action, and of recognizing that the social context we live in influences the work that we do, the questions that we ask, and how we go about answering those questions. The debate between positivism and interpretivism has not been settled, and there are well-regarded sociologists on both sides of the debate, and in the middle. It is important to know where you stand in regards to this debate, as your positioning shapes the kind of research you will conduct.

Within interpretivism, there are a number of more specific approaches. This book adopts a social constructionist approach (Harding, 2003; Walter,

2006b). Often contrasted with an objectivist approach, which 'asserts that social phenomena and their meanings have an existence that is independent of social actors' (Bryman, 2004, p. 16), social constructionism argues that the social world is the outcome of human action, interaction and engagement. Such an approach 'suggests that multiple realities exist, formed within a particular context. The researcher studies how reality is "constructed" by the individual within this context' (Gratton and Jones, 2004, p. 21). As a result, any research about activities in a context such as sport needs to recognize that the context does not exist independently of human action, but is constituted and reconstituted through human actions. This does not mean that individuals are simply free to act and change the world as they like. Indeed, it is vital that, while engaging with individuals, sociologists also analyse social and power structures and the ways in which they either enable or constrain social action on the part of individuals and organizations.

Working within these frameworks of knowledge, when sociologists conduct research, they engage in a process of systematically collecting, analysing and communicating information and explanations of social issues (Hall and Hall, 2004). In other words, social research goes beyond anecdotal information. In addition, social research involves interactions with other people, meaning that it is a relational process. These relations may be formed with interview or survey participants, with people who can grant or deny access to data, such as organizational gatekeepers and librarians, and, when working in a team, with research colleagues.

In considering these approaches, a critical point is that the research methods used should be driven by our research questions. Some questions lend themselves well to being answered through counting and numerical data. For example, if we want to know how many girls and boys play basketball in a particular city, it is essential to use a quantitative approach as a qualitative approach cannot answer that research question. In contrast, if we want to know why girls decide to play basketball, we would need to employ a qualitative approach. The crucial point is that the methods used should be determined by the questions we are asking.

Depending on the goals we are seeking to achieve with our research, one or the other of the dominant approaches will generally be most useful. For example, quantitative research is a frequently used approach for identifying general numerical patterns at a societal level. This may involve measuring levels of participation in particular sports among young people, or counting the types of injuries suffered by competitors at a particular stadium. By contrast, qualitative research is an important approach for researchers who

are interested in 'interpreting culturally or historically significant phenomena' (Ragin and Amoroso, 2011, p. 35) and for 'giving voice' (Ragin and
Amoroso, 2011, p. 35) For example, a researcher may want to find out what
competitors think about the question of sexuality in sport, or how people in
a particular community feel about being excluded from decision-making
processes about a new stadium development proposal. Comparative
approaches are often used for exploring patterns of diversity, which can
cover issues ranging from seeking to understand why different nations have
developed different means of regulating media ownership of sport organizations through to comparing how fans in different locations organize themselves in supporters' groups (Ragin and Amoroso, 2011).

The research process

All research projects involve a research process, which in turn involves the
following (see Ezzy, 2006; Gratton and Jones, 2004):

- Choosing the research question/topic.
- Developing a theoretical framework and literature review.
- Considering the ethical aspects of the project and, if necessary, getting
  ethics approval from an appropriate body.
- Selecting an appropriate research method to answer the research ques-
  tion, including who will be researched (sampling) and how the research
  will be conducted.
- Collecting the information and analysing it.
- Writing up and communicating the results of the research, potentially to
  diverse audiences.

Whatever the approach, all projects will involve these steps. While we list these
here in an order, the actual research process itself involves overlaps and moving
back and forward between these stages. While we do not need to go into each
of these steps in detail for current purposes, we do want to highlight some
issues. First, researchers' own social positions influence not only how they view
the world, but also how they engage with the world. Within this context, a
range of sociologists including Dorothy Smith (1990) and Sandra Harding
(2003), have contributed to the development of standpoint theory, an approach
to research which suggests that we cannot understand or engage with the world
separate from our social location or our standpoint. The approach makes it
clear that researchers do not act independently of the world in which they live,

but rather act within and are shaped by the particular circumstances within which they are working. For example, researchers need to reflect carefully on how their own viewpoints and experiences influence the work they are doing, and to build those viewpoints and experiences into their analysis.

Second, underlying the sociological research process are questions of power and ethics (McGee, 2007). Whenever research is conducted into social worlds, we need to remember that the research will impact on various individuals and groups in the community, and that those impacts may potentially be harmful. While it is rare that sociological research will cause physical harm to participants, the research process has the potential to harm the reputations of individuals or to indirectly cause harm to the feelings and experiences of participants. For example, this may arise when we ask people about issues that are sensitive or which bring up unwanted memories or experiences – such as, around experiences of racism or homophobia in sport. Or, concerns may arise where findings relate to power contests within organizations, where the publication of those findings might impact on the people in those organizations. For reasons such as these, all research involving human participants must take ethical issues into consideration. At the very least, potential participants in research must be made aware that they are being asked to participate in a research project, and must be given the opportunity to consent, or not, to such participation. In much sociological research, it is also common practice not to use real names of people or organizations, but to use pseudonyms, or made-up names, to protect the privacy of participants. It is also important that participants be told who will have access to the data, and how such data will be used. The purpose of such processes is to ensure that people are aware that they are involved in research, that they have consented to participate, and also for the researcher to seek ways to minimize any potential for harm to come to those participants. In many research contexts, including universities, these processes are managed by ethics committees (Bryman, 2004; Walter, 2006b).

A third question relates to the issue of who, or what (if documents are involved), to include in the research. This is the question of sampling (Bryman, 2004). In some cases, for example, if a small organization or community is being investigated, it may be possible to try to include everyone involved as a participant. However, in many cases, it will not be possible to access everyone in the population of interest. In such cases, a sample, or a segment of the population, will need to be selected for inclusion in the project. A question then emerges as to whether or not a representative sample is needed or wanted. A representative sample is one that is an accurate reflection of the broader population from which it is drawn. The importance of a representative sample, in particular for quantitative research, is that it allows the findings to be generalized to the broader population from which the sample was drawn, if properly done. To obtain a representative sample, it is necessary to use probability sampling techniques, such as simple random sampling, where everyone in the population of interest has the same chance of being selected to participate in the research. Such sampling is possible if we have a list of everyone in the population of interest, and we are able to randomly select people from that list in accordance with probability theory. For example, if we are interested in the attitudes of players in a particular league towards drug testing, it may be possible for us to get a full list of the players from the league's governing body. If we cannot survey everyone on the list, we may be able to use random sampling techniques to create our research sample. However, in many cases, it is not always possible to get such a list. For example, if we want to survey supporters about their attitudes towards drug testing, we may not be able to access a complete list of all supporters. Indeed, such a list may not exist. Or, in the case of a league or other organization, privacy issues may mean that we are not given access to lists that do exist. For example, for privacy reasons, a school may not give a list of the names of all of its students to a researcher interested in student attitudes towards sport. In such cases, it may be necessary to undertake sampling which is not representative of the population – that is, non-probability sampling. Examples of non-probability sampling include convenience sampling, snow-ball sampling and purposive sampling. The main point in this context is that, with non-probability sampling, when results are discussed, we can only talk about the people who participated in the project. We cannot generalize to a broader population (Bryman, 2004; Walter, 2006b).

A fourth point to consider relates to the question of resources. In an ideal world, there would be no constraints in terms of what research it would be possible to do. In the world of practice, however, resources need to be considered. Many forms of research involve financial expenditure. This may include travelling to research sites, having access to a recorder, being able to print and post surveys and so on. Once a research project reaches a particular size, these resource issues become significant. At the same time, it is also necessary to think about whether access to relevant information is possible. For example, if historical research is being undertaken on a deceased sports person, are documents available and accessible? In some cases, libraries or families may make papers available. In other cases, however, families may not want to make personal papers accessible, or papers and documents simply may not exist. As another example, it may be desirable to conduct an interview-based research project. As part of the planning, it will be necessary to consider whether people are willing to participate and to be interviewed. For some people, interviews take up time that they do not have, while others may simply not want to be interviewed. While people are frequently willing to be interviewed, as evidenced by the sheer amount of research that has been done, we cannot simply assume that this will be the case. A critical element in the planning stage of any project involves considering what data is needed, whether it can be accessed and what financial and equipment resources will be needed to undertake the research (Ezzy, 2006).

Fifth, the question arises of how to analyse and present the data, once it has been collected. In quantitative research, the most basic way of analysing data is in terms of frequencies, or numbers of responses, and percentages. For example, if we conducted a survey around attitudes towards drug use in sport and asked the question, 'Are you in favour of drug testing in sport?', we may give participants the option of answering yes or no. If 100 people answered our survey, and 60 said yes and 40 said no, we could represent this both numerically (60 said yes and 40 said no) and in percentage terms (60 per cent yes and 40 per cent no). There are many more sophisticated ways in which data can be represented quantitatively, but frequencies and percentages are used with great regularity, and are often sufficient. Results can then also be presented in various visual formats, such as graphs. In contrast, qualitative data is analysed and represented through the use of words and language. One very common approach is to identify common themes, or issues, that emerge in the research, from the perspectives of the participants. Another approach is to analyse the meaning of the language being used, often through an approach referred to as discourse analysis. Yet another approach is identified as narrative analysis, in which we present the data from participants in terms of the individual stories, or narratives, they tell us (Bryman, 2004; Walter, 2006b). Even from this brief discussion, it is clear that there are many ways of analysing and presenting data. The approach we take will be linked to the questions we have asked, the precise form of the data we have collected and what we think will be an effective way of presenting the data for the purposes of the particular research project. Related to this, we also need to think about the forum in which we are presenting our results. For example, the presentation format for an academic journal article may be very different to the format for a policy document or for a media release. Researchers should be aware both of their own needs and of the expectations and demands of their audience (Hall and Hall, 2004).

While this discussion by no means covers all of the issues that researchers need to be aware of, it engages with some important issues that all researchers need to consider. To explore these issues further, there are a wide range of research books and journals available, while it can also be useful to look at particular research articles, books or reports to see how the authors have discussed their research approach (Bryman, 2004; Ragin and Amoroso, 2011; Walter, 2006b).

DISCUSSION POINT

Is there any area of sporting activity that should be considered off limits to sociological researchers? That is, are there any aspects of sport that sociologists should not be able to explore for ethical or other reasons? For example, should sociologists be able to research issues that raise potentially painful memories for participants? Why, or why not?

STUDYING SPORT FROM A SOCIOLOGICAL PERSPECTIVE

Having examined the research process, we are now in a position to discuss some specific research examples from studies of sport. In reading these examples, you may like to consider what you think are the strengths and limitations of the research projects. You may also like to consider whether you would have conducted the research in the same way, or whether you would have used a different research approach. By considering such questions, you can gain insights into the research process and the decisions that need to be made. It is also important to recognize that, while we are discussing these approaches separately, in practice, researchers may combine different approaches, depending on the particular questions they are asking.

Ethnography or participant observation

Ethnography is a qualitative technique that involves studying something through participant observation. '[T]he essential feature of most ethnographic research is that it attempts above all to describe "the nature of social discourse amongst a group of people"' (Edwards *et al.*, 2002, p. 9). To achieve this, ethnographic work typically involves the researcher positioning themselves to a greater or lesser extent as a member of the community, group or organization they are studying, in a process sometimes referred to as participant observation. An important example is the work of Ramon

Spaaij, a Dutch sociologist, who studied football (soccer) hooliganism in the context of six Western European football clubs. His research was based on a combination of 'interviews, participant observation, fanzines, official documents and databases, literature, newspaper reports, internet websites and (official and private) video footage' (Spaaij, 2006, p. 66). The participant observation involved spending time with hooligan and non-hooligan fans, in both football and non-football settings, as a means not only of collecting data but of getting a feeling for fan culture (Spaaij, 2006). In another example, P. David Howe developed an ethnographic study of pain and injury at Pontypridd, a leading Welsh professional rugby union club (Howe, 2001). While conducting his research, Howe 'adopted the role of massage therapist, water-boy and general "gofer"' (Howe, 2001, p. 293), thus enabling him to get close to the players and other members of the club during practice, matches and in the general community beyond the club.

Interview- and document based research

While ethnographic research can provide powerful insights into everyday practices in sport, and in other social worlds, it is a difficult method to work with in a fully fledged manner. It demands that researchers are able to immerse themselves in particular contexts for extended periods of time, something that is not always possible because of time and resource constraints or because participants do not agree to such a level of investigation. For this reason, for research questions that require qualitative methods, interview- and document-based research are much more commonly used. Such approaches involve interviewing participants in particular social and organizational contexts, or analysing documents such as organizational reports and media texts.

In relation to interview-based research, Capling and Marjoribanks (2004; 2008) undertook research, in the 2000s, around organizational restructuring in Australian Football League clubs by conducting in-depth interviews with stakeholders within clubs. While parts of each interview focused on factual information, such as the formal organizational structure of the club, much of the interview engaged with the experiences, perceptions and understandings of the participants. Once the interviews were conducted, they were analysed to uncover common themes that arose among the interviewees, but also to explore differences, and to attempt to explain such similarities and differences. For example, Capling and Marjoribanks found that while all clubs were concerned with the roles of members in clubs, some clubs were more open than others to enabling members to take a participatory role in club governance (Capling and Marjoribanks, 2004, 2008).

Other projects have used document analyses to examine the ways in which race is represented in media coverage of sport. To engage with this issue, Farquharson and Marjoribanks (1) analysed media discourses around race in the context of the 1995 Rugby Union World Cup, which was held in South Africa (Farquharson and Marjoribanks, 2003); and (2) analysed media discourses around an event that occurred in the early 2000s in Australia, when an Australian cricket player racially vilified a Sri Lankan cricketer (Farquharson and Marjoribanks, 2006). In both cases, newspaper articles were collected from a range of newspapers in the particular national context, namely South Africa and Australia, and thematic, discourse and content analyses were undertaken of the material, systematically categorizing the content by discursive theme, and counting how frequently each term was mobilized. The former project found that sport was mobilized as a way to further racial reconciliation in post-apartheid South Africa. The latter project found that there was a perceived Black/White divide in cricketing nations, and how issues of race and racism were dealt with in cricket was shaped by this perceived divide.

Survey research

Surveys, a popular quantitative social science research method, are used for a number of purposes, from capturing the number of times certain events have occurred, through to the perceptions of individuals about particular events. In the sociology of sport, such data has been used to measure items ranging from participation levels in certain sporting activities (ABS, 2007a) through to representations of race in media-sport (McCarthy and Jones, 1997).

While many social researchers using quantitative approaches seek to develop their surveys as a means of collecting their own data, sociologists also work with data that has been collected by others. Organizations such as the United Nations, the International Labour Organization, the World Health Organization and international- and national-level organizations, including sport organizations, and censuses collect information through surveys that can be used by sociological researchers. For example, if we are interested in how many people participate in leisure activities of various kinds, it may well be possible to find such data collected by other organizations (e.g., Department of Sport and Recreation, 2005; ABS, 2007b; ONS,

2001). Or, if we want to know how many people watched a particular event on television, say the opening ceremony of the Olympic Games or the final of the FIFA World Cup, then the relevant television station or the organization hosting the event, may well have the figures.

One of the challenges with using data collected by others is that those who designed the survey probably had different research questions than we might have. While we may be fortunate and the data available might match exactly what we are looking for, in other situations it will be necessary for us to make some accommodations to work with the existing data, perhaps in our research questions or in the populations that we speak about. In addition, just because data exists does not mean that we will be able to access it. In some cases, organizations such as sporting bodies or media organizations may consider their information to be private, and therefore they may not want to provide researchers with the information for fear that competitor organizations may get access to the data. Alternatively, organizations may provide access to data, but put strict limitations on how the researcher can use the data. For the researcher, these issues are ones that need to be managed on a case by case basis – for example, considering whether restrictions put on use of data will still allow them to achieve their objectives, in which case they may accept those restrictions. If the restrictions are too prohibitive, the researcher may decide not to access the information. Of critical importance here is that the researcher does not use the data in any way that has been forbidden by the organization providing the information. To so use the data would be a severe breach of ethical obligations.

Historical research

Historical research on sport is important, not only because of what it tells us about the past but also because of what history can tell us about the present, based on the argument that current social relations and practices are only meaningful and understandable if we locate them within a broader historical context (Hutchins, 2002). For example, C. L. R. James (1993) undertook research on the history of cricket in the Caribbean as a means of providing insights into the experience of colonization, and its continuing impacts on Caribbean societies. Historical research has also played an important role in giving voice to previously marginalized groups in sport, including groups organized around gender, race, sexuality, disability and so on (Booth and Tatz, 2000; Williams, 2001). Historical research can be quantitative, qualitative or both.

CONCLUSION

The ways we conduct research into sport are linked to our social location, including where we stand on the positivist/interpretivist divide, which influences what interests us and how we approach it; the stakeholders involved in the research; and the research question. Research takes place in social, economic and political contexts and these contexts shape the research in fundamental ways. In doing research, we should aim for a clear discussion of what has influenced us and how it has shaped both the questions that we asked and the outcomes of the project. We should aim for research based in evidence that is rigorously collected and analysed in transparent ways, so that others can understand what we did and, if they wish, attempt to replicate it.

CHAPTER SUMMARY

This chapter has shown:

- Sociological research is a process involving interactive relationships with others.
- Sociological research is both systematic and purposeful and, as such, requires researchers to undertake extensive planning before commencing.
- Major approaches available to sociologists tend to be grouped under the headings 'qualitative' and 'quantitative' research, although many sociologists seek to combine approaches.
- In the social research process, the research questions drive the methods we use.
- Questions of ethics are central to all research projects, and raise issues ranging from how we select and engage with participants through to how we write up the results of our research.
- Through adopting a range of social science research methods, sociologists have made important contributions to knowledge of sport.

DISCUSSION QUESTIONS

1 You are a researcher who wishes to understand why people in a particular country support certain teams in a national basketball league. What questions do you need to ask to engage with this problem? What methods would be most appropriate for getting the data you need? What

might your answers reveal about the connection between teams and supporters in the particular country?

2 What does it mean to argue that knowledge is a social construction? What does your answer to this question suggest about the sorts of claims we can make based on our sociological research?

3 Based on the examples given towards the end of this chapter, what do you think are the strengths and limitations of sociological approaches such as ethnography, interview research, survey research and historical research?

4 We don't need sociological research to understand sport. We know enough from our experience and from the media. Discuss.

FURTHER READING

Bryman, Alan (2004) *Social Research Methods*, 2nd edn, New York, Oxford University Press.

Gratton, Chris and Jones, Ian (2004) *Research Methods for Sport Studies*, London, Routledge.

Ragin, Charles C. and Amoroso, Lisa M. (2011) *Constructing Social Research: The Unity and Diversity of Method*, 2nd edn, Thousand Oaks, CA, Sage.

Walter, Maggie (ed.) (2006b) *Social Research Methods: An Australian Perspective*, South Melbourne, Oxford University Press.

Part II

Sport and Societal Processes

Part II of the book examines sport and societal processes. Chapters 4 and 5 look at societal hierarchies around race and gender, arguing that sport is organized to maintain the dominance of White heterosexual men. Chapter 6 discusses the relationship between sport and nation in a context of globalization, asking whether sport contributes to processes of denationalization, or whether it helps to maintain the relevance of nations. The chapter shows that the relationship between sport and nation is not a straightforward one, and that the nation is a contested site through which contemporary sport is constructed. The final chapter of Part II looks at the body in sport, showing that contemporary understandings of the body place it as individual and biomedical, but also that a sociological approach provides insights into the ways in which bodies are influenced by politics and social relations. This chapter highlights the social and political dimensions of sporting bodies by looking at how the body intersects with drugs, pain and technology. In short, this part of the book engages with sport and social hierarchies.

Chapter 4

Sport, Race and Racism

INTRODUCTION

Race is a social construction based on appearance. Skin colour, hair texture and facial features are all markers of race, and it is commonly believed that these markers tell us important things about people. Despite these popular beliefs, race, as a category, actually has no biological validity: geneticists have clearly established that there are greater genetic variations within so-called racial groups than between them (Bamshad *et al.*, 2003). Despite this, commonly held stereotypes assert that Black competitors are naturally better at sport than White competitors, even though there is no biological evidence that this is the case (Carrington and McDonald, 2002). Race might have an impact on sport, but its impact is social, not genetic.

Race can be understood as a process of racial formation (Omi and Winant, 1994). Racial formation is the 'the sociohistorical process by which racial categories are created, inhabited, transformed, and destroyed' (Omi and Winant, 1994, p. 55). Understanding race as racial formation means situating it in its social context, and understanding that social contexts vary over time and space. Racial categories themselves vary around the world, as do the social relations around race. For example, in Australia the word 'Black' refers to Indigenous peoples, whereas in the United States it is reserved for those with at least some African ancestry. In South Africa, Black refers to those believed to have only African ancestry, with other terms for those with some African ancestry. In the UK, Black sometimes refers to people of South Asian background in addition to those with African ancestry. The same word, then, has very different meanings around the world. So, to understand race relations, there is a need to take into account their social context.

This chapter focuses on race relations in Western racialized nations. We have capitalized the racial and ethnic terms we use, for example, Black and White, to signify that they are social constructions. The terms are understood to be contested and to refer to different people in different contexts. Because of this, we take care to place racial and ethnic terms in their national contexts throughout the chapter.

Race and racialized beliefs are particularly important in the context of global sport. People care about race and sports because they are intertwined in a number of important ways. Entire sports are racialized. For example, in the United States more than two-thirds of players in the professional basketball and football (gridiron) leagues are African-Americans despite African-Americans comprising only approximately 12 per cent of the US population. Conversely, swimming and gymnastics are dominated by White athletes, with very few non-White participants. At the individual level, beliefs about racial prowess in sport impact on the everyday experiences of athletes and their career trajectories after their athletic careers are over. In this chapter, we explore the intersections of race and sport, arguing that, although the social institution of race is a construction, it has material effects on how sport is organized, played and experienced. In the following sections we discuss racial stereotypes about athletic ability, and how beliefs in those stereotypes have shaped sport. We next examine the role the media has played in maintaining these racial stereotypes. We then outline racial patterns of participation in sports, racial disparities in pay and racial vilification. The chapter closes by looking at how studies of Whiteness might contribute to a better understanding of racism in the context of sport.

NATURALLY TALENTED?

As race is a social construction, so beliefs about racial prowess in sport are also socially constructed and have no basis in biological realities. There is no evidence that people with dark skin are inherently better athletically than those with lighter skin. There is a great deal of evidence that social structures around sport reinforce racial stereotypes around sporting prowess. Yet, in nations around the world Black peoples are popularly believed to be naturally more talented at sport than White peoples. These persistent myths about the superiority of Black athletes are very powerful, and the beliefs themselves structure sports so that Black athletes participate in ways that reinforce the idea that they are naturally talented and so are able to do well with little effort, while White athletes participate in ways that reinforce the idea that they have to work hard to succeed. The consequence of these myths is that stereotypes around race, intelligence and hard work that place White competitors in a morally superior position to Black competitors are continually reinforced by the structures and the actors in sporting arenas.

Beliefs around Blackness and sporting skill are pervasive around the world, and in many cases have a long history related to experiences of colonialism and colonization, and the beliefs about racial superiority and inferiority that were central to the colonizing experience (Carrington and McDonald, 2001; James, 1993). In the UK, non-White cricket and rugby league players are considered more flamboyant and more talented than White players (Long and Hylton, 2002). In Australia these traits are associated with Indigenous competitors (Hallinan and Judd, 2009). Hallinan and Judd (2009, p. 1227) quote Australian Rules football coach Kevin Sheedy as saying: 'You think you're a coach and you get some really wonderfully talented people and they actually teach you how to coach. Indigenous players, they don't need a compass and a protractor. They know the angle coming into the goals.' The quote suggests that Indigenous athletes possess a special talent for football that others lack. That Sheedy would make such a statement is of particular interest in that he has been one of the most important people in the Australian Football League in taking a politically progressive stance around race. Similarly, in Norway, athletes of African background reported having their sporting success explained by their presumed natural talent, not their hard work and dedication (Massao and Fasting, 2010).

There is US evidence that racial stereotypes are held by novice coaches who then have different expectations of their athletes depending on their race (Rasmussen *et al.*, 2005). Novice coaches are those who have some, but not a great deal of, experience in coaching. They are important because they 'will significantly affect the selection, shaping, and ultimately [the] success of future athletes as well as the persistence of unfair practices such as stacking [positional segregation, discussed below]' (Rasmussen *et al.*, 2005). This particular study of novice coaches found that they expected White athletes to succeed based on environmental factors and Black athletes to succeed based on biological factors (Rasmussen *et al.*, 2005, p. 430).

The study of the novice coaches suggests that when White athletes excel in sport, their excellence is not attributed to their race, but when Black athletes do well, this success is seen as being due to a racially endowed talent. As Carrington and McDonald note:

The fact that for most of the 1990s the white English athlete, Jonathan Edwards, broke all known records for the triple jump ... did not lead people to reconsider their mistake in assuming the 'natural' advantages of black athletes. (Carrington and McDonald, 2002, p. 4)

There was no connection made between Edwards' athletic skill and his (White) race. His success was assumed to be the result of hard work. St Louis (2005, p. 114) argues that there is a: 'subtle qualitative hierarchy between the intellectual and physical that exists alongside the material-structural formation of sport'. This hierarchy places the intellectual above the physical and interacts with the racial stereotypes to place White athletes, associated with the intellectual, over Black athletes, associated with the physical. In this way, sport maintains the racial hierarchy that exists in society more generally. The myth of Black competitors being naturally athletic downplays their achievements while reinforcing the racial stereotype that asserts that White competitors are more intelligent and hard-working.

Why do these myths about race and sporting ability persist? There are a number of reasons. Beliefs about race being a biological category are deeply held, and are held in relation to many aspects of social and political life, not just sport, so merely providing information that race is not biological will not be enough to dismantle the beliefs; the myth has acquired the status of common sense (St Louis, 2004). These beliefs are even held by athletes themselves and are reinforced in the ways players and fans behave. William C. Rhoden recalls playing sports as a child: 'The fate of black civilization seemed to rest on every round, every at bat. "Knock his *white* ass out," or "Outrun his *white* ass" ... Or, worst of all: "You let that *white* boy beat you?"' (Rhoden, 2006, p. 14, italics in original). From an early age both White athletes and Black athletes are taught that Black competitors are better at sport, and the athletes internalize this (Rasmussen *et al.*, 2005). The difference in outcomes is not due to actual physical differences, but to the internalized and reinforced belief in physical differences.

Myths about racial difference in sport are also perpetuated through the media and by coaches, parents and athletes (Azzarito and Harrison, 2008). Although individual Black athletes might resist ideas that their sporting success is due to natural talent, White athletes are unlikely to do so, thus maintaining and reinforcing the myths through discourse (Azzarito and Harrison, 2008; Massao and Fasting, 2010). One study found that:

White males, in particular, were more complicit with the maintenance of the racial order in sport, the 'essentialist project of race', which implicitly upholds the construction of 'normal' White masculinity; a masculinity imagined as threatened by the presence of hypermasculine blacks in sport. (Azzarito and Harrison, 2008, p. 361)

While Black male athletes participated in the discourse of being naturally talented at sport, they rejected the idea that they had an advantage.

These myths have very real consequences for Black and White athletes. By situating the achievements of Black athletes as natural, their achievements are also situated as not being as worthy as the achievements of White athletes, which are constructed to be the result of hard work. They perpetuate the idea that Black competitors are 'intellectually inferior to Whites' (Sailes, 1991, p. 485). St Louis argues that there is a mind/body dichotomy in operation in sport that is racialized (St Louis, 2005). Society values the intellectual over the physical, and sport reinforces this hierarchy. So for Black athletes, their participation in sport reinforces stereotypes about their physicality and lack of intellectual prowess, while for White athletes, their participation in sport emphasizes their intellect. This dichotomy makes it difficult for former Black athletes to move into coaching or administrative positions after their sporting careers are over, maintaining White power structures in sport (St Louis, 2005).

MEDIA DISCOURSES OF RACE AND SPORT

The ways race is portrayed in the media have the potential to both reinforce and contest racial stereotypes. Unfortunately, extensive research into media discourses of race in the context of sport suggests that most discussions of race in the media reinforce the dominant beliefs, discussed above, that the sporting success of Black athletes is due to genetically endowed abilities, while the sporting success of White athletes is due to hard work and intelligence (see Bruce, 2004, for a good review of the literature). This is the case in Australia, South Africa, New Zealand, the UK and the US, and it is likely the case in other racialized places as well.

One example of this is television portrayals of Black football (soccer) players in the UK. In one study, although both Black players and White players were portrayed positively by television commentators, Black players were far more likely to be evaluated in physical terms than White players, who were far more likely to be evaluated using psychological descriptions (McCarthy and Jones, 1997). In addition, Black players were much more likely to be described positively in physical terms than White players. White players were also much more likely to be described positively in psychological terms than

Black players (McCarthy and Jones, 1997). While Black players and White players were both portrayed positively, the types of positive portrayals were different by race. Linking Blackness with sporting ability reinforces the stereotype that Black people are better athletes. As McCarthy and Jones note:

> [B]y excessively portraying the Black soccer player in positive physical terms, it is being implied that any success achieved is due to inherent physical advantage the Black player has over the White player ... Consequently, however much success the Black athlete gains, when his or her performance is being associated with natural ability, the implicit suggestion remains that it should be remembered that the White athlete is competing without the natural ability possessed by the Black athlete. Thus, in a bizarre way, the covert suggestion is made that the White athlete is still superior. (McCarthy and Jones, 1997, p. 357)

This study points to the role of expert commentators, who reinforce the dominant stereotypes (McCarthy and Jones, 1997).

There are numerous other examples of media discourses of race and sport that report similar findings. What contemporary racial portrayals of athletes have in common is that they are no longer openly racist, but the ways that the media portray Black and White athletes 'support existing racial hierarchies' (Bruce, 2004, p. 861).

Everyday practices around race reinforce beliefs about and hierarchies of race through a process that Essed (1991) calls 'everyday racism'. Many sports commentators engage in everyday racism in a variety of ways. In a study of American basketball sports commentators, for example, Bruce (2004) found that the commentators, generally White men, were more likely to call Black players but not White players by their first names only, a less respectful form of address. When asked, the commentators said that they found many of the African-American players' first names to be unique and exotic, and, for some, that is why they liked to use them. Foreign names were also exoticized, and foreign players were often given nicknames as their names were thought to be difficult to pronounce. White players' first names were thought to be too normal and not distinct enough to be used on their own (Bruce, 2004). The everyday practice of using first names or nicknames for non-White players positioned them as others, not part of the supposedly normal group whose first names were too uninteresting to use.

This is not to suggest that journalists and others who work in the media are racist, but rather that the media reflects and reinforces existing racial hierarchies in the ways in which it operates, and everyday practices can have racist outcomes, even when that is not the intention (Bruce, 2004; Essed, 1991). The commentators in Bruce's (2004) study suggested that the pressures on them when calling live games led to the racialized patterns in the coverage. Although the practice of calling African-American players and foreign players by first names and nicknames reinforces them as different from White players, for the commentators it was about providing interesting and memorable commentary (Bruce, 2004). In addition, in pressured situations, commentators are likely to invoke dominant ideologies. In the case of race and sport, dominant ideologies situate Black competitors as naturally athletic and White competitors as hard-working and intelligent, and these stereotypes are drawn upon in the heat of the moment.

RACIAL PATTERNS OF SPORTS PARTICIPATION

Myths about racially based sporting abilities are both reflected and reinforced by racialized patterns of sports participation. Many sports are racially segregated. In the major US college and professional sports, such as men's basketball and football (gridiron), there is an overrepresentation of African-American players, while in US swimming and gymnastics there is an overrepresentation of White participants (Sailes, 1991).

At the professional level, some of the most high-profile team sports in the US and the UK are dominated by Black players. In the United States approximately 65 per cent of all professional football (gridiron) players and 80 per cent of professional basketball players are Black, despite African-Americans comprising only 12 per cent of the US population. In the UK, where less than 2 per cent of the population is Black, at least half of the top basketball players, boxers and athletics squad members are Black, and one fifth of professional football (soccer) players are Black (cited in Rasmussen *et al.*, 2005). Black athletes are underrepresented in American Major League Baseball, comprising less than 9 per cent of all players (Associated Press, 2008b).

Individual sports are also racially segregated. If we look at elite sprinting, Black people very much dominate. In examining the Olympic sprint medallists since 1980, we found that there have been no non-Black men's 100m sprint winners in the Olympics, and only one in the 200m sprint. There have been no non-Black winners in the women's 200m sprint since 1980, and just one non-Black winner in the women's 100m sprint, in 2004. Long-distance running events, conversely, have not been dominated by a particular racial group.

Swimming, on the other hand, is a sport that is dominated by White athletes, with very few non-White participants at the elite levels. Indeed, we found that there has been only one non-White medal-winner of the men's 50m freestyle race, and there has not been a non-White Olympic medallist in the men's 100m freestyle race since 1952, when Japan won the silver medal. The only non-White medallist in the men's 200m freestyle race was silver medallist Korean Park Tae-hwan in 2008. On the women's side, four out of the 19 50m freestyle medallists have been non-White: three were Chinese and one was a Black Frenchwoman. The longer distances are dominated even more by White swimmers, with only three non-White medal-winners (all Chinese) of the 100m freestyle race since 1912, and one non-White medallist in the 200m freestyle race (the bronze medal in 2008) since it started running in 1968.

Although many high-profile professional sports are dominated by Black athletes, the majority of sports are actually dominated by White athletes in the West. In particular, White people are more likely to participate in recreational sports than other races. For example, in South Africa and England, White people are more likely to participate in sports than members of other racial groups (Department of Sport and Recreation, 2005; Sport England, 2005). In South Africa, 37 per cent of people classified as White reported participating in sports, compared with 25 per cent of people classified as Africans, 24 per cent of people classified as Asians/Indians and just 15 per cent of people classified as 'Coloured' (Department of Sport and Recreation, 2005). In England, White individuals were 2 per cent more likely to participate in casual sports than the average and Black individuals were 21 per cent less likely to participate in casual sports than the average (Sport England, 2005). In Australia, migrants from non-English speaking countries were less likely to participate in sport than either Australian-born people or migrants from English-speaking countries (ABS, 2007a). In the United States, Black and Hispanic students were more likely to attend schools with low rates of varsity sports participation than White students, giving them fewer opportunities to participate (Johnston et al., 2007). The domination of professional sports by Black players contributes to the continued beliefs in the racial stereotypes of African ancestry leading to athletic ability (Rasmussen et al., 2005) while masking lower levels of recreational sport participation.

Sport is also segregated at the administrative level. While Black athletes dominate the playing positions in many professional sports, White people dominate the boardrooms (Washington and Karen, 2001). In 2010, out of

30 teams in the US National Basketball Association there was only one non-White owner, African-American basketball legend Michael Jordan, owner of the Charlotte Bobcats, who had then recently taken over the ownership. There were no non-White owners of any of the 32 American NFL professional football (gridiron) teams.

Seven of the 30 National Basketball Association teams in the US have Black executives and 12 teams had Black coaches in the 2007 basketball season (Associated Press, 2008a). In 2009 there were only six Black coaches in the NFL. Given the predominance of Black players in both of these sports, one would expect to find more Black coaches and administrators. The statistics in the US are even worse at the college level. In 2008 it was reported that there were only four Black head football (gridiron) coaches in the 119 NCAA (National Collegiate Athletic Association) universities, despite the fact that 55 per cent of student athletes were not White (Associated Press, 2008c). Such forms of segregation indicate patterns of inequality that might relate to positional segregation.

POSITIONAL SEGREGATION

One of the main sites of racial inequality in sport is in the area of positional segregation. Also known as stacking, positional segregation is where particular positions on and off the field are racialized. That is, stacking or positional segregation is a process whereby people are assigned to certain playing or administrative positions on the basis of the beliefs that other people have about mental and physical capacities associated with their race. Stacking has been documented in the United States since at least the 1970s (Loy and Elvogue, 1970).

Research into positional segregation indicates that non-White competitors are more likely to be given positions on the field of play that require muscle and speed, and White competitors are more likely to be given positions that require decision-making. In American football (gridiron), the position of quarterback, the person who calls the play, has historically been predominantly held by White players, whereas tackles are often African-American players (Loy and Elvogue, 1970; Berri and Simmons, 2009). In their early groundbreaking study of positional segregation in baseball, Loy and Elvogue (1970) found that Black athletes were excluded from central positions on the baseball field, and in football (gridiron), Black athletes were excluded from positions where they would have to exercise judgement such as quarterback or linebacker. They argued that the major disadvantage resulting from this positional segregation was a lack of post-playing career opportunities for Black athletes in professional sports (Loy and Elvogue, 1970).

Positional segregation persists today with arguably similar outcomes (Washington and Karen, 2001; Hallinan and Judd, 2009; Massao and Fasting, 2010). In American major league baseball only 3 per cent of pitchers are African-American even though 9 per cent of players are African-American (Associated Press, 2008b). And there is solid evidence that stacking occurs in American NFL football (gridiron), with few African-Americans playing the leadership position of quarterback, and those that do being less likely to get time on the field than White quarterbacks (Berri and Simmons, 2009). The maximum number of Black quarterbacks with a significant amount of playing time in any given year for 32 NFL teams was 11 (Berri and Simmons, 2009). Given that teams have more than one quarterback, and that 65 per cent of NFL players are Black, the number is very low.

In Norway, one of the participants in a qualitative study noted that 'her racial background influenced the positions she was assigned by her former coach' (Massao and Fasting, 2010, p. 153). In Australia, Indigenous Australian Rules football players are thought to be naturally quick on the field and skilful with the ball but they are not thought to be natural leaders (Hallinan and Judd, 2009). So they are often played in the midfield, where they have plenty of opportunities to run and kick, but they are very rarely given leadership roles. Hallinan and Judd quote one of their research participants as describing Indigenous footballers as being 'simple':

> They just lead a simple life, you come round to our place, we go home, you come round next year, I'll give you the best kangaroo steaks, everybody comes to eat, the neighbours smell what I'm cooking and they're there, and you're thinking: Can they become coaches? They live more day-to-day. (Hallinan and Judd, 2009, p. 1228)

This quote is indicative of a pervasive belief that Indigenous peoples do not have leadership qualities and would not be capable of coaching. Stereotypes around Indigenous peoples of this sort are significant barriers in terms of them moving into administrative roles in sport. In this way positional segregation reinforces ideas about the supposedly natural talent of Black athletes while simultaneously limiting their career prospects.

Interestingly, there is no evidence for positional segregation in the NBA (basketball) in the United States (Kahn and Shah, 2005). Similarly, there has previously been on-field positional segregation reported in British football (soccer), Australian rugby (union and league) and other sports, but in recent years this appears to no longer be practised. However off-field positional segregation remains. Coaches and managers are still most likely to be White. In Australia, there are very few opportunities for Indigenous players in football after their playing careers finish (Hallinan and Judd, 2009), and there are no Indigenous head coaches in the Australian Football League (AFL).

There is evidence that stacking occurs at early levels, including high school (Washington and Karen, 2001) and possibly earlier than that. This is not surprising given that the novice coaches discussed above (Rasmussen *et al.*, 2005) buy into negative racial stereotypes about Black athletes, and they are the ones that groom players for particular positions. The position an athlete specializes in has an important impact on their future career, with coaches and sporting administrators tending to be players who previously played in central field positions. Positional segregation by race reserves the central positions for White players, reducing the likelihood that a Black player will move into a coaching position (Hallinan and Judd, 2009).

RACIAL DISPARITIES IN PAY

The best players in the US National Basketball Association are primarily African-American. Black NBA players tend to be drafted higher and to outperform White NBA players. They have better performance statistics, miss fewer games and are selected more frequently for All-Star teams than White players (Kahn and Shah, 2005; McCormick and Tollison, 2001). Despite this, Black players have shorter contracts than White players and, along with that, receive less total compensation than White players (Kahn and Shah, 2005). In their study of player payment differentials in NBA basketball, Kahn and Shah (2005) found that there were three groups of players: rookies, free agents and contracted players. The majority of players were on contracts, and Black contracted players received less compensation overall than White contracted players, despite their better performance. Rookies (who were on union-mandated salaries) and free agents (whose salaries were protected because employers were competing for them) were not compensated differently by race; it was the mid-career contracted players who were disadvantaged. Kahn and Shah (2005) suggest that unions and competition are potentially important in reducing the racial pay differential.

An alternative explanation for racial pay differentials is provided by McCormick and Tollison (2001, p. 203), who argue that 'NBA owners and executives are engaging in price discrimination across classes of players who have different elasticities of supply.' What they suggest is that Black players can be paid less than White players without the numbers of Black players declining. This could be due to Black players having fewer other options outside of sport, possibly due to discrimination. There also appear to be pay disparities in NFL football (gridiron), where Berri and Simmons (2009, p. 40) found 'evidence of performance-related discrimination in compensation' against Black quarterbacks.

At the administrative level, Kahn (2006) found that Black NBA coaches were not subject to racial discrimination in terms of pay (see also Fort *et al.*, 2008). So once Black individuals enter the pro basketball coaching arena, they appear to earn as much as non-Black individuals. This does not appear to be the case for American NFL football (gridiron) coaches, though. Research by Madden (2004) argues that African-American coaches are held to higher standards than White coaches. As noted above, it is more difficult for African-Americans to become a coach because of positional segregation and its accompanying lack of leadership opportunities, which affect the opportunities for Black athletes to enter into the coaching profession after they finish playing. There also appears to be discrimination at the college coaching level. Although the majority of college gridiron players are Black, just 2.5 per cent of American Football Bowl Subdivision college football coaches, the colleges with high-profile football programmes, are Black (Institute for Diversity and Ethics in Sport, 2008). For those who are able to make the move into coaching, African-American coaches appear to need better win–loss records in order to both secure and keep NFL head coaching positions (Madden, 2004).

Although there are racial disparities in pay for both players and coaches, these do not appear to be evenly spread. Some sports are doing better than others along equity grounds in this context.

RACIAL ABUSE

Non-White athletes frequently report experiencing racism in the context of their sport. One of the most common ways racism is experienced is through racial abuse: 'Racial abuse is a form of coercion: it represents, dehumanizes and objectifies its target. Constructed of and through imaginary stereotypes, it protects both fantasies and fears of difference' (Gardiner, 2003, p. 34).

Racial abuse in sport can be directed at players by players, spectators and/or coaching staff (Long, 2000). Research into racial abuse in UK rugby league in the 1990s found that almost half of spectators, one third of all officials and all players had heard racial abuse directed at Black players (Long, 2000). In Norway, one of Massao and Fasting's research participants reported: 'Most of the time it was players from the opposite team who came out with racist slurs. This happens for example when a black player tackled a white player' (2010, p. 155).

Cricket is a sport that, at the professional level, is dominated by England and its former colonies. British colonialism has shaped the racial formations and local understandings of race in its former colonies. In the world of elite cricket, there is a divide between so-called White and Black nations and between England and its former colonies (Farquharson and Marjoribanks, 2006). Racial formations intersect with understandings of nation and power relations between England and its former colonies. For its former colonies, beating England is a particular source of pride as it symbolizes the overcoming of their colonizers (Mills and Dimeo, 2003). Race is central to these symbolic contests.

Debates over racial vilification in Australian cricket in the early 2000s exemplify the intersections of race, sport and nation. In Australia, cricket is a very White sport, with few non-Whites participating, in particular at the professional level, despite the fact that Australia is a multicultural nation. An Australian cricketer was accused of racial vilification in 2003 during a Sri Lankan tour of Australia, when he was heard referring to the Sri Lankan cricket team by a racial epithet. The Sri Lankan team brought a case against the Australian player, and he was suspended from play for a period of time. Media discourses around the racial vilification case reinforced this Black/White divide (Farquharson and Marjoribanks, 2006). However there were also challenges to the way that race and racism were constructed in cricket and the ways race was mobilized as a symbol of inclusion and exclusion. The meaning of race in Australia was actively contested and developed through these discussions of sport and norms around racialized sporting behaviour.

Farquharson and Marjoribanks (2006) found that, while racial vilification is often condemned, it is also frequently explained away or excused. In the case examined, the perpetrator of the racial vilification was framed in the media as being the real victim of the vilification because he was a *White* perpetrator. The implication of the media coverage was that if he had been *Black* and had perpetrated racial abuse, he would not have been punished to the same extent. Discussions of the case argued that this one incident should be excused because, for example, Zimbabwe, a cricket-playing nation, was perpetrating racism across the society and it hadn't been punished (Farquharson and Marjoribanks, 2006). This equating of societal policies with individual behaviour takes the focus away from the outcome of individual behaviour: the discrimination against someone on the basis of their race.

Racial abuse can be directed in a number of ways, and against local minorities as well as foreigners. When racial vilification in Australian Rules football is perpetrated it is usually perpetrated against local Aboriginal players. And racial abuse need not take the form of racial epithets. Long (2000), for example, discussed an incident where the Sri Lankan cricket team was visiting England and the BBC commentator complained about the Sri Lankan names on the grounds that they were difficult to pronounce, singling them out as racial others.

Racial abuse has also been couched both as a sporting tactic that puts opponents off their game and as a joke that Black athletes and supporters have just got to learn to live with (Long, 2000). Sometimes vilified minorities are advised to go ahead and vilify back. The power differences between White people and non-White minority peoples in Western societies mean that a White person vilifying a non-White minority group is much more insulting than a person from a non-White minority background vilifying a White person, and also that White people are enabled to engage in such vilification in a way that is not available to Black people.

As we will see in the chapter on sport and social justice, there is some evidence that policies against racial vilification do have an impact on its practice (Gardiner, 2003). However, although progress has been made, there is still a long way to go in reducing discrimination in sport on the basis of race (Long, 2000).

DISCUSSION POINT

In 2003, Australian cricketer Darren Lehmann racially vilified the Sri Lankan cricket team. Lehmann's reputation as a 'good bloke' (Knox, 2003) shaped media discussions of the vilification case. Malcolm Knox, an opinion writer with the Melbourne newspaper *The Age*, wrote:

> His defenders cannot reconcile his outburst against his Sri Lankan opponents with his reputation as a 'good bloke'. Teammates and associates have described Lehmann's slur as an 'out of character' act, committed 'in the heat of the moment'

by someone who is 'universally regarded as a nice guy'. Instead, it is the Sri Lankans who are rendered villains, oversensitive and unmanly to complain. (Knox, 2003, online)

What does it mean when a 'good bloke' perpetrates racial vilification? Lehmann was found guilty of racial vilification and given a seven-match suspension. Some media reports suggested this punishment was too harsh. What do you think?

WHITENESS

Research into race in sport has largely focused on Black athletes and the challenges they experience, particularly their levels of participation, discrimination in terms of pay disparities, positional segregation and sport as a vehicle for social mobility (Washington and Karen, 2001) rather than on the structures that maintain the system whereby Black athletes are systematically disadvantaged. Research into Whiteness and sport attempts to understand the racial structuring of sport by analysing how sport is structured to benefit White people, and how White people preserve sporting structures that maintain their power position. As Hartmann writes in the context of sport research, there is a need to engage with 'how Whiteness, a whole set of ideologies, discourses, and identities, serves to produce and perpetuate existing racial hierarchies and White domination more specifically' (2007, p. 56). In societies such as Australia, the UK and the US, while Blackness is visible, Whiteness is largely invisible (Hylton, 2009). Whiteness is the norm and White people are the powerful invisible insiders while Black people are the visible other (Hylton, 2009; Long and Hylton, 2002). By engaging with Whiteness, sociologists are able to engage with a key dimension of power in sport.

In their study of Whiteness in cricket and rugby league in the UK, Long and Hylton (2002, p. 93) found that while the athletes they interviewed were readily able to identify 'racially distinct characteristics' of minority groups, they found it difficult to identify the characteristics of White players. Non-White players were characterized as 'ethnic', while Whites, presumably, were not (Long and Hylton, 2002). Long and Hylton (2002) argue that sport is characterized by everyday White privilege. In other words, they argue that White sportspeople can participate in sport with a realistic expectation that if they play well it won't be attributed to their race; that they won't be racially vilified while playing their sport; that if they have a problem the person they complain to will be of their own race; that they won't be asked to be a role model for their race; and that wherever they go to play their sport people will be neutral or positive about them in terms of race. This is not the case for other racial groups. In these and other ways, Whiteness and its powerful role as the norm are reinforced through sport. Sociologists, by engaging critically with everyday assumptions around race, are able to uncover vital components of the power hierarchy within sport, in this case as organized around race.

CONCLUSION

Sport is an important site for political and social struggles around race. The focus in this chapter has been on issues revealing the ways in which sport produces and reproduces dominant understandings and practices around race. Although Black athletes can challenge racial stereotypes and racism in sport, until White athletes and sports administrators also change their perceptions and behaviour, and until the organizations that constitute sport are also changed, racism in sport will continue (Hartmann, 2003). As Massao and Fasting express it: '[S]port is organized around social, economic, cultural and political structures that historically have privileged, and continue to privilege, dominant groups in society, in this case White Norwegian majorities' (2010, pp.158–9). As the discussion through this chapter has shown, such forms of racial privilege and dominance in the context of sport continue to exist in many other societies around the world as well.

CHAPTER SUMMARY

This chapter has shown that:

- Race and racism are central to contemporary experiences of sport across a range of countries and, in this regard, the concept of racial formation provides a meaningful way of engaging with the relationship between sport and race.
- Race is a feature across all dimensions of the organization and practice of sport, from who participates and how and in what sports, through to who takes up leadership positions off the field.
- Media play a crucial role in representations of race in sporting contexts. While there are exceptions, mainstream commercial media coverage tends to reproduce dominant understandings of race.

■ In contexts where White peoples dominate, it is important to study Whiteness in the context of sport, in particular to uncover ways in which unspoken assumptions around race are manifestations of power-based race relations.

DISCUSSION QUESTIONS

1   What does it mean to argue that race is a social construction? Why is this significant in the context of sport? What does it suggest about the relationship between race, genetics, biology and sporting performance?
2   Think of sport in a country that you are familiar with. What role does race play in sport in that country? Is the place of race in sport ever questioned or discussed, or is it a silent issue?
3   Why does it matter how race in sport is represented in the media? How does the media that you consume tend to represent race in sporting contexts?
4   What does the study of Whiteness add to our understanding of the relationship between race and sport? Why is it important to study Whiteness?

FURTHER READING

Carrington, Ben and McDonald, Ian (eds) (2001) *'Race', Sport and British Society*, London, Routledge.
Hallinan, Chris and Judd, Barry (2009) 'Race Relations, Indigenous Australia and the Social Impact of Professional Football', *Sport in Society*, 12(9), pp. 1220–35.
Long, Jonathan and Hylton, Kevin (2002) 'Shades of White: An Examination of Whiteness in Sport', *Leisure Studies*, 21, pp. 87–103.
St Louis, Brett (2004) 'Sport and Common-Sense Racial Science', *Leisure Studies*, 23(1), pp. 31–46.

Chapter 5

Sport, Gender and Sexuality

INTRODUCTION

Gender is a social institution based on masculinity and femininity. Masculinity and femininity are relational; they only exist in contrast to each other in a system of gendered relations (Connell, 1995). Gender differs from sex because it refers to social differences, not physiological ones. Sex refers to physiological sexual characteristics. Sexual orientation, sexuality, refers to homosexuality or heterosexuality, whether one is attracted sexually to those of the same gender (homosexuality) or the opposite gender (heterosexuality). Gender, more broadly, is a social practice that structures our daily lives in terms of power (patriarchy), divisions of labour and sexual desire (Connell, 1995).

Gender, sex and sexual orientation are all popularly thought of as having two main categories (in binary terms). We think of gender as having two categories: men and women. Similarly, we think of sex as having two categories: male and female, and sexual orientation as having two categories: heterosexual and homosexual. The everyday terminology we use – for example, the opposite sex – both reflects and reinforces our binary understanding of these categories. In reality, though, none of these categories is actually binary. Biological sex can be ambiguous, with a person possessing both male and female sexual characteristics. In terms of gender, many men express femininity, and many women express masculinity. And there are a variety of combinations of sex, gender and sexual orientation, such as a person who is biologically female but considers himself a man. This man may be attracted to other men, so may be homosexual. In addition, how masculine or feminine a person appears may or may not be related to their sexual orientation. A feminine man may be heterosexual, and a feminine woman may be homosexual. Similarly, a masculine man may be homosexual and a masculine woman may be heterosexual. Nevertheless, gender categories are socially constructed as social binaries.

Gender, sex and sexual orientation are embedded in and shape all aspects of sport. Entire sports are gendered, particularly at the professional level, but also at junior and recreational levels, where boys and girls, and women and men, are funnelled into playing particular types of sport. There are social rules around the types of play that are socially appropriate for men and women, and the sports that women predominantly participate in tend to be less valued in society than those that men participate in. In this chapter we discuss gender and sport at a variety of levels. The bulk of the research into gender and sport has focused on masculinity and femininity in sport, and on gender equity (Washington and Karen, 2001). In this chapter we examine how sport is structured by gender and argue that it serves to maintain patriarchy and heteronormativity and their associated gender norms around masculinity and femininity.

PATRIARCHY AND THE SOCIAL CONSTRUCTION OF GENDER

The social construction of gender is ideological. An ideology is a value that has a social actor's interest behind it. Ideologies justify the structuring of social relations in particular ways. In the case of gender, the dominant ideologies in many nations are patriarchy and heteronormativity. Patriarchy refers to the dominance of men. Heteronormativity is the process by which society enforces the dominance of heterosexuality.

In the case of gender, patriarchy justifies differences in the treatment of men and women and the lower value accorded to women. By asserting that it is right and normal for men to be in charge, patriarchy also asserts that it is right for women to be subordinate and to be treated accordingly. Patriarchy justifies allocating the bulk of resources to men's activities. In the case of sport, patriarchy means that the dominance of men's professional sports across the full range of sporting activities is not often questioned because it is expected and considered normal that male sports would get a majority of the attention.

Heteronormativity perpetuates the dominance of heterosexuality and the binaries around gender and around sexual orientation that link heterosexuality with masculine men and feminine women. As Elling and Janssens have written, 'Heteronormativity refers to the fact that "real" men and women are considered heterosexual and that according to the "natural" gender order men possess physical, mental and social power over women' (Elling and Janssens, 2009, p. 72). Sport is one of the few areas in contemporary society where male dominance is hardly contested. To the contrary, sport actually lauds the physical power of heterosexual men as a sign of superiority (Messner, 2002). Sporting heteronormativity marginalizes homosexuality while also maintaining gender hierarchies. It interacts with patriarchy to justify the dominance of heterosexual men over women and homosexual men. Understandings of masculine and feminine in many societies around the world are based on heteronormativity, which values the masculine man and feminine woman. Heteronormativity and patriarchy combine to justify hierarchies around masculinity and femininity.

Because of the dominance of these ideologies, gender differences serve to maintain and reinforce inequality in society in general and in sport in particular. To understand why sports are gendered, there is a need to consider them in the context of patriarchy and heteronormativity. The very way in which sport is organized reinforces patriarchy. The types of sport that men and women play, the relative value accorded those sports, and the ways that gender norms and practices structure sport combine to maintain gender hierarchies in sport, which in turn are reinforced by both patriarchy and heteronormativity.

Messner's work on gender and sport helps to describe these hierarchies and how they are maintained. Messner identifies what he calls 'the center of sport':

> The center of sport is where it all starts, a place that serves as symbolic and economic reference point for alternative images and practices. The center is a position occupied by the biggest, wealthiest, and most visible sports programs and athletes. It is a site of domination and privilege. It is the major focal point of the gaze of millions of fans and spectators. We find sport's center at the core of athletic departments in schools and universities, at the locus of the peer status systems among young people, and at the major nodes of sports media. And sport's center is still, by and large, a space that is actively constructed by and for men. (Messner, 2002, p. xviii)

The centre is a heterosexual masculine space that reinforces patriarchal power relations. It is maintained by the structures of sporting institutions, the practices of participants and beliefs about masculinity and femininity, enabling the wealthy heterosexual men who dominate it to maintain their positions of power (Messner, 2002). Sport's centre as a male-dominated space is long-standing and sportspeople are socialized in such a way that it is maintained.

SPORT AND GENDER SOCIALIZATION

There is evidence that we are socialized into our gender from birth. For example, despite being physically the same in terms of height, weight and health, baby boys and baby girls are thought of and treated differently, with girls being encouraged to play cooperative games and boys, but not girls, being encouraged to play competitive games (see Furze *et al.*, 2008, for a discussion of gender socialization). Children are socialized into gender and they are socialized into the gendering of sport both formally and informally from an early age (Messner, 2002). Children's sports teams are mostly gender segregated, and adult roles in children's sports are also organized by gender. So children learn that boys and girls, and men and women, participate differently in both the playing of sports and in their administration.

Sport itself is gender segregated. There are women's sports, and men's sports. Some sports, such as soccer, tennis, golf, swimming and basketball, are played by both men and women (but usually not against each other). Others, such as softball, netball, football, baseball and ice hockey, are very much gendered. Girls are encouraged to play some sports, and boys are encouraged to play others. In the US context, girls are encouraged to play softball, basketball and gymnastics, while boys are encouraged to play football (gridiron), baseball and basketball. Although boys and girls both play basketball and tennis, they play separately, and the games are thought to be quite different. In Australia, boys play various types of football (Australian Rules, rugby union and rugby league, soccer) and cricket, while girls play netball, softball and basketball. Although some girls play football, it is rare for them to take their football playing into adulthood. And although some boys play netball, it remains uncommon. So children are funnelled into the belief that sport is a gendered activity from the first times they encounter it.

The gendering of sport is not just in the playing, it is also in the administration. At the organizational level, men take most of the decision-making roles while women's roles in sports organizations are often the caring and hidden support roles. If men attempt to take on these roles they are ridiculed for it (Shaw, 2007; see also Messner, 2002). Children see this gendered division of sporting labour and learn the expectation that men will be in charge and women will be in supporting roles as the norm, and they carry this through their lives, reinforcing patriarchy.

Patriarchy and heteronormativity are embedded in sporting practices that start in childhood. One way that heteronormativity and patriarchy are reinforced is through locker room talk among boys. Messner (2002) argues that boys and men bond in sports teams through talk that is both homophobic and misogynistic, and the processes around this bonding reinforce sport as a masculine domain where women are not welcome. The most popular boys and men, the team leaders, engage in 'homophobic and misogynistic verbal sparring' (Messner, 2002, p. 36). The language used by boys in sport values a manly form of masculinity, and negatively situates girls/women and less masculine boys/men. Social control occurs in male sporting contexts when team leaders use language that denigrates women (for example, 'You run like a girl') or gay men to criticize the sporting performance of men or boys. Through the use of this type of language, boys and men learn that women and gay men are marginal, that they do not want to be singled out and described as feminine or gay, and that it is appropriate to denigrate women and gay men. Coad (2008) terms this 'jock culture'. Through these processes, which begin in boys' sports and continue in men's sports, particular forms of heterosexual masculinity maintain their place at the centre.

The masculinity of jock culture also contributes to societal violence in general, and normalizes violence against women and gay men in particular (Messner, 2002; Coad, 2008). Locker room talk can lead to groups of athletes actually perpetrating violence against women (Benedict, 2010; Messner, 2002; Benedict and Klein, 1997). Violence is a normal consequence of jock culture (Messner, 2002), and there is evidence that young athletes are more likely to commit violence than non-athletes (Benedict, 2010). Further, athletes who participate in the most central and mainstream of sports, those at the centres of power, are the ones who are most likely to perpetrate violence (Messner, 2002).

GENDER AND EQUITY

In the past, sport simply excluded girls and included boys, thus making the ideological equation of males with athletic power and of females with physical weakness and passivity seem to appear natural. Now with girls involved in sports in great numbers, a more complicated process of differentiation has replaced simple exclusion. (Messner, 2002, p. xxii)

Previous research indicates that there is little gender equity in sports: men's sports get the lion's share of the resources, and women's participation at all levels, as players, coaches and administrators, is much lower than men's (Washington and Karen, 2001). Politically, women's sports are and have been less valued in society, and most sports around the world are constructed as male. Women's sports are less likely to be professional, and if they are they have fewer spectators and sponsors than male professional sports. Access to and participation in sport has been a part of the women's movement since at least the late 19th century, when women claimed the right to participate (Cahn, 1994), but there is still work to be done if equity is to be achieved.

Social institutions around sport maintain the gender order. Because men have been active participants in sport for longer, in many locales they have priority over sporting facilities simply because they were there first. For example, in some places male sports teams have the first pick of sporting fields and locker rooms, and women's sports teams have to make do with what is left over (Messner, 2002). In some places cultural ideas about gender pay equity say that women coaches should earn less than men even if they have better records, simply because women's sports are less valued than men's sports (Messner, 2002). Messner argues that 'People who are operating at the center of the gender regime of sport – athletic directors, men's basketball and football coaches, and male athletes in high-status sports – are enabled and privileged by virtue of their positions in this institutional structure' (Messner, 2002, p. 66).

Since the 1960s there has been an increase in the number of women participating in sports. Nevertheless, women participate less frequently in recreational sports than men do in most places, and their reasons for not participating differ from those of men. For example, in England, 24.2 per cent of men reported regularly (at least three times per week) participating in sport or active recreation, compared with only 18.5 per cent of women (Sport England, 2009). In South Africa the gender differences were even greater, although this was for any participation not just active participation: 43 per cent of South African men said they participated in sport, but only 11 per cent of women did (Department of Sport and Recreation, 2005). Interestingly, Australian men and women appear to participate in sport and physical recreation in similar numbers, with 66 per cent of men and 65 per cent of women having reported participating (ABS, 2007b). The types of recreational sports Australians preferred did vary by gender: walking and aerobics were twice as popular among women as they were among men, while cycling and golf were twice as popular among men as among women.

Table 5.1 (below) shows the reasons why people said they did not participate in recreational sport in South Africa and Australia. The comparison shows that it is important to look at gender equity in sport in its local context. The reasons for non-participation were different in South Africa than in Australia. For example, the most frequent reason why South African women did not participate was because they were not interested. Relatively few said they were not good at sport, that they were injured, that there were no facilities or that transport was an issue, or that sport is dangerous. South African men were more likely to cite injury, time constraints or age as reasons for non-participation than South African women. We have no way

Table 5.1 Reasons for non-participation by gender (per cent), South Africa and Australia

Reason for non-participation	South Africa			Australia		
	Male	Female	Total	Male	Female	Total
Not interested	18.1	28.1	24.6	19.1	19.3	19.2
Age	21.7	19.2	20.1	16.3	17.7	17
No particular reason	14.1	15.8	15.2	*	*	*
Time constraints	14	11.2	12.2	35.9	35.2	35.5
Opportunities/facilities not available in community	9.7	11.2	10.7	*	*	*
I am not good at sport	8.2	6.3	7	*	*	*
Health/injury/disability	9.1	4.9	6.4	18.7	17.1	18
Other	2.5	1.9	2.1	1.1	2.9	2
Financial constraints	1.6	1.1	1.2	0.9	1.3	1.1
To play sport is dangerous	0.5	0.2	0.3	*	*	*
Transport problems	0.5	0.1	0.2	*	*	*
Already active	*	*	*	8	6.5	7.2
Total	100	100	100	100	100	100

Note: *Question not asked.
Sources: Compiled from Department of Sport and Recreation (2005, p. 7) and ABS (2007b). Australian data from 2005–06. South African data from 2005.

of knowing from this data why women were less interested in participating than men in South Africa. However, the fact that they indicated they were not interested may reflect local social norms around women participating in recreational sport.

Gender differences for non-participation were much smaller for Australia. The differences for all of the indicators listed were relatively small, no more than 2.5 per cent. The most common reason for not participating was time constraints, with over a third of respondents choosing that as their main answer. This is different from South Africa, where fewer listed time as a barrier. This might be due to survey design, as Australians did not have several of the choices South Africans had on their survey. There was more information on types of time constraints in the Australian survey, and there was a gender difference there: Australian men cited time spent at work/study as their major time barrier (27.5 per cent said that was a reason, compared with 18.8 per cent of women), while Australian women reported insufficient time due to family (15.3 per cent, compared with 7.6 per cent of Australian men). So although the overall proportion who cited time constraints was similar, the reasons for the time constraints varied by gender.

SPORT AND SEXUALITY

Sport both reflects and reinforces norms of masculinity and femininity (and patriarchy and heteronormativity) in society. As Elling and Janssens write, 'Since male homosexuality is associated with femininity and mainstream competitive sports with hegemonic masculinity, gay men are regarded as generally unsuited to sports, and to team sports like football in particular' (Elling and Janssens, 2009, p. 72). Conversely, lesbians, being associated with masculinity, are perhaps expected to play sports (Elling and Janssens, 2009). Because sport is so gendered, individuals, particularly boys, who transgress its gender boundaries are sanctioned. Men who participate in female-dominated sports are often marginalized and have their sexuality questioned. For example, American Olympic figure skater Johnny Weir has repeatedly had his sexuality questioned. Those who do not match conventional gender roles and norms around masculinity, femininity and heterosexuality are considered deviant. According to Coad, 'In sports culture, nonnormative sexualities are highly problematic, since sports sex is synonymous with heterosexism and homophobia' (2008, p. 9).

Masculinity and femininity have different associations in sport. Sport encourages a type of hegemonic masculinity that is hypermasculine and actively denigrates feminine men. So for gay men, participating in mainstream men's sport means interacting in a homophobic culture. Manliness is celebrated, and feminine men are likely to be marginalized. It is interesting that, while heterosexuality is virtually compulsory in men's team sport, much of the bonding that occurs involves physical intimacy on the field and in the locker rooms. It is as though in order to freely express their intimacy physically, sportsmen need to be assured that those they are intimate with in this context would not construe that intimacy as sexual. Coad (2008, p. 17) describes this as 'the great paradox of jock culture' which 'is that while subscribing to heteronormativity, it keeps women at bay and keeps the boys together.'

The dominance of heteronormativity in the locker room means that gay athletes who participate in team sports are very unlikely to come out (Coad, 2008). According to Coad (2008), only six professional American sportsmen have ever come out as homosexual, and all did so after they had retired. In the UK, Justin Fashanu, a British footballer (soccer player) came out publicly in 1990, Welsh rugby union and league player Gareth Thomas did so in 2009, and English cricketer Steven Davies did likewise in 2011 (BBC Sport, 2011). The only Australian professional footballer to have come out as gay was rugby league player Ian Roberts, who did so in the 1990s (Australian Story, 2005).

In 2010 there was discussion of homosexuality in Australian Rules football, which resulted in a senior player, Jason Akermanis, saying that he didn't believe gay football players should come out. In an article for a local newspaper, Akermanis argued that if a current player came out as gay it could 'break the fabric of a club' (Akermanis, 2010). He said that locker room nudity was a part of everyday life in football clubs and having an openly gay player would make that uncomfortable, putting pressure on both the gay player and the rest of the club. Akermanis's article was about jock culture and its homophobia. Although there was a great deal of discussion about the issue, no professional Australian Rules football players has come out as homosexual as a result of the discussion.

On the other hand, a number of sportsmen have come out as heterosexual. Heterosexual outings are where players publicly assert their heterosexuality, usually after rumours that they might be gay (Coad, 2008). These outings serve to reinforce heteronormativity by suggesting that sportspeople do not want to be associated with homosexuality and those who are must actively dispute the association. In doing so, the outings contribute to misogyny and homophobia (Coad, 2008).

Metrosexuality, men expressing their feminine side through their appearance, has become increasingly common in elite sport (Coad, 2008). Successful sportsmen such as the swimmer Ian Thorpe and the footballer (soccer player) David Beckham epitomize the metrosexual, with their interest in clothes and grooming, and with their attractive bodies (Coad, 2008). Coad sees metrosexuality as a challenge to heteronormativity because it enables both women and men to be associated with power and with passivity, distinguishing masculinity from heterosexuality. This claim is contestable. One of the key points about metrosexual athletes is their overt heterosexuality. Ian Thorpe, for example, has come out as heterosexual repeatedly in the face of questions about his sexuality due to his metrosexual appearance and interest in fashion (Jeffery, 2009). David Beckham is able to be seen with his glamorous and beautiful wife, Victoria Beckham, and his children, which operates as a marker of his heterosexuality (Cashmore, 2002). For both Thorpe and Beckham, being metrosexual is being heterosexual. Although metrosexuality may allow male athletes to show a feminine side, it does not challenge the expectation that they be heterosexual.

The gender dynamics around sexuality are different for women. Because sport has long been constructed as a masculine pursuit, sportswomen are constructed as not feminine. Perhaps in response to this, women's sport sometimes highlights the femininity of their participants rather than their athleticism. For example, the Women's National Basketball Association (WNBA) in the United States, a professional women's basketball league, is portrayed in the media in such a way that the players' femininity is emphasized. After games the players are shown with their children, reinforcing their roles as heterosexual women and mothers; they are also often shown out of their uniforms, made up and accessorized (Muller, 2007). Male basketballers are not portrayed in the same way.

As with men in female-dominated sports, women in male-dominated sports also have their sexuality questioned. This is because they, just by their participation in masculine sports, are challenging hegemonic masculinity in the sporting arena (Russell, 2007). Women who participate in male-dominated sports, such as rugby union or league, are constructed as masculine or 'butch', linking their sporting prowess with homosexuality (Russell, 2007, p. 107). There is no evidence to suggest that women athletes are more likely to be homosexual than any other women. That they are portrayed that way operates as a means of discouraging female participation in sports and maintaining hegemonic masculinity by representing women athletes as sexually deviant. Athletic success is associated with masculinity, and successful women athletes are often likened to men (Cahn, 1994).

Compulsory heterosexuality is also reinforced through the social construction of desire. Wedgwood (2008) argues that the female sexual desire for sportsmen contributes to the maintenance of the patriarchal gender order. Female sports groupies, although assertive in their expressions of heterosexual desire for sportsmen, are subordinate to the men they pursue. The men have the power to choose, use and discard these women, while the women do not. Research into why women become sports groupies suggests they are attracted by the trappings of money, power and fame that come from being associated with elite sportsmen (Wedgwood, 2008). Those women who actually marry elite sportsmen find that their domestic work supports their husbands' careers to the detriment of their own, as they often have to travel and relocate due to their husbands' work (Wedgwood, 2008). One area where wives and girlfriends often accommodate sportsmen is by tolerating institutionalized adultery. This tolerance 'helps to preserve male privileges' (Wedgwood, 2008, p. 315), perpetuating a sexual double standard around fidelity and maintaining women's subordinate position.

Very few studies have looked at differences in sports participation by sexuality. It is difficult to get information on athletes' sexual orientations, so this is a difficult area in which to do research. One study of sexual orientation in sports participation, conducted in the Netherlands, found that sexuality was linked with sports participation, with mainstream sports clubs being less popular among homosexual men than they were among heterosexual men, while homosexual men were more likely to attend fitness clubs than heterosexual men (Elling and Janssens, 2009). The authors, Elling and Janssens (2009), attributed the popularity of fitness clubs among gay men to a gay subculture that values muscular bodies. They further suggested that mainstream sporting subculture and its homophobia are disincentives for gay men to participate in team sports. Given the dearth of research in this area, further research is needed into how sexuality impacts on sports participation.

The research discussed above indicates that heteronormativity is a dominant organizing principle of sports. Jock culture, organized around heteronormative principles, perpetuates the marginalization of both women and homosexuals in sporting contexts. It also likely prevents homosexual athletes from disclosing their homosexuality.

BODILY SEX VERSUS GENDER: POLICING GENDER BOUNDARIES IN WOMEN'S SPORT

In 2009, Caster Semenya, the winner in the 800m race at the Berlin World Championships, had her sex questioned. Semenya, a powerfully built young South African woman who seemed to emerge from nowhere to start winning international races, was accused of being a man. Semenya's gender is clearly female, she identifies as a woman. The issue was whether she might have biological advantages over other women because of her sexual characteristics (Levy, 2009).

Gender boundaries are strongly policed in sport, especially women's sport. There are physical differences between men and women that are believed to advantage men in sport: men are stronger and bigger than women. Because of this, women's sport in particular is concerned to prevent men from participating as they would be expected to have an unfair edge, making women unlikely to win. So while men's sport does not necessarily check the sex of participants, women's sport particularly attempts to ensure that men do not participate. This has meant that women who play sport may be subjected to sex testing.

Sex testing is not as straightforward as it might seem. This is because sex itself is not as straightforward as it might seem. The goal of sex testing is to ensure that only women participate in women's sports. However, the markers that indicate whether a person is female or male are not always clear. Levels of 'male' and 'female' hormones are variable and a person might quite normally have high testosterone or low oestrogen. For example, a person might have complete Androgen Insensitivity Syndrome (cAIS), where they are genetically male, but develop externally as female because the body does not process androgens. This person would not get any particular athletic benefit from being 'male', in fact she would have lower testosterone, the hormone thought to give athletic advantage, than other women (Dreger, 2010). So genetic sex testing would disadvantage a woman with this condition. A woman with cAIS would probably not have her sex questioned unless she was performing particularly well. Her genetic status would most likely be discovered through routine genetic testing. Because of cAIS, sports officials have stopped using chromosome testing to indicate sex (Dreger, 2010).

Other conditions such as adrenal abnormalities and partial Androgen Insensitivity Syndrome (pAIS) further complicate matters. Women with adrenal tumours or other adrenal abnormalities might naturally have very high levels of androgens. PAIS occurs when a baby is designated a girl because of the appearance of female genitals, but who has a condition whereby they have internal testes, and these testes develop normally at puberty, sending out testosterone and masculinizing the girl's appearance (Dreger, 2010). It is also not clear what levels of androgens are 'normal' for women and men. Women without any complicating conditions exhibit a range of levels of testosterone, as do men. If a woman did have unusually high levels of androgens, Dreger (2010), a scholar who has long studied issues around atypical sex, asks: should she be allowed to use drugs to reduce them in order to compete in sport? Conversely, should a woman with cAIS be allowed (or even encouraged) to take supplements to get her testosterone up to a 'normal' level? Dreger (2010) points out that otherwise healthy men with low testosterone are already permitted to use testosterone supplements for sport. The ambiguities around sex make sex testing problematic. Given these various scenarios, the dividing line between women and men is far from apparent. If there are no definitive markers of sex, it is impossible to make concrete determinations about which sex a person belongs to.

Men athletes are not subject to the same bodily controls over their participation as women. That healthy men with low testosterone should be allowed to use supplements to improve their sports performance is not problematized. Yet women athletes who might have naturally high testosterone are very much constructed as a cause for concern. We can relate this back to patriarchy and the marginalization of women in sports. The idea that women might chemically enhance their sporting prospects could threaten male dominance of sport. It would lead to questions about why sports are gender segregated, whether it is appropriate to maintain gender segregation and about the right of women to participate in sport on an equal footing with men.

Related to that is heteronormativity, which values feminine women and masculine men. High levels of testosterone, even when they occur naturally, lead to a masculine appearance. In discussions of Semenya, she was described as: 'breathtakingly butch. Her torso is like the chest plate on a suit of armor. She has a strong jaw line, and a build that slides straight from her ribs to her hips' (Levy, 2009, p. [2]). Her appearance was regularly masculinized in press reports, likening her to a man and raising questions about her femininity. Nevertheless, someone may look like Caster Semenya, but not have any athletic advantages (Levy, 2009).

Women who perform particularly well, like Caster Semenya, are the ones most likely to have their sex questioned. As Cahn writes, 'Highly skilled female athletes continue to meet with profound scepticism. At times, not only their femininity but their biological sex comes into question' (Cahn,

1994, p. 2). Semenya was raised as a girl, believed she was a woman and her genitals appeared to be female. Despite this, perhaps because of her sporting achievements and her somewhat masculine appearance, her sex was questioned.

Given the ranges of 'normal' and the difficulties in determining one's sex, Dreger (2010, p. 24) suggests that rather than sex testing a better policy would involve gender verification, meaning that anyone who was raised as a girl could play as a woman. The reality is that there are a variety of physiological advantages that individuals bring to sport. Hormones may be one of them, although it is unclear exactly what advantage extra testosterone provides.

Framing sporting success as being due to an unfair biological advantage diminishes that success. It downplays the hard work of the athlete, and also the other variables that might contribute to an athlete's success. It is a similar process to the one whereby athletes of African descent are erroneously believed to be 'naturally' better at sport than those of other backgrounds.

DISCUSSION POINT

In the context of the Caster Semenya case, Lord Sebastian Coe, a former elite athlete and at the time of the case a Vice-President of the IAAF (International Association of Athletics Federations), commented that a solution to controversies around sex verification required a two-part response. First, the IAAF should have the power to stop an athlete temporarily from competing when testing had not been completed, but where there may be an issue around the athlete's sex. Second, there needs to be open debate. Coe was quoted as saying:

> One of the problems we had was that we don't actually have a mature or open discussion about this ... This has been the taboo, not just in track and field or in sport; it is a societal taboo ... You want to protect the confidentiality of the athlete, but we were doing it against the backdrop of a subject that frankly no one really wants to discuss in an open or sensible way. It is the kind of conversation that you have tucked away in corners of offices. There needs to be a broader discussion here. We have to get away from the elephant in the room. (Coe, quoted in Slot, 2009)

What are the key issues raised by the Semenya case? What do they suggest about the relationship between sport, sex and gender? What do you make of Coe's suggested solutions? Do you think his approach would adequately address the questions raised by such cases? Given the discussion in this chapter, is it possible to arrive at definitive answers around the sex of an individual? What are the consequences of your answer for our understanding of the relations between gender, sex and sporting competition?

INTERSECTIONS: RACE, GENDER, SEXUAL ORIENTATION

Although little research has concentrated on how race and gender intersect in sporting contexts, it is clear that beliefs about racial prowess interact with gender norms in sport (Carrington, 1988). In the US context, while Black men are constructed as over-athleticized, Black women are virtually invisible in the media (Hardin *et al.*, 2004). Black women are also de-feminized, as they do not meet White American standards of feminine beauty (Hardin *et al.*, 2004). Black women are believed to be more naturally athletic than White women – this places them as less feminine – and the sports they dominate are also framed as more culturally masculine (Hardin *et al.*, 2004). Beliefs about race and gender, then, intersect in sport to reinforce the place of heterosexual White men at the centre of sport.

CONCLUSION

This chapter has analysed gender and sport, focusing on how patriarchy and heteronormativity organize it so that men's sport has and keeps the bulk of prestige, resources and power. Norms around how boys and girls participate in sport continue to maintain patriarchy in the sporting context. Heteronormativity values the masculine man and the feminine woman, calling into question the achievements of masculine women, while also overtly vilifying and marginalizing feminine men.

How might we alter the gender ideologies that structure sports? These ideologies are embedded in sports at all levels and are seemingly difficult to shift. A first step, which can be implemented in everyday life, might be paying attention to the language we use and not using language that denigrates girls and women, femininity, or homosexuality. Telling boys that they need to 'go out there and play like a man' is telling both boys and girls that it is not okay to play like a boy, a girl or a woman.

CHAPTER SUMMARY

This chapter has shown that:

■ Gender relations in sport are shaped by the ideologies of patriarchy and heteronormativity, which influence how children are socialized into sport, how sport is divided by gender, and how sport is valued in society.

■ In examining gender equity in sport, while women's participation has increased, men's sports still get most attention and resources. Around the world sports participation varies by gender.

■ Sex testing in sport is a particular concern of women's sport. It is structured so that women who do particularly well or who are masculine in appearance are singled out, marginalizing both high achieving women, and women who challenge heteronormativity in their appearance.

■ Gender intersects with other social categories, so that Black men and women experience sport differently from White men and women. It also intersects with ideas of nation and belonging, which are discussed in Chapter 6.

DISCUSSION QUESTIONS

1 Which sports do you automatically associate with men? With women? Why do you think that is the case? How would a sociologist explain these associations?

2 How might a sociological analysis of gender and sports contribute to improving gender equity?

3 This chapter has shown that jock culture, particularly locker room talk, contributes to heteronormativity. Discuss the processes by which language reinforces gender and sexuality norms.

4 Think of a sport you are familiar with or have played. Was the locker room culture similar to the jock culture described in this chapter? How did that culture structure player participation?

FURTHER READING

Coad, David (2008) *The Metrosexual: Gender, Sexuality, and Sport*, Albany, State University of New York Press.

Dreger, Alice (2010) 'Sex Typing for Sport', *Hastings Center Report*, 40(2), pp. 22–4.

Elling, Agnes and Janssens, Jan (2009) 'Sexuality as a Structuring Principle in Sport Participation: Negotiating Sports Spaces', *International Review for the Sociology of Sport*, 44(1), pp. 71–86.

Messner, Michael A. (2002) *Taking the Field: Women, Men, and Sports*, Minneapolis, University of Minnesota Press.

Chapter 6

Sport, National Identity and Nation-Building

INTRODUCTION

Sports and nation are very much connected. As Rowe (2003, p. 285) argues, 'there are few sports that have not – either voluntarily or under duress – been aligned with some conception of nation'. Expressions of nation and nationalism are often played out through sports at local, national and global levels. For example, when the national anthem is played at a sporting event, a sense of nation is evoked, solidifying the idea that those in attendance are a national unity. At local and national levels, ideas of the nation are reinforced when the flag is flown, and when local athletes aspire to represent the national team in their sport. Representing one's nation is the pinnacle of success in many sports. Meanwhile, for supporters, any success achieved by their national team is often understood to be a more general reflection of the status of the nation itself, and of the place of the nation and of the individual supporter in the global context. At the same time, however, it is important to note that these forms of inclusion also carry with them forms of exclusion. By identifying certain people as belonging, other people are identified as not belonging. As such, relations between the nation and sport involve important fault lines, both between and within nations.

The concepts of nation, state, nation-state, nationalism and nation-building are defined in this chapter. The evidence presented in this chapter suggests that sport is an important but contested vehicle for nation-building, providing numerous opportunities for nations to reinforce their sense of identity and invoke national pride, while at the same time also providing a space in which counter-narratives may emerge. Part of this discussion considers the question of whether sport strengthens or weakens national sentiment, while the chapter also explores debates around the relationship between globalization, nationalism and the nation in the context of sport, considering whether or not globalization influences the importance of the nation in sport. Overall, the analysis in this chapter shows the importance of a sociological approach to sport that considers relationships between different dimensions of the nation and the power processes that are integral to those relationships.

NATIONS, STATES AND NATION-STATES

When we think of nations we most often think of nation-states. A state is a territory with a single structure for government. This structure consists of a political system, which includes a parliament and a civil or public service, as well as other institutions such as the armed forces; and a legal system, which includes the court system and the police. The authority of the government is backed up by this legal system, which the government can use to enforce law and order (Furze *et al.*, 2008).

However, we can also consider these concepts in a somewhat different manner, where the emphasis is less on formal structures and more on shared understandings. Anthony Smith, a leading scholar of nations, defines a nation as 'a named human population sharing an historic territory, common myths and historical memories' (quoted in Hawkins, 2006, p. 9). By this definition, states could include multiple nations. Also, by this definition, many nations would not have states. The nations of Wales, England and Scotland are part of the British state, and the First Nations peoples of Canada and the Indigenous peoples of Australia are nations without their own states.

Combining the definitions of nation and state, we can define the nation-state as a state with some sort of national history. It is 'a body of people occupying one territory, organized under one sovereign government, and who share both legal rights and duties, as well as institutions, ideas, and culture' (Hawkins, 2006, p. 83). By this definition, nation-states can have multiple nations within them, but they are a form of umbrella identity.

Further to these arguments, Benedict Anderson (1991) suggested that we can think of nations as 'imagined communities', communities that exist because as a collective we believe them to exist. Nations are imagined because no one in a nation expects to know everyone else personally; however, in each person's mind is the idea that they have their nation in common, 'the image of their communion' (Anderson, 1991, p. 6). Such images are frequently represented through symbols such as national flags; war memorials; in Australia, kangaroos; and in the United States, bald eagles. In sporting contexts, such symbols are also often used to represent national teams. The three lions that appear on the shirts of national teams representing England are a famous example of this, even celebrated in songs such as 'Three Lions', a song originally released as the anthem for the English football (soccer) team in the 1996 UEFA European Football Championship.

Nations are imagined in particular ways, as self-governing or sovereign, limited and as a gathering of equals (Anderson, 1991). Nations all have boundaries and only exist in relation to other nations. No single nation encompasses all of humanity. Nations are also not necessarily unified. They may have internal conflicts between different ethnic, religious, regional, or other groups that are managed within the national umbrella. Nations, then, are the outcome of contested processes where economic, political and symbolic forms of power are mobilized to include and exclude individuals and groups (Anderson, 1991; Anthias and Yuval-Davis, 1992; Gilroy, 1992; Houlihan, 1997; Marx, 2003).

Nation-building refers to the processes through which nations develop and reinforce their national identities. Nations are what their citizens imagine them to be, and nation-building occurs not only through political and economic processes, but also in cultural and symbolic contexts, such as through sport. Ideas of nation are actively reinforced through discourses, such as through the stories that nations tell of themselves, the communal rituals they perform, and the images and other symbols that they hold dear (Hogan, 2003). For example, many Australians reinforce their sense of nation every year on Anzac Day (Hawkins, 2006). Anzac Day, 25 April, is a day of remembrance for those who died in war, particularly in World War I, but also in subsequent wars. Australians observe Anzac Day across the country by attending a dawn service in memory of soldiers lost in war, followed by a parade of ex-soldiers through the town or city (AWM, 2010). The parade is often followed by social events, with many participants gathering to watch the Anzac Day football match, either on a television, or by going to the game. Here, the sporting event is important in itself, but is also significant as being seen to be representative of a critical moment in the history of the nation.

Sport was also a significant site of nation-building when, in post-apartheid South Africa in the 1990s, President Nelson Mandela and Archbishop Desmond Tutu were able to transform the Springbok emblem that adorned the shirts of the national rugby union team from being a symbol of White dominance to becoming a symbol of a new non-racial South African nation (Farquharson and Marjoribanks, 2003). From a more historical perspective, C. L. R. James, in his book *Beyond a Boundary* (1993), revealed how an engagement with cricket could provide insights into the colonial politics of the Caribbean, and into the struggles of the West Indian peoples for liberation from British colonial domination. In examples such as these, sport becomes a site for imagining and reimagining the nation, thereby contributing to nation-building processes.

Nationalism refers to a feeling of identification with and a sense of loyalty to one's nation. Feelings of nationalism can call people to action, and sport can inspire nationalism. In particular, sport is an opportunity for participants and spectators to express their commitment to their nation (Bairner, 1996). The kinds of nationalism that sport inspires can vary. On the one hand, when one nation competes against another nation, sport can be a unifying influence for the supporters of a particular nation. On the other, sport can also highlight internal divisions within a nation, 'providing an important channel for the expression of alternative nationalist sentiments' (Bairner, 1996, p. 315). For example, Catalan football (soccer) supporters have used football games involving the Spanish national team as a venue for expressing a regional identity that contrasts with what they see as the unjust dominance of Madrid in Spanish political and economic affairs. Further to this, in some contexts, sport becomes a site through which conflicts between nations are expressed as, for example, when supporters of different nations clash with each other, sometimes through chants and symbols, and sometimes through the use of physical violence.

DISCUSSION POINT

Sport can be used in some contexts as a means to promote forms of nation-building that create a sense of national belonging and inclusion among members of the nation. In other contexts, however, sport may operate to exacerbate pre-existing conflicts, or even to create new conflicts. For example, the success of the Australian men's cricket team in international competition is frequently represented in Australia as a positive reflection on Australian society as a whole. At the same time, the continued domination of elite men's cricket in Australia by White Anglo men is problematic in the context of a multicultural and multiracial nation in terms of processes of exclusion and inclusion. And, further, while both the men's and women's national teams are very successful, it is the men's team that gains the overwhelming majority of attention and praise in the context of nation-building.

In the context of a nation with which you are familiar, can you think of positive and negative examples of the relationship between sport and nation-building? What role do you think sport plays in nation-building processes? Should it play such a role?

GLOBALIZATION, SPORT AND NATION

While the nation and the nation-state, and associated concepts, have been central to sociology and to sport, in more recent times, debates around globalization, by which is meant the 'increasing interconnectedness of societies' (Macionis and Plummer, 2008, p. 40) around the world, have raised questions about the continuing relevance of the nation-state. Such questions have arisen both at a theoretical level, and in terms of seeking to understand everyday experiences around sport. In particular, debate arises around the purpose of the nation-state in a globalized world. On one side of the debate are those who argue that globalization has led to a weakening of the nation-state. Giddens (1999) has gone so far as to call the nation-state a 'shell institution', one that looks the same on the outside but is hollow on the inside. He argues that the global and the local are now the important levels of governance, while the nation-state is becoming less relevant and is no longer able to fulfil many of the functions it used to carry out. From this perspective, globalization has reduced the significance of the nation. On the other side of the debate are those who argue that nations remain important and that, while globalization may be occurring, it is not the revolutionary process that many believe it to be. From this view, nations remain critical as sites for the organization of political and social activity.

In sport, there is a similar debate. There are those who argue that '[n]ationalism and globalization are intertwined' (Lee and Maguire, 2009, p. 8). From this view, the local and the national are transformed by global culture, but the relationship is not necessarily straightforward. In particular, globalization processes can strengthen, weaken, or broaden national and local culture (Lee and Maguire, 2009). On the other side of the debate are those who argue that sports nationalism is countering globalization (Rowe, 2003). Indeed, sport may be 'seen as stubbornly resistant to the "harder" forms of globalization because of its dependency on the robustness of the *idea* of the sporting nation' (Rowe, 2003, p. 285). In other words, while globalization may be occurring in many social and political contexts, and may be challenging the nation in those contexts, the nation remains a critical site in sport, both for participants and for supporters. These varying viewpoints suggest the importance of sport as a site for investigating the extent to which globalization does result in the transformation of the nation (Rees, 1996). As such, this is an example of the more general sociological argument that it is important to consider sport as intimately connected to broader societal processes, and as an activity that can have an influence on how those societal processes emerge and are transformed over time.

For international sport to exist, nations must also exist as a basis for competition. So it is in the interest of at least three parties – nations, sports and the corporations that sponsor sports – for sport to reinforce the idea of nations, nation-building and nationalism. For example, without nations, an event such as the Olympic Games would be completely different. While alternatives may be imaginable, such as athletes competing as individuals or competing for corporate organizations, as in the Tour de France bicycle race or in Grand Prix motor racing, such versions of the Olympic Games would have a completely different feel and meaning, and would involve radically different forms of organization. In other words, although many sports operate in a global context, and involve global corporations and international movements of competitors, they also require nations in order to exist and to have the meanings we commonly associate with them.

Denationalization and the global movement of athletes

A question that sociologists ask about sport in the context of debates around the relationship between globalization and the nation is whether sport is contributing to denationalization. Related to the idea that nations are now shell institutions (Giddens, 1999), denationalization refers to the incorporation of the global into what was previously considered national (Sassen, cited in Poli, 2007). In other words, formerly nation-based processes and practices become connected into global processes and practices. In the sporting context, to give one example through which processes of denationalization may be occurring, the global sports labour market provides incentives for athletes, particularly those from developing nations, to ply their trades in elite leagues outside of their home nations (Poli, 2007). One of the issues that this global movement of sportspeople raises is that those athletes who have migrated may be faced with the decision of which nation to compete for, either their country of origin or their country of adoption. Although individuals can be dual nationals, in the sporting context a person cannot be loyal to more than one team, they must choose. In some cases, this means that an athlete who was born in one country may take out citizenship in another country, if permitted, so that they can compete for that nation. For example, a number of cricket players born and raised in South Africa have taken out British citizenship and subsequently competed for England, without having previously competed for South Africa. An athlete may also compete for their country of birth, subsequently move and take out citizenship in another country, and then compete for that nation. Merlene Ottey, the highly successful Olympic athletics sprint champion, for example, competed for many years for Jamaica, before moving to Slovenia, becoming a Slovenian citizen and competing for that country (Chandler, 2010).

Related to these general processes, an athlete who is selected to represent a new country can, according to Poli, contribute to a 'de-ethnicization of the nation in sport' (Poli, 2007, p. 654), which Poli also refers to as a form of denationalization. Poli (2007, p. 654) defines the de-ethnicization of sport as 'the progressive disconnection between the geographical origin of sportsmen [*sic*] and the nation states that they are supposed to represent according to the traditional conception of the nation as a homogenous ethnic and cultural entity'. Embedded in this traditional conception of the nation as a monocultural entity is the idea that the presence of migrants weakens national identities. In the following sections we will explore this issue further by discussing the ways in which athletes are geographically mobile while considering the idea that migrant athletes can contribute to the de-ethnicization of national sports teams.

Professional athletes often relocate to pursue their sports (Elliott and Weedon, 2011; Magee and Sugden, 2002). Teams in the leading European football (soccer) leagues, for example, sign up the best footballers from around the world, and are able to do so because of their financial resources and because of the high standard of play, which is attractive to players. Footballers who play in the leading European leagues benefit from the standard of competition personally and the nations that they represent may also benefit from their improved play when they select them to represent the nation in international competitions. Interestingly, as this suggests, while footballers from around the world aspire to play European football at a club level, most who do move to Europe from elsewhere maintain their affiliations with their countries of origin. For example, Didier Drogba has been a football player at Chelsea in England for many years, but still represents the Cote D'Ivoire, while Lionel Messi, a superstar of the game, plays for FC Barcelona in the Spanish League, La Liga, but represents Argentina at the national level. In other words, while players may be mobile in terms of their professional careers, elite players still tend to represent their country of origin at the international level. Indeed, for many such players, representing their country is an important means through which they keep a connection with their homeland even as they earn a living in an often distant nation. In such contexts, it may be possible to see a process of de-ethnicization occurring at the club level connected to the international movement of players, as clubs become multiracial and multiethnic, which in turn has the potential to influence understandings of the nation, and of who is seen as belonging. In this regard, denationalization may in fact be better understood as a reconfiguration of the nation to include greater diversity. This is, however, a contested process, as often such players continue to be seen as foreigners – for example, by supporters, other players and the media – no matter how long they play in a different country. Further, at the level of the national team, such a process of de-ethnicization does not occur unless mobile players shift their allegiances and represent their new country.

In contrast to team sports such as football (soccer), tennis is a sport where individuals primarily compete in private competitions for themselves, but may also represent their nations both as individuals and in team competitions, such as the Davis Cup and the Federation Cup. Tennis players are renowned for travelling globally for most of the year, living out of their suitcase, and some, such as former Australian tennis star Pat Rafter who lived in Bermuda, maintain tax homes outside of their official national affiliation. Nevertheless, they are associated with their nations of origin when they compete. Rafter's Australianness has never been questioned. Indeed, he is celebrated as an Australian success story and is embraced in Australia, even to the point of being an advertising figure for the iconic Australian underwear brand, Bonds. While Rafter lived and worked internationally as a professional athlete, he has remained Australian in the eyes of the public (Merritt, 2001).

The case of Jelena Dokic, a Serbian migrant to Australia and professional tennis player, highlights some of the flexibility around national origin that athletes may have (John, 2009; Newman, 2009). Dokic moved to Australia as a child, where she pursued a professional tennis career and represented Australia. After some difficulties, at age 17 she elected to represent Yugoslavia, and then Serbia and Montenegro nationally, which she did for five years; then she became Australian again. In terms of de-ethnicization, could Dokic's representation of Australia be considered part of a process of de-ethnicization? When can one genuinely claim to be a particular nationality? These processes are not straightforward. Dokic went to Australia as an eight-year-old child, and was educated there. Nevertheless, she had Balkan roots. As such, she could lay claim to both Australian and Serbian ethnicity. In countries such as Australia, where a large proportion of the population are migrants, the idea that having migrants on a national team might de-ethnicize the nation does not make sense, as part of the national identity is being multicultural. Alternatively, and working with Poli's framework, perhaps Dokic de-ethnicized the Yugoslavian team with her Australianness, although given her Serbian background her right to represent Yugoslavia (and later Serbia and Montenegro) was not questioned.

While the global movement of athletes may contribute to processes of de-ethnicization, in some cases it may lead to new forms of nation-building. An illustrative example here is Qatar, which regularly recruits elite athletes from elsewhere to compete on its behalf (Campbell, 2011; Poli, 2007). Counter to the idea that global movements of athletes can lead to de-ethnicization and denationalization, Campbell (2011) argues that transnational sports labourers in contexts such as this can actually contribute to projects of nation-building by representing their new nation as citizens. In the case of Qatar, 'the Qatari sport model builds a national team based on commercial power, selling national identity to athletes where other nations sell sport' (Campbell, 2011, p. 56).

As these examples show, de-ethnicization and the related concept of denationalization are highly contested issues, both sociologically and socially. They are important concepts insofar as they allow us to engage with critical questions around the place of the nation in contemporary sport, based on the international movement of players. At the same time, the varying dimensions of de-ethnicization that the above examples highlight also show that the relationship between globalization, the nation and the sporting athlete is in a state of flux.

Sport and nationalism

Regardless of the side of the debate around globalization on which you fall, nations and nationalistic sentiment remain prevalent today, and are particularly relevant in the sporting arena. Nations compete with each other in global competitions, and in many sports it is the national team that is the most revered. As Rowe *et al.* (1998, p. 120) suggest, sport is a site for the 'symbolic binding of the people of the country through culture'. In this context, the media play a critical role in facilitating the connection between sport and nationalism, and in presenting particular versions of national identity. For example, in their analysis of media coverage of the semi-final of the

1996 European Football Championships (soccer) between England and Germany, Maguire and his colleagues found that the English print media tended to emphasize supposed divisions between England, or Britain more broadly, and mainland Europe, while bringing up previous hostilities between the nations, in particular in the context of World War II, and also highlighting previous sporting successes of English teams (Maguire *et al.*, 1999). By contrast, the German print media did not focus on the past, but preferred to engage with the contemporary context of Europe, emphasizing the significant place of Germany in current politics, economics and sport, and notably in comparison with England. In both cases, therefore, but in different ways, the media presented particular images of the nation, clearly linked to specific forms of nationalism and supposed national superiority over a rival (Maguire *et al.*, 1999).

The connection between sport, nationalism and national identity also emerges in a range of other contexts. Bairner and Hwang (2010) have noted, for example, the important role that sport is playing in the context of the emergence of a new Taiwanese identity, in which the people of Taiwan seek to distinguish themselves from mainland China. In this context, sport becomes a significant site for struggles that have broader political and social ramifications, and for highlighting divisions in national and international contexts. Further to this, Alan Klein has written, in the context of professional baseball in the Dominican Republic and the United States, of the ways in which 'Dominicans everywhere view the numbers of their countrymen that play [base]ball in the United States as a major accomplishment, boosting cultural and national pride' (Klein, 2008, p. 124). In the context of highly unequal relations between the Dominican Republic and the United States, the success of Dominican baseball players in the elite MLB competition becomes of huge symbolic and economic significance, and a source of national pride.

Global sport, transnational corporations and nation

Those who question the value and contemporary relevance of the nation-state point out that the actions of transnational business and non-governmental organizations have led to an interlinking of nations along a variety of axes, economically, culturally and politically. Transnational corporations like Nike, Adidas, Panasonic, Kellogg's and others sponsor sports and it is in their interest to have large audiences exposed to their products. These corporations are critical players in the relationship between global sports and the nation, bringing sports fans into the equation as the consumers of the goods they are selling. An important part of this dynamic is that, as sports are played in local contexts, transnational corporations using sports to sell products must engage with the local (Silk and Andrews, 2001). In other words, corporate activity combines the global with the national and the local in the sporting context. A case illustrating this process, and the relations involved, concerns the marketing of Adidas products in an advertising campaign that utilized the Maori *haka* (Jackson and Hokowhitu, 2002). The *haka* is a traditional Maori dance in New Zealand and is performed by athletes, particularly the New Zealand All Blacks rugby union team, as a national sporting ritual prior to international matches. The *haka* serves to intimidate the opposition while celebrating Maori culture (Jackson and Hokowhitu, 2002).

Adidas began to sponsor the New Zealand All Blacks in 1999, a welcome sponsorship in financial terms and in terms of international exposure, and with this sponsorship sought to utilize the *haka* in its advertising campaigns, which showed the All Blacks performing the *haka* while incorporating other Maori traditions (Jackson and Hokowhitu, 2002). The advertisements were widely seen, but led to questions being raised about whether Adidas was misappropriating Maori culture for commercial gain, while also essentializing Maori peoples. Adidas was sued by a Maori tribe who claimed compensation for the use of their culture (Jackson and Hokowhitu, 2002).

The case shows that the relationships between global corporations, the sports they sponsor and nations are often contested. The Maori nation, which arguably sits within the New Zealand nation, was at odds with both the transnational corporation and the New Zealand nation in this case. It was also at odds with the All Blacks, a Maori-dominated sporting team. As this suggests, the intersections between commodity, sport, culture and nation in this case were not straightforward. Maori culture was being used by Adidas to promote both the All Blacks and their products. The consequence of this was a depiction of Maori as a particular type of indigenous culture, an image that some Maori reject, in order to promote a product for commercial gain.

The relationship between products, nations and fans was also contested in the case of the introduction of the FoxTrax puck in televized coverage of the National Hockey League in 1996. The puck, which had electronics inbuilt so that it would leave a visible trail of its path, was introduced by the US-based Fox Broadcasting Company, the television network which had the rights to broadcast the NHL, in order to make ice hockey easier to watch on television (Mason, 2002). In Canada, hockey is strongly associated with Canadian identity, both in its own right and as a point of contrast with the United States, its neighbour to the south. Many Canadians, being mistrustful of what they perceive to be US cultural imperialism, 'tend to be wary of the influences of American media products and couch these concerns in terms of cultural dependency and a loss of local identity' (Jackson, cited in Mason, 2002, p. 141). When the FoxTrax puck was introduced, it was criticized in the context of concerns that Canadian national identity was being marginalized to the benefit of Fox and its parent company News Corporation (Mason, 2002). Because hockey was seen as central to Canadian identity, innovations like the FoxTrax puck that originated outside of Canada were seen as tampering with the game. Canadian reactions to the FoxTrax puck were almost universally disapproving of Fox and its US audience, characterizing the FoxTrax puck as a type of Americanization (Mason, 2002). The introduction of the FoxTrax puck was couched in nationalist terms as the Americans and their transnational corporation versus the Canadians trying to protect their national culture. Here, a global media corporation came into conflict with questions of national and local identity. Eventually, near the end of the 1998 season, when the television rights for broadcasting the NHL went to another media company, the FoxTrax puck was no longer used.

As suggested by these examples, despite the dominance of transnational corporations, sport is still anchored by the idea of the nation (Rowe, 2003). While these corporations by definition operate globally, they ultimately function in national and local markets. This necessity of gaining local markets has led companies to incorporate ideas taken from local cultural practices, such as the New Zealand *haka*, into their global marketing campaigns. But when global corporations act in ways that are perceived to be counter to national identity, they can encounter forms of opposition. These processes can thereby serve to reinforce national identity even as there is an attempt to sell globalized products to local markets.

Sports fans and nationalism

Sports fans are also part of the sport and nationalism picture. Dedicated sports fans often follow their national team around the world. The English Barmy Army, a group of English cricket fans, follows the England cricket team on all of its international tours. It offers organized tours, merchandise and other enticements for members, all grounded in the idea that it is good and desirable to support the national team and, by extension, the nation (Barmy Army, 2010). There are also avid groups of tennis fans that travel to tournaments to support their compatriots, such as the Swedish tennis fans who don Swedish colours and attend all the Swedish players' matches at major tournaments, an overt expression of Swedish nationalism (Bairner, 1996). Australian tennis fans even have their own name, the 'Fanatics', and website, www.thefanatics.com. Even though the professional tennis players are most often playing for individual glory and personal wealth, they are still perceived as representing their nations. For such fans, supporting national teams or individuals considered to be representing the nation is a way of providing actual and symbolic support for the idea of the nation itself.

An interesting variation on this theme has been identified in the work of Anthony King, who conducted research with a group of Manchester United Football Club (soccer) supporters in the 1990s (King, 2000). One specific focus of King's work was on the question of how these supporters were constructing their identity at a time when Manchester United was successful in both domestic and European competition, and at a time when the city of Manchester was reinventing itself as a European city in the context of debates around the relationship of England to Europe. King's research revealed that, while these supporters still considered the English competition to be important, there was also a movement towards conceptualizing Manchester United as a European team. These supporters were constructing their social identity as supporters of the club around its movements into Europe, and they were creating an identity through their relations with supporters in non-English European cities. Interestingly, for the supporters that King interviewed, there was also an emerging view that 'the city of Manchester itself should also strive to integrate itself and compete as fully as possible with the other cities in Europe' (King, 2000, p. 433). The imagined community of these supporters was undergoing an expansion into new domains, fuelled by the success of the club and by the regeneration of the city of Manchester. For these supporters, while national identity was important, there was also an emerging connection to a community imagined to be European, rather than purely national. The role of fans in sport is discussed in more detail in Chapter 12.

MEGA-SPORTING EVENTS, NATIONS AND NATION-BUILDING

Large-scale international sporting competitions, sometimes called sports 'mega-events' (Horne and Manzenreiter, 2006a, 2006b; Roche, 2000) are high-profile events where nations compete on the world stage. Their defining features include mass participation and global media coverage and audiences. The Olympics and the FIFA Football World Cup (soccer) are perhaps the most prominent examples of mega-events, but the Commonwealth Games, the Rugby Union World Cup, the Tour de France and Grand Prix racing are other examples of sporting events which can be understood as mega-events.

While we discuss mega-events elsewhere in this book in the context of debates around the global organization of sport, it is also notable that sports mega-events are structured in particular ritualistic ways that promote nationalism and related feelings of loyalty toward one's nation. Most are characterized by opening and closing ceremonies, which particularly highlight the host nation's culture, often in relation to their founding myths (Mewett, 2007). For example, the 2000 Sydney Olympics opening ceremony included references to Australia's Indigenous peoples, and to settlers conquering the land, but omitted stories of dispossession, colonization and other less than flattering aspects of the nation's history (Mewett, 2007). These ceremonies are a form of nation-building, emphasizing collective accounts of how the nation came to be, and invoking national symbols, while downplaying sources of potential internal conflicts. As Hogan puts it (2003, p. 102):

> Olympic opening ceremonies in their current form are elaborately staged and commercialised narratives of nation … This narrative serves not only as an affirmation of national identity but also as an extended advertisement for the host nation.

Those groups which are culturally dominant in a society will dominate its opening ceremony, potentially legitimating the existing social order and its associated ethnic, racial and gender hierarchies, while downplaying intranational debates and contests (Hogan, 2003). In other words, a particular form of imagined community emerges from such processes, shaped by power relations in the broader society.

Alternatively, opening ceremonies can also incorporate counter-narratives to the dominant myths of how the nation came to be formed. In her study of the 2004 Athens Olympic Games, Traganou (2010) investigated how 'Greekness' was represented in the opening ceremony. She found that although the dominant narrative portrayed was one of the continuity of the Greek nation, the ceremony also indicated that the Greek nation was a multicultural one that had been influenced by newcomers from elsewhere. So viewers of this opening ceremony around the world saw, perhaps, a particular vision of Greekness that gave a different picture of Greece than the dominant narratives would suggest.

The opening ceremony sets the stage for further nationalistic symbolic evocations of nation embedded in these mega-events. Each individual contest is marked by its own rituals, such as the parading of flag-bearing athletes onto the sporting ground and the playing of the national anthem. In the Olympics, the Commonwealth Games and other similar mega-events, at the end of each contest the top three contestants walk ceremoniously to a winners' podium. The flags of the medal-winning nations are raised and the national anthem of the country of the gold medal winning athlete is played. Most often, the winning athlete proudly sings along with their anthem. The athlete is present as the embodied national representative, and they are usually honoured to be selected to compete on behalf of the nation. In this regard, sports mega-events can be thought of as a 'ritual of cohesion' (Hong, 2005, p. 517), a process through which there is the creation of a sense of belonging embodied in sport.

Case study: cricket in the British Commonwealth

Research on the relationship between sport and nation-building suggests that the symbolic and institutional manifestations of the relationship are context-specific (Jarvie and Walker, 1994). Sporting competitions take place within local, national and global political contexts. The case of England and its former colonies, many of which now form the Commonwealth of Nations, highlight the processes through which sport can foster a sense of national pride both for the colonizer and formerly colonized. For English sporting teams and their supporters, victory over former colonies on the sporting field is symbolic of a continuity of a more general English superiority, even in the post-Empire age. To the same end, the power dynamic whereby England, the former colonizer, is overcome on the sporting field by its former subordinates is a powerful symbol of the end of colonialism. In this overall context, the dominance of former British colonies over teams from Britain, and in particular England, in quintessentially British sports such as rugby union and league, cricket and netball has been both a source of national shame for Britain, and a source of pride for its former colonies (see Brookes, 2002; Mills and Dimeo, 2003).

Cricket is a sport where nationalistic sentiments between England and its former colonies have played out over the years. Perera's (2000) research into Australian and Sri Lankan cricket shows that sporting victories are celebrated as national victories that reinforce a sense of nation. Tensions between England and Pakistan during test cricket are a further example, with cricketing success for Pakistan being understood as 'an assertion of Pakistani national identity, part of the attainment of decolonisation' (Williams, 2003, p. 100). Similarly, Scalmer has argued that 'Australians, Indians, and West Indians have always drawn special comfort from cricketing victories over English teams' (Scalmer, 2007, p. 437). In such contexts, the previous connections between nations based on Empire which continue into the present through the Commonwealth and through initially imposed, but then shared and recreated, cultural and sporting practices, provide a space in which ideas about the nation, and about relations between nations, can be both developed and challenged.

CONCLUSION

The discussion in this chapter has shown the continuing relevance and importance of the nation to sociological analyses and understandings of sport. In particular, the nation is a site through which critical dimensions of contemporary sport are constructed, ranging from the way in which people experience and give meaning to sport through to the ways in which multinational corporations operate. As such, even in the context of debates around the hollowing out of the nation and around processes of denationalization and de-ethnicization, the nation remains a critical domain within the contemporary world of sport.

CHAPTER SUMMARY

This chapter has shown that:

- While the nation and related concepts such as nation-state, state and nationalism have been central issues in sociology, recent developments in globalization suggest that the nation is under threat as a core unit of social analysis and experience.
- Despite such developments, the nation remains a critical dimension of contemporary sport. However, the nation should be analysed not as an isolated entity, but in terms of its relationships with global and local processes.
- Examples such as de-ethnicization and denationalization show the continuing significance of the nation in sporting contexts, even as it is being challenged by global processes.

■ As examples such as player migration, nationalism and nation-building reveal, a sociological approach to the study of the nation in the context of sport requires an engagement with contested and unequal power relations.

DISCUSSION QUESTIONS

1   To what extent do you think the nation is still important in the context of sport? Is there any evidence to suggest that globalization is challenging the importance of the nation in sport?
2   Do you think it is appropriate for professional sports people to be able to represent more than one country over the duration of their career? What issues, if any, does this possibility raise? For example, can an athlete be loyal to more than one country over their career?
3   Why are some supporters so fanatical about supporting their national team, or individual athletes from their own country? Is there anything problematic about such support, or is it to be applauded?
4   Benedict Anderson coined the concept of 'imagined community'. Can you think of examples where sport has contributed to the construction of an imagined community? What about examples where sport has contributed to divisions within an imagined community?

FURTHER READING

Horne, John and Manzenreiter, Wolfram (eds) (2006b) *Sports Mega-Events: Social Scientific Analyses of a Global Phenomenon*, Malden, MA, Blackwell.

Jackson, Steven J. and Andrews, David L. (eds) (2005) *Sport, Culture and Advertising: Identities, Commodities and the Politics of Representation*, New York, Routledge.

Lee, Jung Woo and Maguire, Joseph (2009) 'Global Festivals through a National Prism', *International Review for the Sociology of Sport*, 44(1), pp. 5–24.

Poli, Raffaele (2007) 'The Denationalization of Sport: De-ethnicization of the Nation and Identity Deterritorinalization', *Sport in Society*, 10(4), pp. 646–61.

Rowe, David (2003) 'Sport and the Repudiation of the Global', *International Review for the Sociology of Sport*, 38(3), pp. 281–94.

Chapter 7

Sporting Bodies

INTRODUCTION

In everyday life, the body is represented as being natural. However, as sociological research reveals, the body is a social and political entity. Nowhere is this more apparent than in sport. At many levels of sport, there is an increasing focus on highly sophisticated management and control of the human body. At a practical level, management of the sporting body of the athlete by organizations includes the employment of specialized training and medical teams, including psychologists, educators, and personal trainers as well as religious and lifestyle advisors. It also involves the construction of discourses around the meaning of the athlete's body, and how it should be managed or controlled. This chapter will use three examples to show how sociological approaches can contribute to understandings of the athlete's body:

- Drug use in sport.
- Management of sport injuries and pain.
- Debates around cyborg athletes.

Before moving on to these specific examples, the chapter outlines ways sociologists have analysed the body, and how a sociological approach differs from the dominant biomedical approach.

SOCIOLOGY OF THE BODY

While sociologists have long focused on relations between people, the body itself was not always a focus of study. However, the work of theorists such as Michel Foucault (1995), Emily Martin (1987) and Bryan Turner (2008) indicated the importance of analysing the body as a site that both carries and can transform power relations. At the same time, researchers engaging with issues around gender, race and disability, among other social relations, have argued that we cannot understand human society without analysing the body and its place in society. Not surprisingly, the body has become an important site of research in sport, although discussion of the body is dominated by the medical sciences.

Understandings of the body of the athlete are dominated by medical and scientific frameworks of knowledge, termed 'biomedicine'. The body in this framework is understood as biological, natural, 'isolated and individual' (Magdalinski, 2009, p. 33). That is, the body is understood as existing independent of and outside of social and political relations (Good, 1994; Magdalinski, 2009; White, 2004). One way that the body has been understood in medicine is as a machine (Martin, 1987). In this context, the human body is understood in functional terms, as working and functioning well, as having broken down, or as experiencing some form of malfunction that needs to be repaired with appropriate medical intervention (Martin, 1987). Such language and understandings are often present in sporting discourses around the body. For example, injured players are often referred to as having broken down, and as needing to be fixed or repaired. Located within this form of discourse is an argument that the goal of medicine is to use scientifically tested and proven methods to cure illness, disease and injury as they affect the individual body (Coakley and Pike, 2009; Bilton *et al.*, 2002).

The modern ideal of the body as a machine in sport was on display in 2003 when English footballer (soccer) David Beckham was transferred from Manchester United in England to Real Madrid in Spain. As part of the transfer process, Beckham had to undergo a 90-minute fitness test, standard procedure across a range of professional sports. Yet, what was taken to an extreme on this occasion was that the fitness test became a media and public relations event, with more than 500 reporters from 25 nations reporting on the event. The test was screened live on Real Madrid TV, and beamed around the world, and a Spanish health company paid £250,000 to sponsor the medical exam. Through such processes, a critical dimension of a player's career and prospects is the question of whether their physical body is considered to be functioning to appropriate biomedical levels (Cockerill, 2003; BBC Sport, 2003). It is considered normal to utilize the biomedical model of the body in sport, thinking of the body as a machine. This is not only the case in professional sport, but in all forms of sport, and often from a very young age. As a result, individuals engaging in sport from a young age are exposed to biomedical discourses almost from the moment they begin playing.

It is evident that sport competitors themselves often work within this model of the body, and what it requires in the context of injury. For example, during the 2008 Olympic Games in Beijing, news reports revealed that Lauren Jackson, captain of the Australian Opals basketball team and one of the best players in the world, was playing with an ankle injury, attributed to wear and tear built up over her career. One report on Jackson's injury (McIlveen, 2008) read:

> The tough as nails Jackson, who has played much of her career with lower leg complaints, said she wanted to break the news so there would be no surprises when she took time off from the game after the Olympics.
>
> She revealed she had played through the Olympics with painkilling injections, but the effects were starting to wear off. 'I'm used to playing injured, it won't stop me from getting on the court. There's a bit of pain when I take off and land a bit but I'll have to play through that', Jackson said.

For Jackson, playing injured and with pain was a normal part of being an elite athlete, and something to be worked through. As her body was experiencing problems with its functioning, the appropriate response was to take painkilling injections to manage the pain so that she could continue to compete. Her machine was malfunctioning, and she was treating it with medication to enable her to compete. She would attempt to heal her body after the Olympics.

These understandings of the body, and of related issues around health and illness, are important in drawing attention to the embodied dimensions of athletic life. Biomedicine has made crucial contributions to the duration and quality of human life, particularly in relation to acute, or short-term, illnesses and infectious diseases. Biomedicine and related scientific fields have also made significant contributions to the well-being of competitors in sport. For example, many injuries that were once career-ending are now treatable through medical intervention. Increasingly sophisticated medicalized management of diet, injuries, recovery after competition and the like have also improved the well-being and health of players.

Nevertheless, from a sociological perspective, to view the body only as an individual biological entity is limited. There is also a need to recognize the interaction of the biological and the biomedical with the broader social, political and economic contexts within which people live. Medical anthropologists

Nancy Scheper-Hughes and Margaret Lock have identified three types of body that can be usefully mobilized by sociologists, and that go beyond a biomedical understanding of the body (cited in Lupton, 2005, p. 196).

First, there is the individual body, 'or the lived experience of the body as an everyday reality for the individual', as captured in the concept of embodiment (Lupton, 2005, p. 196). Here, for example, we could consider how athletes such as David Beckham and Lauren Jackson experience their body at an individual level, when going through medical tests or seeking to play through pain or to recover from injury. In this context, an important research approach would be to ask them as individuals how they experienced their bodies in the context of injury.

Second, there is a notion of the body as a 'social body' (Lupton, 2005, p. 196). Here, the body is understood to represent other aspects of society and of social relations, and is used in particular by social scientists interested in the relationships between culture and society. For example, the individual body of a successful athlete may be used to represent the achievement of excellence in a society where ideals of individual achievement are paramount (Duina, 2011). In the case of Jackson, the social body would indicate the pressure on her to play injured and the cultural expectation that she would not let down the team.

Third, there is the notion of a body politic, particularly connected with the work of Foucault. This concept of the body is used to refer 'to the social regulation, surveillance, and control of groups or populations of bodies' (Lupton, 2005, p. 197). Forms of regulation of athletes' bodies, such as drug testing, can be seen as attempts to manage and control the population of athletes (Lupton, 2005, pp. 196–7). For Jackson, pressures to fulfil obligations to sponsors and pressures placed on her to play by staff are part of the political aspects of her body. From a more historical perspective, the emergence of muscular Christianity in England and its colonies in the nineteenth century, with its promotion of physical activity as an important part of religious moral development, can be understood as an attempt to manage the body at the level of the population (Booth and Tatz, 2000).

Thinking of these three types of bodies (individual, social and political) can help to develop an understanding of the importance of bodies and sport. The following sections examine the body and three specific sports context: drug use in sport, management of pain and injuries, and cyborg bodies. The argument proposed is that although the biomedical body is important, it is also useful to consider the subjective individual, social and political dimensions of bodies in sport.

DRUG USE IN SPORT

One of the most controversial issues for sport over many years has concerned the use of drugs in sport, particularly since the use of anabolic steroids became common in the 1960s (Sjoqvist *et al.*, 2008). Whether at the level of the individual athlete or of entire national teams, one of the critical concerns about drug use in sport is the argument that performance-enhancing drugs remove sport from the level playing field. Those who take such drugs are considered to be placing themselves at an unfair advantage, thereby removing one of the cornerstones of sporting competition, namely the belief that any advantage that players have in a competition should come from their own endeavours, and not from artificial sources. Whether it is disgraced Olympic athletes such as Ben Johnson and Marion Jones, or entire teams such as the Festina cycling team in the Tour de France, the use of drugs in sport is widely condemned, and the consequences for the careers of those found to have used drugs are often severe.

When considering the use of drugs in sport, Nixon and Frey (1996, p. 116) make a useful distinction between three types of drug use. These are:

- Restorative drug use.
- Recreational drug use.
- Additive or performance-enhancing drug use.

Restorative drug use refers to the use of drugs to help an athlete recover from injury (Nixon and Frey, 1996). Being injured, playing while injured, and using restorative drugs have become normalized within much sport. Such drug use is largely considered unproblematic, ranging from the use of headache tablets through to the taking of vitamin supplements available over the counter from the pharmacy. In some instances, however, questions arise about restorative drug use if very powerful pharmaceuticals are used in an attempt to get an athlete back on the field of play at a rate that is quicker than expected. And, in some instances, there are concerns over whether the health of the player may be at risk if they return to competition too soon after undergoing drug enhanced recuperation. Here, power relations are important: who is arguing for the use of restorative drugs – coaches, managers, players themselves? Who benefits when injured athletes play? For example, the injured Lauren Jackson was playing for her nation, and she was committed to seeing through the Olympics even though it would require her to recuperate afterwards. Playing on the national team puts pressure on players to play injured as they are at risk of losing their place as well as of letting down the nation.

Recreational drug use relates to the use of drugs for pleasure and is common throughout society, not just among athletes (Nixon and Frey, 1996). In the context of a celebrity culture, however, the recreational use of drugs by athletes can become a mediatized scandal, whether the drugs involved are legal – for example, in cases of alcohol consumption – or illegal – as, for example, with the use of cocaine or speed. In such cases, questions arise around whether or not use of the drugs will have an adverse, or beneficial, impact on the player's performance and therefore on their value to their team. Questions also arise around whether or not the use of drugs diminishes the place of the player, and of the sport, as a role model in the broader society. In the context of discussions around players and recreational drug use, a moralistic media discourse often emerges, condemning players for not living up to societal expectations. The response from players and their agents, in turn, often focuses on questioning whether or not players are being held to higher and inappropriate standards compared with other members of society (Kelly and Hickey, 2008).

While these first two forms of drug use raise considerable concerns, arguably the third form of drug use, the use and administration of performance-enhancing drugs, has raised the most controversy in sport. While leagues and players often attempt to downplay the use of performance-enhancing drugs, they have in many sports become both widespread and entrenched (Nixon and Frey, 1996). This can be attributed to at least two reasons: first, the ease of access to drugs and, second, the pressure to win (Nixon and Frey, 1996). The pressure to win comes both from external sources – for example, expectations from supporters, coaches, family and so on – and also from within, as athletes internalize and normalize an understanding that the primary goal of competition for an elite professional athlete, in particular, is to win. Athletes may justify their own use of drugs because they believe their competitors are using the drugs, or they may argue that their team or organization encouraged them to use the drugs, either by implication or overtly. For many supporters and other people associated with sport, one of the main problems with the use of performance-enhancing drugs is that it is seen to shift the ground of fair competition. While supporters and competitors admire athletes who are able to outperform their rivals, based on their disciplined training and personal sacrifice, drugs are seen as a cheater's way of trying to secure an unfair competitive advantage.

Within sport, concerns about drugs have led to varying forms of regulation that aim to control and eliminate drug use among athletes. In the 1960s the International Olympic Committee established a Medical Commission, initially with the goal of identifying the level of doping within sport, and later with the goal of protecting the health of athletes. Nevertheless, until the 1990s, individual nations remained largely responsible for drug policies (Magdalinski, 2009). After the 1998 Tour de France scandal, however, in which a team was expelled on the basis of drug-related charges, a World Conference on Doping in Sport was organized by the International Olympic Committee (IOC) and held in Lausanne in 1999. One outcome was that:

> the World Anti-Doping Agency (WADA) was founded in 2000 to 'harmonise' anti-doping policies, though the zeal with which this organisation has pursued its mission has created something of a global 'police force' charged with arresting athletes for 'crimes against humanity', prompting many to question the degree to which individual and civil rights are being infringed. (Magdalinski, 2009, p. 47)

Despite such reservations, WADA is now very much part of the international sport landscape, and plays a significant role in regulation of drug use.

At the same time, questions arise around exactly what it is that WADA and other organizations actually do, and what they should do. Here, work by Bob Stewart and Aaron Smith (2008) is helpful. In considering current and possible arrangements for the management and regulation of drug use in sport, and in particular for performance-enhancing drugs, they identify four options available to policy-makers:

- 'Accept the problem and hope it goes away.'
- 'Address the problem head-on by implementing a raft of coercive measures.'
- 'Education.'
- 'Understand the realities of elite sport competition.'

(Stewart and Smith, 2008, p. 289)

While Stewart and Smith (2008) recognize that previous unsuccessful attempts to regulate drug use suggest that the first option is sensible, they also argue that it is irresponsible, given the potentially serious negative health outcomes associated with drug use. Similarly, while the third option of education is important, by itself it will not be enough, given the environments within which athletes live and compete. The second option, of addressing the problem head on through punitive measures, is the dominant approach taken by WADA. As Stewart and Smith (2008) argue, this is a deterrence-related approach in which the focus is on the individual and on implementing measures to change behaviour. In the context of sport, this model is based on an argument that, if the penalties are severe enough, then athletes will alter their behaviour in relation to drug use, or will not use drugs, because they will realize that the costs of using drugs outweigh the benefits. For Stewart and Smith, this focus on the individual is limited because it does not acknowledge the broader context within which athletes live and compete.

They suggest a fourth option, whereby drug policy needs to take into account three other factors that contribute to the place of drugs in sport. These are, first, globalization and commercialization; second, sport culture; and third, identity. Such factors have an important impact on whether or not athletes will take drugs, and therefore need to be factored into regulation efforts (Stewart and Smith, 2008). In other words, they argue that there is a need for more research that 'considers the contextual factors ... that affect athlete beliefs and decision making and how these factors can be managed to make drug taking less attractive and less harmful to athletes' (Stewart and Smith, 2008, p. 294). As part of such a process, there is a need for policy that 'focuses more on the health and well-being of athletes and less on the need to remove cheaters from sport and maintain a level playing field' (Stewart and Smith, 2008, p. 294).

The arguments of Stewart and Smith identify the need to consider the broader contexts within which athletes compete. While athletes are individuals, they compete in an organizational context where there are pressures and structures which constrain the range of options available to them. The social and political bodies shape drug use; it is not just an individual issue. This is not an argument to excuse the behaviour of athletes. Rather it is an argument for recognizing both the complexity of the worlds that athletes live and compete in, and the structural and contextual pressures that exist which may lead them to seek to improve their performance through drug use.

DISCUSSION POINT: DRUGS, SPORT AND THE BODY OF THE ATHLETE

In 2005, the former Major League Baseball star Jose Canseco released a controversial autobiography entitled *Juiced: Wild Times, Rampant 'Roids, Smash Hits, and How Baseball Got Big* (2005). In the book, which went onto the *New York Times* best-seller list, Canseco openly discussed the use of steroids in baseball, including both his own use and the use of steroids by other stars in the game. While this led to a number of controversies, with named players having to defend their own personal history around whether or not they had used drugs, what is of particular interest are the arguments that Canseco made about the use of steroids in baseball, and by implication in sport more generally. The following are two quotes from his book. As you read them, consider: (1) are you persuaded by Canseco's argument? (2) why or why not? (3) what issues does his argument raise in the context of our understanding of sporting excellence?

I have no doubt whatsoever that intelligent, informed use of steroids, combined with human growth hormone, will one day be so accepted that everybody will be doing it. Steroid use will be more common than Botox is now. Every baseball player and pro athlete will be using at least low levels of steroids. As a result, baseball and other sports will be more exciting and entertaining. Human life will be improved, too. We will live longer and better. And maybe we'll love longer and better too. (Canseco, 2005, p. 2)

People want to be entertained at the ballpark. They want baseball to be fun and exciting. Home runs are fun and exciting. They are easy for even the most casual fan to appreciate. Steroid-enhanced athletes hit more home runs. (Canseco, 2005, p. 9)

MANAGEMENT OF PAIN AND INJURIES

Part of the reality of life for athletes is that, at some time, they will be injured. In some instances, injuries may prevent them from playing – for a short time, perhaps for a season, or, in rarer situations, injuries may be so serious as to end a career. In addition to injuries which prevent a player from playing, another dimension of the career of the athlete is playing or competing in pain. Indeed, in some instances, players would never play if they waited until they were fully injury and pain free. So, for players, and for their managers and teams, a central element of being an athlete is playing with, or through, pain while injured. The following quotes from three elite athletes in three different sports in different parts of the world provide insights into personal experiences of injury and pain:

Olga Korbut, gymnastics

Olga Korbut, a highly successful gymnast who won gold for the Soviet Union at the 1972 and 1976 Olympic Games, wrote about the period after the 1972 Munich Olympics in the following terms: 'My strongest memories of that entire period are fatigue, pain, and the empty feeling of being a fly whose blood has been sucked out by a predatory spider' (Korbut, quoted in Waddington, 2000, p. 415).

Andre Agassi, tennis

In the opening chapter of his autobiography, *Open*, US tennis superstar Andre Agassi writes about leaving the court after a big match, which he has just won:

> I meet Baghdatis [his opponent] at the net, take his hand, which is trembling, and hurry off the court. I don't dare stop. *Must keep moving.* I stagger through the tunnel, my bag slung over my left shoulder, feeling as if it's slung over my right shoulder, because my whole body is twisted. By the time I reach the locker room I am unable to walk. I'm unable to stand. I'm sinking to the floor. I'm on the ground. (Agassi, 2009, pp. 24–5)

Matthew Lloyd, Australian Rules football

Reflecting on the place of injuries in the careers of Australian Rules football players, former Essendon player Matthew Lloyd wrote:

> Players will go to extraordinary lengths to ensure they can play the next week. A typical week for me towards the latter part of my career included the hyperbaric chamber, particularly if I had a corked thigh, hot and cold plunge pools most days, standing in the icy water of Port Phillip Bay in the middle of winter, physio, and constant massage. As you get older, you often didn't feel you ever recover to 100 per cent from the previous week's game. It then becomes a mental battle, which separates the greats from the also-rans. (Lloyd, 2010)

What these quotes suggest is that pain is a central part of the experience of being an athlete. While not all athletes will experience pain of the sort described here, or will be willing to play through such pain, these descriptions suggest that pain is not a peripheral element of being an athlete, but is central to the everyday experience of competing.

Related to these personal narratives of pain and injury, the management of injuries and of pain has become an important element of contemporary sport. In addition to the traditional biomedical doctor, many teams and sports now employ, or engage with, a wider range of other health care professionals, including physiotherapists, psychologists and chiropractors, among others. While many issues arise in the context of the management of pain and injury in sport, here we identify three.

First, while health care professionals work to the best of their ability to ensure as far as possible the recovery of the player, they also face a range of pressures from stakeholders in the game, who may have varying objectives in mind. As Magdalinski suggests, 'the aims of medicine and the aims of sport are not always in concert, particularly when physicians are employed by teams rather than engaged by players' (Magdalinski, 2009, p. 79). In such contexts, the needs of the team may predominate at the potential expense of longer-term health issues for the individual player.

Second, players often take extreme measures to enable themselves to play, measures that would by and large be unthinkable for people in other employment contexts. For the individual player, there is the fear that if they are injured and do not play, they will lose their place in the team or their capacity to compete as an individual. In the fiercely competitive world of professional sport, for example, an injury to one player is an opportunity for another player. All but the most outstanding of players recognize that to miss too many games or events through injury is to risk their professional livelihood. Players seek to do everything they can to play because of a genuine commitment to their team. There is a fear that to miss a game through injury is to risk letting the team down. In this context, players face a conflict, because if they play when injured and do not perform to their usual standards, they may be accused of playing when they should have rested.

Third, another feature of pain and injury in sport is that they become rationalized. That is, pain and injury, and the risk of pain and injury, are taken to be part of the game, and something that players should accept. For example, Rex Ryan, the 2009 New York Jets coach, in the (US) National Football League, was reported in the *New York Times* as saying that football (gridiron) is inherently risky to one's health. 'The game is meant to be played physically,' Ryan said. 'It's meant to be played at a violent level, but not cheap.' 'I love the fact that we try to get rules to protect the players; the equipment is better. But at the end of the day, there's some inherent risk in this game' (Rhoden, 2009).

It is also notable, however, that what may be considered to be acceptable can change over time. In particular in contact sports, but also in non-contact sports, and in light of research emerging suggesting a link between sporting head injuries and long-term health problems such as Alzheimer's disease and other memory-related diseases, an emerging trend has been to clamp down on actions on the field that may lead to head injuries (Schwarz, 2009). Playing with pain and injuries is a social expectation especially associated with elite sport and it can have short- and long-term effects on athletes' bodies. While pain and injury can be managed medically, if it is bad for athletes in the long-term to play injured, the social expectation that they should do so needs to be addressed.

CYBORG ATHLETE

A number of significant social science contributions have emerged around the relations between the body and technological innovations, with some theorists suggesting that we need to rethink our understanding of what it is to be a human. Leading this discussion for many years has been Donna Haraway (1991). She has mobilized the concept of the cyborg, 'a hybrid of machine and organism' (Haraway, 1991, p. 149), as a means for suggesting that we need to rethink human/non-human relations – for example, the relations between humans and machines such as computers. It is important to ask the question: if we become linked to, or dependent on, machinery, does it still make sense to distinguish between a so-called natural human body and a technologically enhanced body? Haraway argues that as social practices and technologies change, so they have an impact on all aspects of human life, including the body. A key dimension of her argument is that we need to move away from some supposedly natural image of what we understand the human body to be, and to recognize that the human body can and does change. In this regard, change may arise from internal processes, or may come from outside of the body, for example, as we interact with varying technologies. The implications of this for sport can be considered in light of the example of Lance Armstrong, not just because of his record-breaking performances as a road cyclist, but because of what those record-breaking performances suggest about our understanding of the human body.

Case study: Lance Armstrong

Lance Armstrong is a US road racing cyclist, famous for winning the prestigious Tour de France bicycle road race seven times in a row, from

1999–2005. Although he retired from racing in 2005, he returned in 2009, and finished third in the Tour de France that year. Notably, he was diagnosed with testicular cancer in 1996, which had spread to other parts of his body, including his brain and lungs. As part of his treatment regime, he underwent chemotherapy as well as brain surgery, and the cancer then went into remission (Butryn and Masucci, 2003; see also Sparkes, 2004). While certain to go down in the record books as one of the all-time great sporting athletes, his career has also attracted controversy in areas related to the relationship between technology and sport performance. What is of interest here are the ways in which Armstrong embodies critical aspects of the emergence of the cyborg as a prominent figure in contemporary sport. Butryn and Masucci (2003) identify important ways in which Armstrong embodies a cyborg form. In particular, the world of cycling has a clear connection with technological advances in cycling equipment, whether that be in the form of the bike itself, clothing or helmets. At the moment of competition, the athlete and the bike become indivisible. Cyclists are also linked very closely to computer technology:

> Cyclists are computer slaves, we hover over precise calculations of cadence, efficiency, force and wattage. I [Armstrong] was constantly sitting on a stationary bike with electrodes all over my body, looking for different positions on a bike that might gain mere seconds or a piece of equipment that might be a little more aero-dynamic. (Armstrong, quoted in Butryn and Masucci, 2003, p. 129)

In the context of discussions around the cyborg body, what is critical here is the seamless integration between human body and computer technology. While it is clear that Armstrong would be an elite performer without technology, the actual levels he has reached were made possible by his engagement with and connections to technology. Further, through both the anti-doping regime in professional sport and through his cancer treatment, 'Armstrong's body has also been subject to omnipresent surveillance by the medical profession' (Butryn and Masucci, 2003, p. 131). As an elite athlete in a sport in which there has been significant drug use, the body of the competitor has become integrated into a technologically sophisticated and interventionist drug-testing regime on an almost continual basis.

The importance of the cyborg argument is that it requires us to recognize that the experience of Armstrong as an athlete who has achieved incredible success through his high levels of commitment, work ethic and skill, both individually and as part of a team, cannot be separated from his interaction with a range of technologies.

DISCUSSION POINT

Oscar Pistorius is a South African sprinter, who was hugely successful at the 2008 Paralympics in Beijing, winning the men's 100m, 200m and 400m events. Born without the fibula in his legs and with two toes on each foot, at the age of 11 months both of his legs were amputated below the knee. As a high-performing athlete today, Pistorius uses prosthetic limbs, 'a pair of j-shaped blades made of fiber carbon and known as Cheetahs' (Longman, 2007). Seeking to compete in the 2008 Olympics, Pistorius was initially banned by the IAAF from doing so, on the basis that the Cheetahs provided an advantage for Pistorius not available to other athletes (Jones and Wilson, 2009). Pistorius appealed to the Court of Arbitration for Sport, which overturned the IAAF's decision. Pistorius then competed in the trials for the 2008 South African Olympic team, but did not qualify. As noted above, however, he was soon to be successful in the 2008 Paralympic Games. In the context of the discussion in this chapter, Pistorius's case raises vital questions around our understanding of the human body. The journalist Jere Longman has asked the following questions, specifically in the context of Pistorius, but they are questions that have a broader resonance. How would you answer these questions? What do your answers suggest about your understanding of the human body, both in the context of sport and more generally?

> What should an athlete look like? Where should limits be placed on technology to balance fair play with the right to compete? Would the nature of sport be altered if athletes using artificial limbs could run faster or jump higher than the best athletes using their natural limbs? (Longman, 2007)

For more discussion of the Pistorius case, see Longman (2007), Robinson (2008), Jones and Wilson (2009), McHugh (2007).

CONCLUSION

The body is a critical element that we need to consider when analysing sport. While the biological elements of the body are of clear importance, sociological research indicates the need to consider also the societal contexts of the body, from the level of individual embodiment through to the body politic. In this way, the body becomes a site for relational power struggles within the world of sport, from modes of managing pain through to techniques for regulating interactions between the body and technologies, and between the body and drugs. As such, the relationship between body and sport becomes an important empirical example underlining the significance of the theoretical model proposed in this book.

CHAPTER SUMMARY

This chapter has shown that:

- Contemporary understandings of the body are dominated by a biomedical and scientific discourse, in which the body of the athlete is understood primarily as an independent biological entity.
- Sociological approaches to the body suggest that, in addition to considering the biological elements of the body, it is important to consider the body as a social entity. The social dimension of the body operates in particular at the levels of the embodied individual, the social body and the body politic.
- Drug use, managing pain and injury, and the cyborg body are all examples which reveal the importance of considering the body not just as a biological entity, but as a social entity located within a series of social relations.
- An understanding of athletes needs to engage with the societal location of their bodies.

DISCUSSION QUESTIONS

1   To consider the body as a social entity is to take away from our primary focus when considering player welfare, which should be the biological body. Discuss.
2   Drugs in sport are here to stay, and we will never get rid of them. Discuss. Should sporting organizations let athletes use whatever performance-enhancing drugs they like? Why, or why not?
3   Read a website for a sporting club, or of a media organization covering sport. Look for examples where they discuss player injuries. What sort of language is used? Are there any key words or phrases that are used to discuss injuries? What understandings of the human body emerge from this language?
4   Why is the question of the cyborg athlete so controversial? What do you think of this concept?

FURTHER READING

Butryn, Ted M. and Masucci, Matthew A. (2003) 'It's Not About the Book. A Cyborg Counternarrative of Lance Armstrong', *Journal of Sport and Social Issues*, 27(2), pp. 124–44.

Lupton, Deborah (2005) 'The Body, Medicine and Society', in John Germov (ed.), *Second Opinion: An Introduction to Health Sociology*, 3rd edn, South Melbourne, Oxford University Press, pp. 195–207.

Magdalinski, Tara (2009) *Sport, Technology and the Body: The Nature of Performance*, London, Routledge.

Turner, Bryan S. (2008) *The Body and Society: Explorations in Social Theory*, London, Sage.

Part III

Regulating Sport

Part III focuses on the regulation of sport, revealing the broad range of organizations involved in governance and their similar and competing interests, while also discussing conflicts around governance of sport. Regulation is an area of central significance for sociology, and for social sciences more generally, in that it highlights the formal and informal rules and processes that seek to create forms of social order, including around power and authority in sport and society. Chapters 8 and 9 engage with governance and regulation at the club, league, national and global levels. Chapter 10 considers the contribution that sport can make to social justice initiatives and, in so doing, considers forms of regulation involved in such processes. Through these three chapters, this part of the book reveals how the organizations involved in the regulation of sport are sites of social and political power and conflict.

Chapter 8

Governing Sport: The Club, League and Global

INTRODUCTION

While clubs and athletes in sport compete with each other to win games and competitions, sports also need systems of governance to ensure the continued viability of competitions. Rules that some leagues develop to attempt to ensure that forms of competitive balance and cooperation exist between competitors such as salary caps are an example. The need for such rules is based on the idea that real and sustained competition is required to ensure that supporters and sponsors remain interested in the league. And at the international or global level, forms of governance are required for decisions such as where major international events, such as the Olympic Games, are going to be hosted.

This chapter unpacks some of the tensions around governing sport, including challenges that confront governance processes at the club level. The chapter argues that processes of governing sport involve politically motivated organizational struggles both within and between organizations. As such, examining organizational governance in sport is a good way of engaging with one of the main claims of this book, that sport involves contested power struggles among individuals and organizations. The following sections first define governance in the context of sport, and then discuss sport governance at the club, league and global levels.

GOVERNING SPORT

Organizational governance refers to the structures and processes that direct and regulate an organization. It includes strategic planning, running the day-to-day operations of the organization in order to achieve the organization's goals (both short term and long term), and developing and implementing the policies which guide the actions of members of the organization (Hoye and Cuskelly, 2007). In short, '[o]rganisational governance is the system by which the elements of an organisation are directed, controlled and regulated' (Hoye and Cuskelly, 2007, p. 3).

Sports organizations include teams, clubs, leagues, player management companies, sporting product companies, local, state and national regulatory bodies and international sporting bodies. There are both for-profit and not-for-profit sport organizations, with differing aims. For-profit sport organizations are fundamentally concerned with financial matters and profit-making, and with serving the interests of shareholders – that is, people with a financial investment in the organization. By contrast, not-for-profit organizations, the majority of sports organizations (Hoye and Cuskelly, 2007), have a diverse range of goals that are not necessarily directly financial, such as serving a range of community-based stakeholders.

While not-for-profit organizations remain central in sport around the world, including in professional sports, the emergence of corporate sport is a global trend (Shilbury *et al.*, 2006, p.151). Corporate sport involves paid professional athletes who play sports with considerable entertainment and income-producing potential (Shilbury *et al.*, 2006). Corporate sports organizations have well-developed administrations which coordinate their relationships with a range of other organizations, including sponsors and the media (Shilbury *et al.*, 2006).

As sport becomes increasingly professionalized and corporatized, money and other financial resources come to play increasingly larger roles. Trends towards corporatization and professionalization have an influence on the governance of the game at all levels, including at the junior and club levels, whether or not a sporting organization is formally for profit or not. This creates tensions for sporting organizations, because it is the 'dual mission of clubs – to promote sporting success and to operate as commercial businesses – that distinguishes them from standard businesses' (Hamil *et al.*, 2004, pp. 45–6). In other words, while commercial trends are increasingly significant in sport, the reason for the existence of sporting organizations and measures of sporting success are not only defined by financial returns.

Sports clubs, whether professional or amateur, differ from other types of organizations in several ways (Hamil *et al.*, 2004). They have cultural connections to their communities. Related to this, the relationship between fans and clubs is not a provider–consumer relationship. Rather, supporters volunteer their time and feel passionate about their club (Hamil *et al.*, 2004). Sports clubs, unlike other businesses, are also not aiming to put other clubs out of business – they need competitors to exist. So there has to be an element of cooperation as well as competition among clubs for sporting leagues to be successful (Hamil *et al.*, 2004). In other words, success in sport, even in corporate sport, is not measured only in financial terms, but by forms of connections and relationships with a diverse range of individuals and organizations. While there are important formal and everyday differences between for-profit and not-for-profit sport organizations, they also face some similar challenges, linked to the specific nature of sport as a social activity.

Three important sites of governance in sport are: at the club level, at the league level and at the global level. Each of these levels has its own governance needs, structures and challenges. In the following sections we examine governance at each of these levels.

GOVERNANCE IN CLUBS

While clubs are often equated with the teams that compete on the field of play, contemporary sport clubs are much more than that. Indeed, in many instances, the sporting activity is just one among many activities undertaken by a club. For example, in addition to a team or teams, a club may have a social club, dining facilities and a sports store, and it may also engage in community-building programmes or other forms of community engagement. Key issues relating to club governance include their ownership structures and management, along with how they deal with former players and with supporters.

Ownership

In analysing governance in clubs, a critical issue relates to ownership structures, which are important when considering how control is exercised within clubs, and which interests are represented by the club. Nixon and Frey (1996, p. 189) identify five forms of ownership in professional sport. While writing from a United States vantage point, these models exist in other national contexts, albeit with some variations. The five forms are: the 'corporate subsidiary' model; the individual owner; 'public owner'; 'entrepreneurial owner'; and the joint 'public–private' partnership (Nixon and Frey, 1996, pp. 189–91).

- In the 'corporate subsidiary' model (Nixon and Frey, 1996, p. 189), a club or team is owned by a larger and often non-sport organization. Important examples of this model include the various teams owned by media organizations such as Major League Baseball's Atlanta Braves (owned by Liberty Media) and the Melbourne Storm in Australia's National Rugby League (owned by News Corporation). Some Formula One Grand Prix teams are owned by automobile companies such as Ferrari and Renault, while others are owned by companies such as Red Bull (an energy drink manufacturer).
- The individual or family ownership model, where ownership of the club is the primary business of the owner, has a long history in the US and is closely identified with people such as Al Davis, owner of the Oakland Raiders in the NFL (gridiron), and the O'Malley family, famous for their ownership of the Dodgers in Major League Baseball (Nixon and Frey, 1996).
- 'Public ownership' (Nixon and Frey, 1996, p. 190) includes organizations that are traded in public on the stock or share market, such as the Boston Celtics in the US (basketball) or Tottenham Hotspur Football Club in England (soccer), and community-owned, non-profit organizations such as the Green Bay Packers in the NFL (gridiron) and clubs in the Australian Football League. From an international perspective, it could be argued that these forms of ownership should be separated out, along the lines of whether or not the primary purpose of the organization is to make a profit.
- 'Entrepreneurial ownership' (Nixon and Frey, 1996, p. 190). In this model, an individual owns a club, based on investing financial resources they have gained in other industries. While this model is associated very strongly with much professional sport in the US, it is becoming increasingly prominent in other sports around the world. For example, Chelsea Football Club in the English Premier League (soccer) is owned by Russian oil magnate Roman Abramovich, and the South Sydney Rabbitohs (in the Australian National Rugby League) are co-owned by actor Russell Crowe and businessperson Peter Holmes à Court.
- Joint 'public–private' (Nixon and Frey, 1996, p. 114) ownership. This is a rarer model, but is one that involves both private individuals or organizations and public organizations being involved in ownership. For example, the MLB team the Pittsburgh Pirates was at one time 'jointly

owned by private investors, corporations and the City of Pittsburgh' (Nixon and Frey, 1996, p. 190).

Some sports leagues, such as the English Premier League (soccer) and the US National Football League (gridiron), have different models of ownership within the league. For example, FC Barcelona in the Spanish Football League (soccer) and the Green Bay Packers in the NFL (gridiron) are membership-based organizations that co-exist in leagues alongside other forms of ownership (Hamil *et al.*, 1999, 2000, 2001; Morrow, 2003).

Ownership structures are important because control and influence at a club ultimately rest with the owner, within the confines of an overall league structure. This can have a series of effects, some predictable and others which are less predictable. One of the most dramatic forms of uncertainty in the context of sport teams, and related to private ownership, is when teams move from one part of a country to another. One famous example of this occurred prior to the beginning of the 1958 MLB season, when the Brooklyn Dodgers (in New York City) were moved to Los Angeles, under the majority ownership and control of Walter O'Malley, and became the LA Dodgers (Quirk and Fort, 1999). Sometimes such moves cross international borders. For example, in 1996 the Canadian NHL team the Winnipeg Jets was relocated to Phoenix, Arizona in the US and became the Phoenix Coyotes, competing in the same league (Scherer, 2001). Privately owned clubs can also be sold, which may also lead to uncertainty. At the other end of the spectrum, clubs that are membership-based, so are not owned by a single individual but are controlled by members, have a different set of concerns, particularly relating to how much members can participate in club governance.

One question that emerges from a discussion of forms of ownership is why people would want to own a sporting team. Nixon and Frey (1996, p. 191) suggest that '[f]un, excitement, ego gratification, public visibility, the chance to be close to elite athletes, vicarious identification with athletes, and community service' are among the reasons why individuals may become interested in team ownership. People also purchase teams in order to make money, so along with the personal reasons there may be economic ones (Nixon and Frey, 1996). Motives for not-for-profit club ownership are less clear, but would likely include the psychological and social rewards outlined by Nixon and Frey.

Management

In examining the organizational structure of sport clubs, both professional and amateur, it is evident that such organizations involve much more than simply putting a team on the field to compete against another team. Clubs have become increasingly sophisticated in their organizational structures. While coaches, training staff and players are critical participants in a club, so too are people located in positions such as administration, managing sponsorship, community relations, membership or supporter relations, finance, medical, media and communications and so on. There are also positions related to the hosting of sporting events such as catering, stadium management, security and parking personnel. And when required, clubs will call on a range of other skilled personnel, including lawyers and medical professionals. In other words, the range of people involved in the everyday running of a sport club is extensive and diverse. To manage the necessary variety of participants, clubs establish formal organizational structures with lines and flows of responsibility and accountability. One such organizational model is as follows (this model is based on research undertaken by Capling and Marjoribanks, 2004, 2008. For variations on this model, see Smith and Stewart, 1999; Stewart and Smith, 2000; Hoye and Cuskelly, 2007; Hoye *et al.*, 2006):

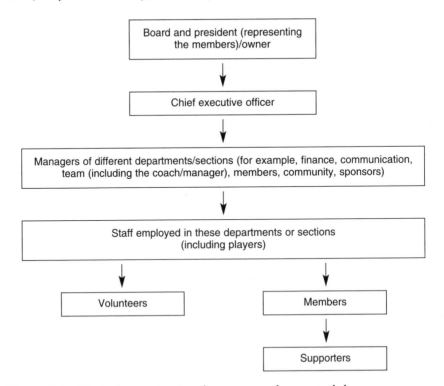

Figure 8.1 Typical organizational structure of a sport club

Although organizational models like this establish clear lines of authority and command, these soon become blurred in everyday organizational practice. Tensions can arise between different parts of the organization, for example, in the relationship between the board and the president (Hoye, 2004). Challenges can occur in the everyday management of sporting organizations when the previously undisputed authority of the playing side of the organization is required to engage with newly emerging but important non-playing dimensions of the organization. While a CEO or other senior organizational leader such as a president or an owner may seek to impose their authority on conflicts or tensions that arise within an organization (Capling and Marjoribanks, 2004), such attempts will not always be effective.

Three issues that have been particular sources of controversy in terms of internal club governance are the place of former players, the role of supporters and the role of communication processes.

The place of former players

Until relatively recently, there was an understanding that, in many areas of activity of a sport club, those with previous playing experience were best positioned to be effective managers. However, this view, while very strongly entrenched, has been challenged (Lewis, 2004). So the expectation that managers have elite playing experience has become less important. It is recognized that management tasks within a club are highly specialized, and that a person with education, training and experiences in those roles and issues may be of more value to the organization than a person with playing experience. In other words, in particular in contemporary professional sporting organizations, non-playing staff with MBAs, accounting, communications or law degrees may be of critical importance. The need for these professionals challenges the norm that former players should hold key positions and is often a source of tension (Capling and Marjoribanks, 2004, 2008).

The role of supporters, members and volunteers

Another challenge in relation to club governance is the extent to which supporters should be involved in it, if they should at all. In some instances, in particular in membership-based clubs, supporters who are members can potentially be involved to a great extent. Members may have the opportunity to run for election to the board of a club, or even to run for President, and thereby take a significant role in the governance of the club. At a lower level of the club hierarchy, there may be an opportunity to become involved in a range of volunteer activities, including participating in membership recruitment drives or working in the club shop, or providing a home for new recruits to the club. The importance of these positions is that they make a contribution to the functioning of the club, while also allowing members and supporters to take an active role in its operation. In contrast, in some sports, supporters and members are given very little or no opportunity to either take on leadership roles or provide voluntary services, with all tasks being undertaken by professional staff. For clubs as organizations, this may be based in a view that it is preferable to have professional staff, because the employer–employee relationship gives the organization greater control over what they can expect from, and demand of, professional staff (Capling and Marjoribanks 2004, 2008). Questions of control play an important role here, with the greater or lesser involvement of supporters in club organizational practice tied to the degree of control that clubs seek to have over people working within the organization (Hamil *et al.*, 2001, 1999). The knock-on effect of this varies by sport and locale, but being involved on a voluntary basis gives fans a greater sense of connection with their team.

Role of communication processes within organizations

While organizational charts set out lines of authority and communication in apparently uncontroversial ways, in practice, communication is also a site of power within organizations. Communication is a means through which power relations are established and curtailed within sporting organizations. For example, in the 2010 FIFA World Cup (soccer), leading player and former captain of the English team (soccer), John Terry, gave a press conference in which he publicly questioned the manager and team decision-making processes, and suggested that a number of players were unhappy. In doing this, Terry was attempting to assert power he perceived he had as a successful and popular player to effect changes in team management. The response from the manager, Fabio Capello, was swift, noting that Terry had made a big mistake by criticizing him in public. This response was a very public assertion of Capello's power in his officially sanctioned role. It was also an assertion that there are communication norms that need to be followed. Terry was perceived to have by-passed formal team channels of communication in a bid to boost his own position in the team (Fifield, 2010). As such, he was subject to censure.

GOVERNANCE OF SPORT AT THE LEAGUE LEVEL

Thus far, the discussion in the chapter has focused on governance at the club level. Clubs, while important, only have a meaningful existence in the context of leagues. Without a league in which to compete, sport clubs lose their reason for existence. In this regard, one of the features of many contemporary sports is that clubs operate within national, and sometimes international, league structures. In some instances, the governance role undertaken by league organizations is extensive. Important examples here include the Australian Football League and the National Football League (US) (gridiron), which regulate their sports extensively. Key features of these league structures include the introduction and regulation of salary caps, the maintenance of strict rules about selecting (drafting) new players, and control of team and player movements. The central goal of such regulation is to try to maintain a level playing field, so that all teams in the organization have the potential to win the league each year, or at least to be competitive. From the perspective of these league organizers, an ideal world is one in which each team would win the competition almost on a rotating basis. So the regulations aim to make the competition as even as possible, keeping the competition exciting. At the same time, while the league ostensibly serves the teams that constitute the league, the league organization also has its own interests. These interests may conflict with the interests of clubs, or may raise tensions in the relations between the league and the clubs. Successful clubs may feel that their success is overlooked or downplayed by a league with a focus on equalization, which is seen as unfairly rewarding poorly performing clubs. For example, a typical draft model in such leagues is one in which the bottom clubs are given the opportunity to select first from the pool of players at draft time (Capling and Marjoribanks, 2008).

Salary caps are an important example of a form of governance that provides challenges for leagues and for the clubs that constitute those leagues. Salary caps are an organizational mechanism put in place to limit how much money teams are allowed to pay the total of all the players on the team. Many of the major professional sport leagues in the United States and Australia have instituted salary caps as a mechanism for seeking to create a competitive environment within the league. From the viewpoint of leagues, salary caps are a means of seeking to ensure that one or two teams do not become overly dominant, based on their capacity to pay players much more than other teams. For governance practices in league contexts, significant challenges emerge if it is discovered that a breach of rules, such as a salary cap infringement, has occurred. In particular, the question arises of how severe any punishment should be if a breach does occur.

In 2010, the National Rugby League, the league organization for rugby league in Australia, discovered that one of its most successful teams, the Melbourne Storm, had been engaging in systematic breaches of salary cap restrictions. The response of the league was severe. The league imposed monetary fines on the Storm and stripped the club of the two premierships (championships) it had received during the period it had breached the salary cap. More controversially, the league ruled that the Storm could not be awarded any points for games in the 2010 season, effectively meaning that the club would finish bottom. Not surprisingly, this ruling resulted in mixed responses. From one viewpoint, it was considered to be appropriate, given the severity of the findings against the Storm. From this perspective, a severe penalty was required to ensure the integrity of the league and its regulations. From another viewpoint, the penalty, and in particular the ruling that the club could not win any points in the 2010 season, was considered to be too harsh, potentially resulting in players leaving the club (NRL, 2010).

DISCUSSION POINT: SHOULD LEAGUES USE SALARY CAPS AS A MEANS OF PROMOTING COMPETITIVE BALANCE?

In the aftermath of the Melbourne Storm salary cap infringement, a debate occurred around the desirability or otherwise of salary caps. In *The Age*, a daily newspaper in Melbourne, an argument against salary caps was presented by Paul Kerin (2010) of the Melbourne Business School, and was followed a week later by a response in favour of salary caps from Hans Westerbeek (2010) of the Royal Melbourne Institute of Technology (RMIT). Here, we present some of the main points in their respective arguments as a means of reflecting on the contested role of salary caps, and in a more general sense, on what role leagues should play in governing club activity.

For the no side, Paul Kerin

Kerin's starting point was that sport leagues should not impose salary caps. He suggested that salary caps hurt competitive balance, because they distort the operation of the market. The market would otherwise operate to ensure balance among the clubs while also acting as a means of weeding out the poorer and less successful clubs. In other words, Kerin's analysis was grounded in a business argument about not interfering to excess in the operations of the market. Among his claims were the following (Kerin, 2010):

If caps help poor clubs stay in the game, they also perpetuate competitive imbalance by impeding adjustments that would ultimately improve balance and financial viability.

Survival of the fittest works in nature and in business. In sport, it works at the player level; if we let it work at club level, it would raise the overall quality of on-field performance.

Caps also distort spending between player and non-player resources. As player payments are constrained, clubs try to improve on-field performance by spending more on other resources.

Kerin's argument is one which posits that, in essence, sporting competition and leagues should operate in the same way as other sectors of industry, and that the market is the best means through which to regulate organizational behaviour.

For the yes side, Hans Westerbeek

In responding to Kerin, Westerbeek made two important arguments. First, he argued that salary caps have contributed to competitive balance which is crucial in sport contexts. Second, he argued that sport cannot be considered to be the same as any other business in terms of the operation of the market. Unlike many industries where the financial failure and closure of one organization is a measure of success for a competitor, in sport, the financial failure and closure of one organization threatens all clubs, as they require competitors to exist. Among Westerbeek's claims were the following (Westerbeek, 2010):

One of the main characteristics of marketing sport is that clubs are required to compete and co-operate at the same time. Competition on the field can only exist if there is consistent and sustained co-operation off the field.

The required level of co-operation – of keeping each other in business to compete – cannot be guaranteed at club level.

The introduction of mechanisms such as the salary cap and the player draft increased the level of competitive balance. This in turn led to more spectators and followers of the game and, to this day, an ever-increasing value of media rights. To argue that increasing revenue from media rights should not be capped and left free to spend on players rather than non-playing resources is folly.

In contrast to Kerin's argument, Westerbeek's main claim was that sport organiza-tions are not the same as other sectors of business, and that forms of cooperation off the field are needed to support competition on the field. As clubs will not or are not able to develop this cooperation off the field by themselves to enhance sustainability, leagues must do this. This then requires that leagues implement measures such as salary caps to ensure the long-term survival of the competition.

Having read the arguments of Kerin and Westerbeek, do you find one of them more convincing than the other? And, if so, why? Are there other arguments that you would make to support either side?

In debates around salary caps, the point is often made that while salary caps may work in leagues such as the Australian Football League or the National Football League (gridiron) in the United States, where in effect there is one dominant league and no challengers, the situation is different in sports that operate more fully at an international level. For example, it is argued that if the English Premier League (soccer) used a salary cap independently of other leagues, the best players would move to the Spanish or Italian leagues. What do you think? Is there a way around this? Do you think it would be possible for major football (soccer) leagues to cooperate and put in place a trans-European salary cap, or even a global salary cap, for all football leagues?

In addition to activities such as those discussed above, sport leagues are also involved in activities such as organizing game schedules, also known as fixture lists, managing and organizing referees or umpires, and setting standards in relation to stadiums regarding seating, safety, catering and so on. While such activities tend to go on in an unremarked manner, save for when problems arise, they are essential to the functioning of the game and the competition. Without such activities being managed, the game could not go on. History has shown that clubs are not able to create effective organizational practices of these sorts without some form of league structure (Michie, 2000).

GOVERNANCE OF SPORT AT THE GLOBAL LEVEL

For many sports, governance at the international and global levels is significant as a form of control. Many of the organizations that work at these levels including, for example, the International Olympic Committee (IOC), FIFA (Fédération Internationale de Football Association) (soccer) and the IAAF (International Association of Athletics Federations) are recognizable the world over, in particular to everyday sport fans but also to many who watch sport only at the time of major international events.

Global sporting bodies such as the IOC, FIFA and the ICC (International Cricket Council) usually consist of a body of professional employees and representatives from member nations who contribute to the organization's policies and decisions. These organizations serve a number of functions such as organizing international sporting competitions like the Olympics or the FIFA World Cup (soccer), promoting the sport they represent, while also promoting the sporting ethos they represent. These organizations often hold themselves up not only as caretakers of the sport, but as organizations responsible for ensuring that the sport has an overall positive impact on the broader world around it. For example, an important tenet of FIFA is its mission statement: 'Develop the game, touch the world, build a better future' (FIFA, 2010). The roles of the IOC include: '[t]o encourage and support the promotion of ethics in sport as well as education of youth through sport and to dedicate its efforts to ensuring that, in sport, the spirit of fair play prevails and violence is banned', and '[t]o encourage and support a responsible concern for environmental issues, to promote sustainable development in sport and to require that the Olympic Games are held accordingly' (IOC, 2009). Such statements show the broad scope of activities that the IOC and FIFA see themselves as engaging in. While sport is at the heart of their endeavours, these objectives also create a strong link between sport and a range of broader social and political issues such as education, the environment, peace and social justice. For organizations such as the IOC and FIFA, sporting governance goes well beyond the organization of sport as a competition among athletes.

There is much formal and informal politics involved in sport governance at the global level. This is particularly noticeable with organizations such as the IOC and FIFA. As these organizations are powerful global actors, their politics are played out in various ways. At one level, there is significant overt and covert lobbying that occurs when nations compete with each other to host major events such as the Olympic Games or the Football World Cup (soccer). Political activity also occurs within these organizations in the everyday business of managing and running global organizations. To this extent, while organizations such as the IOC and FIFA are primarily sport organizations, their spheres of influence extend further to areas including relations with national governments, global sport product manufacturers and a range of other powerful industries. In the process of developing and negotiating these relationships and connections, the politics behind the reality of everyday practice often results in a different picture than is evident from mission statement claims, such as those mentioned above (Allison, 2005). For example, the IOC faced a critical challenge in the face of a bribes scandal in relation to the 2002 Winter Olympic bid, where it emerged that members of the IOC had accepted bribes, in the forms of gifts, from members of the Salt Lake City Olympic bid committee. Some years later, it also emerged that the successful bid by the Japanese city of Nagano to host the 1998 Winter Olympic Games had been helped by the giving of excessive gifts to members of the IOC (Miller, 2003).

In addition to such activities, organizations such as the IOC and FIFA are influential at an international level, both in sport and beyond, and so become key sites for internal struggle, as people compete with each other for leadership positions within the organization (BBC Sport, 2010). As Trevor Slack (2004) and Alan Tomlinson (2005) have identified, the IOC and the Olympic Games as institutions are now so massive that they are much more than a sporting organization and event. In Tomlinson's analysis (2005, p. 61), the significance of the Olympics 'is not so much about what is on the agenda of Olympic competition and activity programmes. It is more about the global profiling of places and the worldwide expansion of consumer markets.' He argues further that, 'The Olympics operate therefore as a focus for the articulation of serious national and global political dynamics, and as a giant billboard for the elite crop of multi-national corporations that are the preferred sponsorship partners of the International Olympic Committee' (Tomlinson, 2005, p. 49). Within this context, the IOC and sport are not merely reflecting general societal trends, but are rather 'pointing the way towards new cultural formations' (Tomlinson, 2005, pp. 48–9). From this viewpoint, the Olympic Games are intimately connected to questions of power and influence in global capitalism.

The IOC is not the only international sport organization where questions of governance are intimately connected to issues of power and politics. Another body that is frequently embroiled in both overt and covert politics is the International Cricket Council (ICC), the international governing body for cricket. The ICC governs cricket on behalf of 96 member nations, with a complex hierarchical system of organization (Hoye and Cuskelly 2007, pp. 37–43). Particularly notable here is that, while there are 96 members, this is broken down into ten full members, 32 associate members and 54 affiliate members. The decision-making body is the ICC Chief Executives' Committee, which 'comprises the CEOs of the 10 Full ICC Member countries plus three elected representatives from the Associate Member countries' (Hoye and Cuskelly, 2007, p. 39). The full members are those nations that engage in professional (Test) cricket. In this way, the interests of the dominant countries are built into the structures of the organization.

Political challenges also emerge in contexts where people are elected to positions of influence within the organization. For example, former Australian Prime Minister John Howard was nominated as ICC Vice-President in 2010, with the position of President to follow in 2012, by the Australian and New Zealand cricket boards, but only after intense lobbying, with New Zealand believing they had put forward a candidate with stronger expertise in cricket administration. Indeed, the former CEO of British Airways, the Australian Sir Rod Eddington, had to be brought in to mediate between the two countries. Once Australia and New Zealand had nominated Howard, they encountered strongly negative reactions from a range of other cricketing nations, including India, South Africa, the West Indies and Zimbabwe. Despite strong and concerted lobbying, including from Howard himself, in an unprecedented outcome, Howard's nomination was ultimately rejected. This process showed the intense politics that can accompany selection decisions in major sport organizations (Roebuck, 2010).

CONCLUSION

Sport governance is important at the club, league, national and global levels, but the different levels have different governance needs. At the club level governance structures are required at minimum to enable team selection and coaching to occur. As sport becomes increasingly professionalized, both the number and diversity of club personnel required increase.

Leagues provide key governance structures for sports. They generally organize playing schedules and venues, and oversee the rules that teams follow. As discussed above, some leagues are very interventionist in their interactions with clubs, while others are less so. Context is important. As the examples discussed show, leagues that oversee localized sports such as the National Football League (US gridiron) and the Australian Football League (Australian Rules football) are able to implement competition-levelling strategies such as salary caps, while leagues whose sports are global such, as the professional football (soccer) leagues in Europe and South America, have to take into account leagues in other nations. Leagues representing global sports are reluctant to implement policies such as salary caps that might limit their ability to attract the best players from around the world.

Sport governance also happens at the global level. Transnational sports organizations such as FIFA and the IOC provide structures for global sporting contests while promoting a range of activities related to the sports they represent. As with the other levels of sport governance, global sport governance is political, with individual nations competing within the structures of these organizations for positions that benefit their constituents.

Through the examples discussed in this chapter, it is evident that governance and regulation are important aspects of the sporting world, and that they involve contested power relations. While clubs, leagues and other organizational actors set up clear and well-defined organizational maps and goals, in everyday practice the precise dimensions of such maps and goals can quickly become contested and subject to challenge. This is not to suggest that such formal processes are unwarranted. To the contrary, they are essential. But what a sociological framework provides is a means to go beyond such formal processes to analyse how they play out in everyday practice.

CHAPTER SUMMARY

This chapter has shown that:

- Governance is a key dimension of the organization of sport.
- Without governance at the club, league and global levels, sport as we understand it could not exist.
- While governance is set up formally, through organizational maps and the like, organizational struggles raise crucial questions around the influence of power in everyday practice.
- Struggles around governance within sporting organizations raise crucial questions around the overall goals and objectives of sporting organizations.

DISCUSSION QUESTIONS

1　Do you think that leagues add an unnecessary level of bureaucracy to sport? Would it be better to leave the organization of sporting competitions to clubs?

2　Some criticisms of global sport organizations such as the IOC and FIFA suggest that those organizations have become too powerful and that, rather than promoting the best interests of the sport, they focus on promoting their own interests. What do you think? How could the criticisms be addressed?

3　In relation to the everyday running of sport clubs, some argue that there is an important role for volunteers, whereas others argue that clubs need to be staffed entirely by professional employees. What is the basis for these different viewpoints? What do you think?

4　The central objective of corporatized sporting clubs should be to make money for their owners. Discuss.

FURTHER READING

Capling, Ann and Marjoribanks, Tim (2004) 'Connecting Commerce and Culture in Third Sector Organisations: The Case of Australian Football League Clubs', *Third Sector Review*, 10(1), pp. 61–76.

Hamil, Sean, Holt, Matthew, Michie, Jonathan, Oughton, Christine and Shailer, Lee (2004) 'The Corporate Governance of Professional Football Clubs', *Corporate Governance*, 4(2), pp. 44–51.

Hoye, Russell and Cuskelly, Graham (2007) *Sport Governance*, Amsterdam, Elsevier.

Michie, Jonathan (2000) 'The Governance and Regulation of Professional Football', *Political Quarterly*, 71(2), pp. 184–91.

Chapter 9

The Politics of Sport Regulation

INTRODUCTION

Chapter 8 was concerned with how sport organizations govern themselves. This chapter shifts the focus from governance of sport to state regulation. An important debate in contemporary political science, policy studies and sociology concerns transformations in the role of the state in societies around the world. The 1990s and 2000s have witnessed an increasing role for the state in regulating many aspects of sport. Engaging with debates around the role of the state in society, this chapter explores the roles that the state is taking in sport, the range of organizations it engages with in taking on these roles and the struggles associated with government regulation of sport. The chapter does this through an extended case study of the attempted takeover of Manchester United (football/soccer) by BSkyB in the late 1990s and into the 2000s, followed by two shorter examples: regulating tobacco advertising and regulating sports mega-events. These examples reveal that organizational relations are important in the outcomes of contests around the politics of sport regulation.

CONCEPTUALIZING THE STATE AND SPORT POLICY

From a sociological perspective, the state can be analysed as the set of institutions that have been formally empowered to regulate and govern society. The state includes political institutions (for example, parliament), the legal system and a range of regulatory bodies and other similar organizations. In the context of sport, the most important organizations of the state include:

- **The Parliament,** or similar body, as the organization that creates and enacts legislation.
- **The court system,** as the set of organizations that enforce the law and also create their own laws, through common or civil law processes.
- **The police force.** In particular, on game day, the police are often a highly visible manifestation of the state. For some people who transgress the law, the courts and prison system may also be part of their interaction with the state.

In addition to these organizations, a range of other state organizations are becoming increasingly important in regulating sport. Competition authorities are taking an active interest in the commercial dimensions of sport, in particular as sport interacts with other industries such as the media. Competition authorities are concerned both that sport organizations do not engage in anti-competitive behaviour, and that other organizations engaging with sport do not engage in anti-competitive behaviour. Other parts of the state may also become involved in sport at various times. With the international flow of sports persons between countries, immigration authorities become involved in terms of the rules around who is allowed to enter countries, for how long and under what conditions. Similarly, because professional sport organizations are important economic entities, a range of organizations within the state that regulate business and enterprise, such as the tax department, employment department, or their equivalents, and so on, will also be involved in regulating sport at various times (Daly, 2003; Jessop, 1990; Skocpol, 1992; Wilks, 1999a, 1999b).

A critical issue to note about the role of the state is that, because it includes so many organizations, there is a chance that different parts of the state will have different interests (Skocpol, 1992). As such, regulation may not always flow in a smooth or predictable path: different organizations within the state may come into conflict with each other. It is also important to note that the state does not act in a vacuum or in isolation. At various stages, a range of other organizations including political parties and leaders, organizations from the private and non-profit sectors and the leagues themselves will become involved in regulating sport, meaning that an analysis of the role of the state in sport requires an engagement with a broad range of organizations, both within the state and external to it.

In an ongoing contribution to our understanding of the politics of sport regulation, Barrie Houlihan has focused extensively on policy processes in the context of sport. His research (Houlihan, 2005) shows that governments have interacted with sport in a number of ways, including:

■ Regulation of sport, around issues including broadcasting rights, drug use and even 'licensing of coaches' (2005, p. 164).
■ Government funding of sporting events and codes.
■ The use of sport as a means to promote particular social objectives, such as reducing obesity and moves towards social inclusion.

Houlihan (2000) argues that, across time, we can see a number of forms of policy intervention and motivations for such intervention. First, governments may seek to 'control or outlaw particular sports' (2000, p. 215). Second, at least in the period prior to World War II, governments sought to intervene in sport to improve military preparedness. Third, governments may intervene in sport through policy as a means of promoting social integration, an issue we discuss in greater detail in Chapter 10. Fourth, governments may seek to 'use sport to build a sense of national identity' (2000, p. 216) and, fifth, as a means of 'project[ing] a positive image of the nation abroad' (2000, p. 216). Sixth, governments may seek to regulate sport as a means of promoting economic development. And, finally, the state may engage with sport as a tool of international diplomacy. It is clear that the state is heavily involved in sport, either directly or indirectly, and that such relations have been ongoing over an extended period of time and in many countries. Any argument that sport and politics do not mix has not considered the evidence!

Within this overall context concerning the role of the state and of politics in governing sport, this chapter takes a different approach than in previous chapters. While discussing a number of examples of regulation that bring politics to the surface towards the end of the chapter, most of this chapter analyses a series of events that occurred in the late 1990s and into the 2000s, when the media organization BSkyB attempted to purchase the English Premier League football (soccer) club Manchester United. This particular case provides in-depth insights into a range of ways in which the state seeks to regulate sport, and into the ways in which the state interacts with a range of other actors.

MANCHESTER UNITED, BSKYB AND THE BRITISH STATE

Through the 1990s and into the 2000s, the satellite broadcasting company British Sky Broadcasting (BSkyB) has been a key player in the context of

English football (soccer), and of sport more generally (BSkyB, 2010d). Indeed, by 2010, BSkyB had sought to position itself as 'the first choice for entertainment and communications' (BSkyB, 2010a). BSkyB is partly owned by News International, the British arm of global media conglomerate News Corporation, and while BSkyB operates across a diverse range of entertainment and communication areas, this case study investigates three stages of its strategy in the context of sport: first, its success in securing the rights to broadcast live football in the 1990s; second, the attempted and ultimately unsuccessful merger between BSkyB and Manchester United Football Club in 1998–99; and, third, BSkyB's subsequent reformulation of its corporate strategy regarding sport to a model of developing strategic alliances with a number of football clubs. In developing this analysis, the chapter focuses on the relationship between the strategy formation of BSkyB and its interactions with the government.

BSkyB and English football: strategy one – securing football broadcasting rights

As a broadcaster British Sky Broadcasting (BSkyB) embodied the faith in the market and the ideology of citizens as consumers that emerged in Britain in the years of the Thatcher Conservative Party governments (King, 1998; Williams, 1994). Historically, free to air television in Britain was constituted by analogue terrestrial stations including the public BBC and independent ITV, followed by the emergence of newer channels in the 1980s and 1990s. Television owners gained access to all programming by paying an annual television licence fee. The establishment of BSkyB in 1990, and its earlier manifestations in British Satellite Broadcasting and Sky Television in the 1980s, amounted to an important shift in broadcasting practice and ideology, based on an opening up of television to the market by providing channels to individual consumers through a subscription-based user-pays system (Saundry, 1998; Williams, 1994). It is an indication of how quickly the world of the media is changing that, while subscription-based satellite and cable television is now commonplace in the UK, as recently as the 1990s it was a new phenomenon.

Since these early days, BSkyB has been hugely successful in promoting this subscriber-based form of television consumption, particularly in sport broadcasting. It is recognized as providing a quality product and, as of 30 June 2010, it had 9,860,000 customers in the UK and the Republic of Ireland, and 16,000 employees (BSkyB, 2010b). In 1998, BSkyB expanded into digital service delivery, with the establishment of Sky Digital. Among programming options made available by BSkyB, sport is central, with Sky Sports carrying more sports programming than any other UK platform across a network of five sports services. In 2010, for example, Sky Sports claimed it 'will broadcast more than 40,000 hours of sports across five core channels and four HD channels' (BSkyB, 2010c).

In developing a corporate strategy that builds on new broadcasting technologies and the ideology of citizens as consumers, BSkyB has been involved in a number of crucial struggles, one of the most important involving broadcasting rights for English football (soccer) (Cowie and Williams, 1997; Findlay *et al.*, 1999; Williams, 1994). The relationship between television and football in England has been, and continues to be, one that is both mutually beneficial and simultaneously fraught with tension for both broadcasters and sporting organizations. In particular, the Football Association and the Football League, the two main governance organizations of professional football in England prior to 1992, were historically resistant to live broadcasting of matches, fearing that such coverage would reduce attendances. When live broadcasting finally began in 1983, it was on a limited basis only, with deals between the Football League and the BBC and ITV from 1983 to 1987, and with ITV from 1988 to 1991.

The 1980s were traumatic for English football, with concerns about crowd behaviour, crowd safety and declining attendances, and the decade culminated in the handing down of a report on football by Lord Justice Taylor in 1990 (King, 1998; Taylor, 1990; Williams, 1994). The Taylor Report recommended that grounds provide only seated accommodation, and that football authorities should look to television revenues as a major means of raising the money needed for stadiums' improvements. In this societal context, negotiations among elite clubs about the establishment of a new Football Association Premier League focused centrally on television revenues and their distribution. The rules of the new league, which was established in 1992, subsequently contained regulations regarding the distribution of television revenues among the clubs and granted the league the right to negotiate on behalf of the clubs in relation to broadcasting rights (RPC, 1996). As a result, clubs were to sell their television rights collectively through the Premier League, rather than on a club by club basis (MMC, 1999). This rule and its effects were to be significant in the unfolding struggle for broadcasting rights.

The Taylor Report and the establishment of the Premier League amounted to a transformation in the power structures of football, with the clubs and broadcasters beginning anew in negotiations for television rights (King,

1998; RPC, 1996; Williams, 1994). Following a protracted series of negotiations involving BBC, ITV and BSkyB for exclusive rights to the broadcasting of live matches and highlights until 1997, a bid made by BSkyB for live matches in conjunction with the BBC for highlights for £214 million was accepted. This was a major increase from the £55 million that had been paid by ITV for rights to the coverage of the previous four seasons and also included a significant increase in the number of live games to be shown. The agreement ensured that television broadcasters were to be significant financial players in the new league. A second round of bargaining commenced in 1996, with BSkyB succeeding again on the basis of raising its bid in conjunction with the BBC to £743 million for a further four years until 2001 (RPC, 1996).

The outcome of these bidding wars was that BSkyB established a dominant position as the broadcaster of live football matches. While BSkyB argued that its position was due to the quality of its product, state institutions including the Office of Fair Trading (OFT) claimed that the dominance came about through the inclusion of restrictions in broadcasting contracts (RPC, 1996). The first set of broadcasting contracts, for example, included a 'matching rights clause' which guaranteed BSkyB and the BBC the capacity to secure the rights for the renewal of contracts if they matched the highest bidder's offer, and in 1997 the Premier League agreed not to sell television rights to any other broadcaster for programmes in the UK. Indeed, the OFT first began investigating the Premier League broadcast agreements with BSkyB in 1992 on the basis that they were anti-competitive and against the public interest.

The matter was ultimately referred by the OFT to the Restrictive Practices Court in April 1996 (OFT, 1996). Central to the case of the Director General of Fair Trading (DGFT) was that the Premier League broadcast agreements had taken the form of a cartel because all the clubs joined together to sell their rights collectively. According to the DGFT, the result was that there was unsatisfied demand among consumers as only 60 out of a total of 380 Premier League games were televized each season. In addition, because of its monopoly over Premier League rights, the DGFT argued that BSkyB had secured a dominant position which was harming competition and the development of broadcasting, thereby operating against the public interest. Ultimately, the Court ruled against the DGFT, stating that the broadcasting agreements had been secured by BSkyB through open competition, and that competition would again be open for the 2001 contract. To the extent that this was the case, the agreements were not contrary to the public interest, although the Court did decide that the matching rights clauses were contrary to the public interest (Hamil *et al.*, 1999; MMC, 1999; RPC, 1996).

An outcome of this case, and of other hearings (see, for example, OFT, 1996), was that BSkyB was required to give undertakings concerning its strategies to ensure that it would not engage in anti-competitive behaviour. As such, the state was actively involved in regulating the strategies available to the broadcaster. At the same time, BSkyB, in conjunction with the Premier League and its club members, engaged in activities that challenged both the formal and informal rules organizing the media–sport economy, including the networks of relations between the organizational actors. For example, the decision of the Restrictive Practices Court that the Premier League and its clubs were not engaging in anti-competitive behaviour by negotiating for broadcasting contracts as a group with individual broadcasters upheld the increasing closeness of the relationship between football and television, both financially and promotionally. The decision also ensured that, at least for the duration of specific contracts, individual broadcasters such as BSkyB would be influential in the unfolding of the sport–media dynamic.

BSkyB and English football: strategy two – the attempted merger of BSkyB and Manchester United Football Club

In 1998 BSkyB attempted to implement a strategy intended to consolidate its relationship with football by announcing a proposed takeover of Manchester United for £623 million. As well as being the most successful team in England in the 1990s, Manchester United was then, and remains, financially very powerful in the context of world football. In stating its reasons for the proposed takeover, management at BSkyB argued that sport was an accepted part of BSkyB's brand-building strategies; that acquisition of Manchester United would be an important part of BSkyB's development of content ownership; that it would allow BSkyB to take advantage of digital technology developments; and that a takeover would be financially beneficial to both organizations (MMC, 1999). Similarly, the board of Manchester United, in recommending acceptance of the offer, suggested that it would secure the long-term future of the club; that it represented a natural extension of the club's business and of its involvement in media; and that the corporate goals of both organizations were similar in emphasizing expansion, marketing and innovation in technology (MMC, 1999). The stance in favour of the takeover received strong support from a number of leading clubs, which argued that the financial and promotional resources of the media were essential for the future of the game (Hamil *et al.*, 2000; MMC, 1999).

The announcement of the takeover bid also led to the mobilization of anti-takeover groups among supporters, who organized in groups such as the Independent Manchester United Supporters' Association and the Shareholders United Against Murdoch (Brown, 1998, 2000). Also expressing opposition to the takeover were the Football Association and the Football League, a number of clubs from lower divisions and a number of media competitors. These organizations were concerned that the takeover would impact negatively on competition, both in relation to future contract negotiations by giving BSkyB a guaranteed and powerful insider position, and in relation to competition on the pitch by giving Manchester United access to resources unavailable to any other club. There was also concern that a successful takeover would transform the existing relations between clubs and the media by allowing News Corporation to control the content of the sporting product through its ownership of Manchester United, in addition to its control of distribution of programming through broadcasting (Branston *et al.*, 1999; Chadwick and Palmer, 1997; Hamil, 1999; Lee, 1999; Michie and Walsh, 1999).

In this early drawing of battle lines, it was not clear how the government and relevant state institutions would align themselves. The Labour government, which had been in office since 1997 under Prime Minister Tony Blair, had attempted to develop links with News Corporation and Rupert Murdoch, both before and after the election. While such links suggested that government figures would support the takeover, significant opposition arose from within Parliament, and an inquiry was ultimately launched to establish whether the takeover would be anti-competitive and against the public interest.

Analysing this period of initial reaction to the proposed takeover, a number of themes can be identified, reflecting the perceptions of the actors involved at the time of the events. Among those who opposed the takeover, the overall perception was that football was the people's game. From this perspective, the most readily apparent theme to emerge was vehement and personalized anti-News Corporation and anti-Rupert Murdoch sentiment. In particular, there was concern that a successful takeover would mean that future decisions regarding Manchester United would be made on the basis of the global corporate interests of News Corporation. Another theme to emerge among those opposing the takeover was that football is a tradition central to the identity of local communities. It was argued that this tradition was experienced in bonds of solidarity and emotional attachment between fans and clubs, but that corporate ownership would destroy such traditions. A number of voices also emerged commenting more specifically on what were perceived to be the anti-competitive commercial aspects of the case. For all these reasons, those opposing the takeover argued that it was against the public interest (Branston *et al.*, 1999; Chadwick and Palmer, 1997; Lee, 1999; Michie and Walsh, 1999; MMC, 1999).

The dominant theme of those in favour of the takeover, by contrast, was that football was part of the entertainment industry and should be treated as any other business. It was argued that News Corporation and BSkyB had been beneficial to football, both by promoting and financing the game. Opponents of the takeover were considered to have a sentimental and anti-competitive vision of the game that did not accord with the reality of contemporary sport and entertainment. It was argued that Manchester United was a major economic and commercial actor, and that permanent relations between media and sport organizations of the type proposed were essential if clubs were to remain competitive in a global sporting and enter-tainment market. In addition, it was suggested by those in favour of the takeover that a decision to stop the merger would be politically motivated, and inspired by opposition to Murdoch, rather than ruled by the needs of business, competition and the public interest (MMC, 1999).

While the voices of these different actors were important in shaping the context of the proposed takeover, the central institution at this stage of corporate strategy formation was to be the Monopolies and Mergers Commission (MMC) (since 1 April 1999 the Competition Commission). The discourse just outlined, which also emerged in submissions made to the MMC, indicates that there was a great deal of public debate around the issue, and it was the MMC that provided the forum in which these voices could take effect. While the MMC could not initiate inquires, it acted on referrals made by officials including the Director General of Fair Trading and the Secretary of State for Trade and Industry (Competition Commission, 1999; Doern and Wilks, 1996; Wilks, 1999a, 1999b). In this case the MMC was mainly concerned with whether the matter referred was against the public interest, as detailed in the Fair Trading Act 1973. From the 1980s the 'effect on competition' (Wilks, 1999b, p. 15) of any proposed merger had become the main criteria in defining notions of the public interest (Wilks, 1999a, 1999b).

The proposed takeover of Manchester United was referred by the OFT to the MMC in October 1998 and the report of the MMC was handed down in April 1999. The MMC ruled that the takeover would be anti-competitive. This ruling was subsequently supported and enforced by the Department of Trade and Industry which blocked the takeover. The reasons given by the MMC (1999, pp. 3–5) for the ruling were:

1   The takeover would impact negatively on competition among broadcasters. It would operate against the public interest by concentrating too much market influence in the hands of BSkyB, by giving it access to information not available to other broadcasters, resulting in an unfair advantage in negotiating broadcast rights to Premier League games.
2   The proposed takeover would impact negatively on football by reinforcing the growing inequality already evident in English football between rich and poor clubs. A takeover would also give BSkyB additional influence over the organization of football, with the possible outcome that Premier League decisions would be made according to the corporate interests of News Corporation rather than in the interests of football as a whole.
3   There were no 'public interest benefits from the proposed merger' (MMC, 1999, p. 5).

Given the success of News Corporation and of other media companies in entering the sport industry globally, through broadcasting, team ownership and sponsorship, the outcome of the Manchester United takeover bid was unexpected. For those in favour of the merger, the ruling represented an economically misguided and politically motivated decision which would have negative outcomes for the media and football industries in England. For those who opposed the takeover, the decision was a vindication of their argument about the unique status of football. The decision also led to a reformulation of the strategy of BSkyB.

BSkyB and English football: strategy three – developing relationships with multiple clubs

Following the decision of the MMC, and its acceptance by the government, an alternative strategy to outright ownership emerged in which media corporations purchased smaller, but still important, shareholdings in football teams in a process of forming 'strategic alliances'. Adopting this strategy, and in accord with Premier League regulations limiting individual shareholders to less than 10 per cent interest in a club, BSkyB purchased 9.9 per cent stakes in Manchester United, Leeds United, Chelsea and Manchester

City, and a 5 per cent stake in Sunderland, while NTL purchased a 6 per cent stake in Newcastle United and Granada had a 9.9 per cent stake in Liverpool.

In each instance the shareholding involvement of media corporations in football was welcomed by the Chairs of the clubs involved. The alliances were presented by the clubs and by BSkyB as securing the financial future of the clubs concerned while also allowing both parties to benefit from formalizing direct links between media and sport (BSkyB, 1999, 2000; Guardian, 2000). What was not discussed by the clubs or by BSkyB were the attempts by BSkyB to position itself for negotiations regarding television rights. This goal did not, however, go unnoticed. Adam Brown, a member of the Government Football Task Force Working Group, argued that by forming strategic alliances BSkyB had adopted a 'Plan B' in which it sought to gain strategic advantages within clubs, including access to information not available to other media corporations, which would assist it in negotiations over broadcasting rights (Brown, 2000; see also Harris, 2000; Teather and Brodkin, 2000).

This process of strategy reformulation by media and sporting organizations was an indication that a new stage had been reached in the relationship between media and football. While the planned full integration of sport and media resulted instead in the defeat of the proposed takeover of Manchester United by BSkyB, the emergence of a new strategy of strategic alliances revealed that the contest for power between sport and media was continuing, and that the state and its organizations were critical players in these processes.

Reflections on the case

In the context of this chapter, this case study is important for a number of reasons. First, it reveals the ways in which politics is central to the everyday practice of sport. While sport and media organizations were at the centre of these processes, the framework in which they operated was developed and enforced by state institutions. Second, it shows how the state, as a regulator, engages with a complex set of relations in the world of sport. Sport regulation involves regulating sporting organizations along with a range of other organizations including, as in this example, media corporations and supporter groups. Third, the case shows the importance of analysing the relations and interactions within the state. In addition to leading political figures, including the Prime Minister, this case also involved various competition authorities and other legal institutions. Having discussed this case in depth, we now consider more briefly two other examples that provide further insights into the politics of sport regulation.

REGULATING TOBACCO ADVERTISING

An important example of the role of the state in terms of regulating sport concerns tobacco advertising, and the more general place of tobacco in sport. If you take a look at major sporting events from the 1960s and into the 1970s through an online video site, or if you look at television programmes or newspaper photographs from those times, or even earlier, tobacco advertising is a ubiquitous feature of the landscape. Tobacco companies advertised heavily through sport, including sponsoring major international and national sport events and competitions. For tobacco companies, advertising at sporting events and sponsoring competitions was an excellent way of securing high-level exposure for their product. For sport organizations, the money paid by tobacco companies for advertising and sponsorship rights was significant financially (Amis and Cornwell, 2005).

If you perform the same test and watch broadcasts of sporting events in the 2000s, a very different picture emerges. Tobacco advertising is either completely or almost non-existent, and, indeed, in many contexts now, smoking at stadiums, and even around stadiums, is prohibited. For example, in Australia, the Federal Government banned all tobacco sponsorships in the 1990s. Related to this process, in the Australian state of Victoria, 'the Victorian Health Promotion Foundation (VicHealth) was set up to offer an alternative source of sponsorship money to sporting and other organisations' (VicHealth, 2002). In Europe, the success of tobacco control groups in ending the sponsorship of the ATP Swiss Indoor tennis tournament by Davidoff, a cigarette brand owned by Imperial Tobacco, has been hailed as bringing 'about an end to the last high profile tobacco sponsorship of sport in Europe' (ASH, 2010).

How did this change come about? It is linked in part to changes in social attitudes around smoking, part of a broader trend based on medical and societal recognition of the adverse health outcomes linked to smoking. But also very much tied up in this process are challenges to the place of tobacco in society from governments around the world. Just as governments have acted around the world to ban smoking in workplaces, restaurants and other venues on health grounds, so too governments have acted to ban cigarette advertising in sporting stadiums and in sport-related events. In addition, smoking itself has been banned in many sporting stadiums, a stark change from even a generation ago when the smell of tobacco filled the air at grounds. At the same time, this has been a contested process, with tobacco companies arguing against such regulations. Nevertheless, the evidence about the harmful health consequences of smoking has been so overwhelming that governments have been able to legislate to control and regulate the advertising and presence of tobacco in sporting contexts on public health grounds. Sport organizations have also taken this path, even in the face of concerns about the loss of sponsorship money from tobacco companies. In many cases, however, other major corporations have stepped in to provide required sponsorship and funding. The significance of this example is that it shows how, within a matter of years, a combination of state regulation, league action and societal change has resulted in a transformation of the sporting landscape in terms of the removal of a group of companies that used to be a financially significant presence in professional sport. At the same time, it is important to remember that tobacco sponsorship of sport and of sport-related activities continues to exist in some parts of the world, and in some sports, while concerns also arise around subliminal advertising on the part of tobacco companies, even in contexts where advertising is banned (Hagon, 2010; Ling *et al.*, 2010, QUIT, 2010).

DISCUSSION POINT

Consider the following three claims:

- The banning of tobacco advertising by governments is going too far in terms of regulation.
- Sports should be allowed to accept advertising and sponsorship money from any organization or individual.
- Governments, leagues and clubs are infringing on the rights of individuals when they ban smoking inside stadiums.

List three points that you could make, first, to support these claims and, second, to dispute these claims. On balance, which side of the argument do you find more persuasive, and why? What do your answers suggest about the appropriate role of the government in sporting contexts such as this?

To bring the analysis in this chapter to a close, one final example is discussed that raises questions around regulation and the role of the state – namely, major global sporting events or mega-events.

REGULATING MEGA-EVENTS

Chapter 6 discussed sports mega-events. In the context of the discussion in this chapter, there are three significant dimensions of sporting mega-events (Horne and Manzenreiter, 2006a, 2006b):

■ First, they 'have significant consequences for the host city, region or nation in which they occur' (2006a, p. 2).
■ Second, they 'attract considerable media coverage' (2006a, p. 2).
■ Third, they raise contested regulatory issues.

The 2010 FIFA World Cup (soccer), hosted in South Africa, highlights some of the regulatory issues that such mega-events raise. For example, in 2008, a so-called 'Temporary Relocation Area (TRA)', named Blikkiesdorp, was built on the outskirts of Cape Town, to provide emergency housing for people who had been illegally occupying buildings (Smith, 2010). In the lead-up to the World Cup, however, hundreds of people were forcibly relocated there away from hostels and settlements they had been living in, because they were deemed to be in the way of World Cup infrastructure developments. Conditions in Blikkiesdorp, or 'Tin Can Town' as it is known, were reported to be appalling, with high levels of illness, inadequate and overcrowded accommodation, high unemployment and few prospects of change. Yet, people were moved there under the threat of force from the police. While local government officials disputed these claims, it seems evident that people were being moved against their will, in the context of South Africa hosting the World Cup. The infrastructure needs of the World Cup took precedence over the housing needs of the people (Smith, 2010; see also, Raghavan, 2010).

In another significant move, prior to the World Cup, South Africa established 56 World Cup Courts across the country (Byrne, 2010). Staffed by more than 1,500 personnel, the courts were set up to dispense speedy justice during the World Cup. While intended officially to promote the legal system in South Africa, and to show the positive face of South Africa in terms of law and order, in practice they were understood as a means of attempting to control the population during the World Cup. Related to this, in 2006,

South Africa put in place the '2010 FIFA World Cup South Africa Special Measures Act'. One controversial case involving this Act arose in the World Cup when a number of Dutch women attending a game were charged with ambush marketing, and with promoting a product that was not officially endorsed by FIFA, by wearing orange-coloured dresses that were reputedly associated with a particular beer brand that was not an official FIFA sponsor. As Marina Hyde (2010) reported, two of the women were subsequently 'accused of contravening two sections of this law, namely the parts that prohibit "unauthorised commercial activities inside an exclusion zone" and "enter[ing] into a designated area while in unauthorised possession of a commercial object"'. As Hyde goes on to note, a radical feature of the legislation was that it made the offences criminal rather than civil offences, meaning they could potentially result in jail terms. While the women were ultimately let off, it is critical to note that this appears to be a situation in which national governments are enacting legislation to meet the demands of global sporting organizations. And, this is not a one-off situation. As Hyde notes, 'similar legislation is in place in New Zealand ready for next year's [2011] Rugby World Cup' (Hyde, 2010; see also Hughes, 2010).

What these examples suggest is that, in the context of mega-events, national governments are very quick to act in accord with the demands of the global sporting organization. As such, non-accountable sporting organizations are influencing the policy-making processes and decisions of governments at the national level, playing on the desire of governments to host these events. The impacts on the people living in the host nation can then be felt directly. As such examples show, sport is anything but apolitical. Politics is at the heart of, and inseparable from, sport.

CONCLUSION

This chapter has argued that the state plays a critical role in the context of contemporary sport. Both by itself and in its relationships with other organizations, the state fulfils important roles in creating the landscape within which sport exists. At the same time, the state can, and does, have a direct influence on sport, whether this is in the context of broadcasting rights, regulation of activities such as tobacco advertising, or regulating global mega-events. As this chapter shows, to understand contemporary sport requires engagement with the contested role of the state in regulating sport.

CHAPTER SUMMARY

This chapter has shown that:

■ The state, and its constituent organizations, have a crucial role to play in the regulation of sport.
■ The role of the state can vary depending on particular contexts, from directive forms of government to more facilitative forms of governance.
■ The example of BSkyB's attempted takeover of Manchester United reveals that, to understand the role of the state in sport, there is a need to consider how it interacts with other organizations.
■ Examples such as tobacco regulation and regulation of mega-event contexts show that the state's role in sporting contests can be highly contentious.

DISCUSSION QUESTIONS

1 In this chapter, we have made the argument that state institutions play a crucial role in regulating sport. Do you think this is an appropriate role for the state to play? Or should sport leagues be left to govern themselves?
2 The case study of BSkyB's attempted takeover of Manchester United reveals how particular state institutions, along with supporter groups, were influential in preventing the takeover of the club. Do you think it was right that BSkyB was prevented from purchasing the club? Why would this situation be any different than, say, Roman Abramovich's successful takeover of Chelsea Football Club (soccer)?
3 What do you make of the concept of sport mega-events? Do you think it is a useful concept? Why or why not? What challenges do such events raise in terms of sport regulation?

FURTHER READING

Amis, John and Cornwell, T. Bettina (eds) (2005) *Global Sport Sponsorship*, Berg, Oxford.
Cowie, C. and Williams, M. (1997) 'The Economics of Sports Rights', *Telecommunications Policy*, 21, pp. 619–34.
Daly, Mary (2003) 'Governance and Social Policy', *Journal of Social Policy*, 32(1), pp. 113–28.

Houlihan, Barrie (2005) 'Public Sector Sport Policy: Developing a Framework for Analysis', *International Review for the Sociology of Sport*, 40(2), pp. 163–85.

Saundry, Richard (1998) 'The Limits of Flexibility: The Case of UK Television', *British Journal of Management*, 9, pp. 151–62.

Chapter 10

Sport and Social Justice

INTRODUCTION

Sport is about much more than competition on the field of play between individuals or teams. This chapter explores the social role of sport and the extent to which sport can contribute to the attainment of social justice. Such a discussion is important because it will: (1) provide insights into the social and political roles of sport; (2) provide examples revealing how sport can have a potential influence on social justice processes; and (3) show how sport is a site of social, political and regulatory contestation. To engage with these issues, this chapter explores four dimensions of the social justice role of sport in society:

- Sport, Social policy and Social Inclusion.
- Sport and Human Rights.
- Sport and Corporate Social Responsibility.
- Ethical Governance in Sport Organizations.

These issues are connected to each other through the concept of social justice. While social justice is a politically contested concept, here it is used in the general sense as expressed by the Secretary-General of the United Nations, Ban Ki-moon, in his message on World Day of Social Justice, 20 February 2010. In that message, the Secretary-General commented that:

> On the World Day of Social Justice, we recognize the importance of tackling poverty, exclusion and unemployment, in order to promote solidarity, harmony and equality of opportunity within and between societies. ... Social justice is based on the values of fairness, equality, respect for

diversity, access to social protection, and the application of human rights in all spheres of life, including in the workplace. (Ki-moon, 2010)

In mobilizing this understanding of social justice, a critical set of questions emerge around how it is to be achieved. The four dimensions identified above are specific means through which sport can contribute towards the promotion of social justice. This is not to suggest that the achievement of any one or more of these goals will result in the attainment of social justice in itself, either now or in the future. Nevertheless, these are important dimensions in the context of broader struggles for social justice.

SPORT, SOCIAL POLICY AND SOCIAL INCLUSION

In many national contexts, social policy has emerged as a means of seeking to achieve social justice goals. Social policies are government policies that aim to improve individual lives while also recognizing that this will benefit society as a whole. They include policies such as the provision of income support, disability support, education, training and health care. Governments around the world vary in the numbers and types of social policy they implement, but the provision of social welfare is an issue for all societies.

From this perspective, social policy can be considered a manifestation of the idea that all members of a society should be enabled to survive at certain minimum standards, relating to issues such as income, health care, housing and the like. If people fall below this minimum, then social policy should provide various forms of support. The emergence of the welfare state in many capitalist societies in the post-World War II period, for example, was based on a belief that society needed to support its members, in particular when they were going through difficult times caused by issues such as unemployment or illness. From the late 1970s onwards, however, many of these same nations experienced a neo-liberal revolution in which the state became a symbol of mistrust, and in which there was a renewed focus on the market as the main organizing mechanism in society (Daly 2003; Smyth 2010).

With ongoing market failures in the 2000s, and with recognition that many people in society were being marginalized and excluded unjustly, the notion of social inclusion, and its related concept of social exclusion, have entered into policy discourse and practice (Smyth, 2010). A crucial point here is that forms of inclusion and exclusion in social contexts cannot be measured by income levels alone, as has historically been done with measures such as the poverty line. Rather, as Smyth has argued, social inclusion can be recognized as 'a banner heading for a new social policy paradigm' in which 'the wider society has to ensure that disadvantaged members have access to high quality education, housing, health, employment and other services' (Smyth, 2010, p. 7). It is here that sport has the potential to play an important role, in particular in providing pathways for people who have been marginalized to reconnect with society. At the same time, while not explicitly coming under a social inclusion heading, it is notable that many sport clubs and organizations are now participating in and developing corporate social responsibility programmes, ranging from seeking to operate in environmentally friendly ways through to engaging more deeply with people in their local communities.

Many nations around the world have been developing social policy initiatives within a social inclusion framework. In this context in which government departments are seeking partnerships and relations with organizations outside of the state, sporting organizations have become sites for the development of social inclusion initiatives. In his article on football and social inclusion, for example, Richard Tacon (2007) argues that a range of policy-driven projects have emerged in the UK that have sought to engage with football (soccer) as a means of promoting social inclusion. Such programmes range from those that seek to create participation in clubs through community coaching programmes through to initiatives that seek to use the popularity of sport as a means for achieving a range of social inclusion objectives. At a more specific level, in 1995 the British Labour Party set out a Charter for Football, which in turn was the basis for the emergence of the Football Taskforce, a body charged with engaging with, among other issues, the policy dimensions of sport (Tacon, 2007). The Football Taskforce published four reports, on '*Eliminating Racism from Football* (1998), *Improving Facilities for Disabled Supporters* (1998), *Investing in the Community* (1999), and *Football: Commercial Issues*' (Tacon, 2007, p. 3). While Tacon identifies a number of limitations associated with such projects, in particular in terms of evaluating programmes emanating from such reports, the critical issue is that sport, football in this case, is being proposed and mobilized as a legitimate site for social inclusion and social policy initiatives.

Still in the UK, Waring and Mason (2010) have analysed social policy initiatives aimed at promoting social inclusion at a community level through sport, under the heading of New Opportunities for PE [Physical Education] and Sport (NOPES). As they argue, such initiatives show the importance that the Blair Labour government, with its social inclusion agenda, was placing on sport as a site through which such social policy objectives could be achieved. At the same time, based on a series of case studies, the authors show that there is a need to problematize any assumption that 'social inclusion will follow directly from increased opportunity for participation through increased sporting opportunity' (Waring and Mason, 2010, p. 517). In particular, they show that providing access to facilities is not the same as developing use of those facilities, and that there is a need for multifaceted programmes that can engage with the wide range of social, political and economic factors that influence whether or not people participate.

An important dimension of social inclusion is that it does not only refer to economic factors, but also focuses on other forms of social relationship such as race, gender and class. As discussed in Chapter 4, questions of race and racism have been central to the history of sport around the world. Historically, while many sports condoned racism, either explicitly or implicitly, or denied its existence altogether, in recent years, and at least in some sports, there has been not only a recognition of racism but also movement to engage critically with racism. One example is the active stance taken by the Australian Football League (AFL), in response to the struggles of Indigenous players and others, to address racism within the game, both within clubs and among supporters. At present, the AFL is involved in a range of programmes aimed at supporting Indigenous footballers and communities, with programmes ranging from promoting healthy lifestyles and the importance of education through to personal development and leadership programmes (AFL, 2010).

Another example comes from the United Kingdom, where a campaign currently operating under the name of 'Kick It Out' has been running for almost 20 years (Kick It Out, 2010a). The Kick It Out campaign in the UK emerged in response to ongoing racism, both within football (soccer) itself and among supporters, based on recognition that pro-active steps were required to challenge racism. As the organization's website indicates:

Kick It Out is football's equality and inclusion campaign.

The brand name of the campaign – *Let's Kick Racism Out of Football* – was established in 1993 and Kick It Out established as a body in 1997.

Kick It Out works throughout the football, educational and community sectors to challenge discrimination, encourage inclusive practices and work for positive change. (Kick It Out, 2010a)

In seeking to achieve these goals, the organization undertakes a range of initiatives, including holding education campaigns, lobbying political and policy actors, providing grants for grassroots initiatives and raising awareness in the general public. Importantly, the organization at the national level is linked into a network of other organizations both within and outside of the UK, including organizations such as FARE (Football Against Racism in Europe), which operates at the European level, and governments at various levels. These organizations have also become involved in struggles against other forms of discrimination and exclusion in sport – for example, struggling against homophobia and sex discrimination. Kick It Out has established an Equality Standard for Professional Clubs, the goal of which is to encourage clubs to undertake internal structural and organizational reform 'to ensure that individuals are not discriminated against on the grounds of any of Race, Religion, Age, Gender, Disability and Sexual Orientation' (Kick It Out, 2010b). This struggle against racism, homophobia, sex discrimination and other forms of social exclusion provides an important example of how sport and sport organizations can play a crucial role in the contemporary policy context, sometimes in collaboration with government organizations but often independently.

While such initiatives are vital, it is important not to assume that these policies and programmes automatically have the expected outcomes and results (Lusted, 2009). The process of translating policy into practice is a fraught one, linked to issues such as the resources invested, political will and the broader social context. In this regard, and returning more directly to the role of government in the context of policy, social inclusion and sport, the work of Fred Coalter (2007) in Britain uncovers and analyses the explicit links that governments have made between social policy, social inclusion and sport, and also engages with the challenges that these relations can confront. In his discussion of the active citizenship approach of the New Labour government, which was in office from 1997 until 2010, Coalter notes that the concept of active citizenship means that people should not expect to have rights without taking responsibility – for example, 'to work or seek to work, to provide for family, to behave responsibly, to take responsibility for personal health, to contribute to the solution of community problems and so on' (Coalter, 2007, p. 16). Here, sport, along with other cultural activities, is seen as having a critical role. Coalter provides two quotes from government documents that exemplify this approach. First, Policy Action Team 10's action plan stated:

> Participation in the arts and sport has a beneficial social impact. Arts and sport are inclusive and can contribute to neighbourhood renewal. They

can build confidence and encourage strong community groups. However, these benefits are frequently overlooked both by some providers of arts and sports facilities and programmes and by those involved in area regeneration programmes. (quoted in Coalter, 2007, p. 17)

Along similar lines, the Scottish Office, a department of the UK government until the creation of the Scottish Parliament in 1999, in 1999 proposed:

Arts, sport and leisure activities ... have a role to play in countering social exclusion. They can help to increase the self-esteem of individuals; build community spirit; increase social interaction; improve health and fitness; create employment and give young people a purposeful activity, reducing the temptation to anti-social behaviour. (Scottish Office, quoted in Coalter, 2007, p. 15)

Underlying such claims is a list of often assumed benefits that sport provides, including better physical and mental health; increased social connection (social capital); better social skills; and self-confidence (Coalter, 2007).

While Coalter is sympathetic to these claims, one of his main arguments is that the presumed outcomes associated with sport 'have rarely been articulated systematically, and even less frequently monitored and evaluated' (Coalter, 2007, p. 21). As in many other areas of social and public policy, the effects of various programmes and policies are frequently assumed without being fully tested or examined. Nevertheless, and despite such limitations, it is evident that sport is considered an important domain for social inclusion policy processes.

Some research does support the potential of sport to act as a site of social inclusion and as a vehicle for promoting related social policy objectives, although this research also makes it evident that it is not an unproblematic relationship. In his research on sport-based intervention programmes aimed at achieving social mobility for youth in Brazil, Australia and the Netherlands, Ramon Spaaij found both benefits and limitations to such programmes. While his research found some evidence that 'sport can be a useful tool for achieving social mobility of socially disadvantaged youth' (Spaaij, 2010, para. 45), he also found a number of barriers. Among these barriers were (Spaaij, 2010):

■ The 'cultural expectations and social norms associated with masculine sporting culture' (2010, para. 47).

- The competitive dynamics of sport.
- The 'financial cost of participation and transport' (2010, para. 49).

Spaaij (2010) also found that the ideals of 'sport for all' were not 'fully achieved in practice' (2010, para. 46).

As this discussion shows, there exists a strong potential for sport to contribute to social inclusion initiatives. At the same time, a tension arises around the extent to which sporting organizations and clubs do, or do not, prioritize such programmes. As in many areas of organizational activity, the danger is that sporting organizations may take on such activities when times are good – for example, when the club or organization is successful and has strong finances. The concern is that when economic times get harder, or when a sporting organization is less successful, such programmes may be wound up. Similarly, concerns arise around the level of ongoing commitment of governments to pursuing social inclusion policy initiatives, in particular in the period following their initial introduction.

Despite these challenges, social inclusion programmes are of tremendous significance. However, they are not the only way that sporting organizations, clubs and sport in general can influence social justice processes. At a broader level, a number of examples exist which show how sport has made a contribution to human rights struggles around the world.

HUMAN RIGHTS AND SPORT

While not always linked explicitly in popular discussions, there are clear connections between sport and human rights. Although working in the context of health, and in particular in relation to HIV/AIDS, the arguments of Jonathan Mann and Daniel Tarantola around the significance of human rights in promoting human well-being are important here in connecting concerns with social justice to human rights issues (Mann and Tarantola, 1996). Mann and Tarantola note that the modern era of human rights began in the aftermath of World War II, with the creation of the United Nations in 1945 and in response to the Holocaust in Europe. As they argue, the Universal Declaration of Human Rights (UDHR) was adopted by the UN General Assembly in 1948 as:

> a global bill of rights – 'a common standard of achievement for all peoples and all nations'. For the first time in history, a set of norms was defined at the international level, providing a universal, secular description of the

preconditions for human well-being, and international and national institutions and organizations were created to promote and protect human rights. (Mann and Tarantola, 1996, p. 468)

Grounded in the idea that 'all human beings are born free and equal in dignity and rights', the UDHR contains a list of rights extending across a range of areas of human activity. For example, the UDHR promotes the liberty and security of individuals, while also promoting rights to health, education, work and so on. Underlying these rights are a number of core principles. These are:

- Rights inhere in people simply because they are human.
- Rights are inalienable; they cannot be granted nor taken away by a government.
- Rights are universal, applying equally to all people in all places at all times ...
- Rights are individual and focus on the relationship between individuals and their governments.
- Governments must strive to realise and protect rights.
- Rights are generally inviolable; they predominate over other social goods ...
- Rights are inseparable and indivisible.

(Mann and Tarantola, 1996, p. 468, bullets in original)

At this point, the question arises as to what these rights have to do with sport. In response, Kidd and Donnelly (2000) identify a range of areas in which the mobilization of human rights has been significant in the context of sport. These include the anti-apartheid movement, women's human rights, and athletes' rights. They also argue that a human rights framework could be applied to sport in the areas of children's rights, workers' rights and the public sphere (Kidd and Donnelly, 2000).

People engage in activities related to sport across all of these areas, and often in problematic or exploitative conditions. For example, many sporting goods and products, ranging from bats and balls through to the latest shirts, are produced by workers, often children, in sweatshop conditions. In addition, while some athletes are well compensated for their activities, many are not. For those that are not well compensated, not only is the life of being an athlete a struggle, but life after retirement can be psychologically traumatic and financially disastrous if they have limited other skills (Kidd and

Donnelly, 2000). Across all of these areas, an opportunity exists to use human rights as a means for seeking to promote social justice, both within sport and in the areas of human activity closely linked to sport. In this regard, the argument of Kidd and Donnelly is that:

> Those of us committed to advancing opportunities for humane sport and physical activity ought to resort more systematically to the strategy of establishing, publicizing and drawing upon charters, declarations and covenants that enshrine codes of entitlement and conduct. To be sure, legal codes and statements of rights are not realized in themselves, but through the efforts of many people in their concrete historical conditions. (Kidd and Donnelly, 2000, p. 135)

Importantly, what underlies the UDHR is that it recognizes the international dimensions of rights. While there have been significant critiques raised around assumptions of universalism within the UDHR, at the same time, in a period of globalization and a thickening of networks of relations that cross national boundaries, mobilizing around human rights perhaps provides a means for engaging with some of the challenges of social policy-making which often still occur at the national level, even in contexts such as the European Union (Mann and Tarantola, 1996).

In another example, Jarvie (2006) makes an important set of observations around the role of human rights in sport in his analysis of the connection between the 2008 Olympic Games, hosted by China in Beijing, and human rights. In particular, he notes that the issue of human rights in China was a point of debate in the bidding process for the Games. Those in favour of awarding the Games to China 'argued that staging the Olympics would help to narrow the gap between China and the rest of the world' (Jarvie, 2006, p. 366). By contrast, opponents of the bid argued that 'China's history of human rights violations should have meant that one of the other contenders for the 2008 Olympics should have been victorious' (Jarvie, 2006, p. 366). From this view, the evaluation of bids for all major sporting events, not just as in this case with China, should have a human rights dimension. In other words, nations with a history of human rights violations should not be rewarded with the staging of global events. Whatever our views on this particular example, or others like it, it reveals that a human rights analysis can provide important insights into sport, and into the possibilities for social justice associated with making the connection between sport and human rights.

DISCUSSION POINT

In the example discussed above, Jarvie provides two different perspectives on whether China should have been allowed to host the 2008 Olympic Games, in the context of a human rights analysis. Which view do you find more persuasive, and why? Think of the country in which you are currently living. Would it pass a human rights test of this sort? What evidence would you use to support your argument? Do you find this form of human rights analysis relevant to sport? Why, or why not?

SPORT AND CORPORATE SOCIAL RESPONSIBILITY

Corporate social responsibility (CSR) has become a key and much contested concept in contemporary business practice. For many years, and in particular in the context of companies in the private sector, the argument was proposed that the primary, or even sole, purpose of private industry was to focus on making money, or on achieving financial success. However, based on a recognition of the power and influence of private companies in global capitalism, an argument has emerged that corporations need to behave in a socially responsible manner. This has resulted in arguments that businesses should focus not only on financial concerns, but also on social outcomes and environmental outcomes – the so-called triple bottom line (Margolis and Walsh, 2001).

Not surprisingly, many of these issues have been taken up in the organizational context of sport. In particular, sport clubs are not only organized around winning contests, but are involved in a whole range of activities involving provision of services to members of the community. Within this context, it is important to recognize that sport teams have for a long time been involved in a range of philanthropic activities, through which they seek to contribute to the community. Here, the language of CSR provides a framework through which such activities can be undertaken in a systematic manner, rather than on an ad hoc basis (Babiak and Wolfe, 2009). Corporate social responsibility can be understood as a set of ideals and practices that organizations adopt as they seek to become good citizens in their local contexts. At one level, on the business side, this means that organizations not only focus on their profit levels, or the bottom line, but also focus on being socially and environmentally responsible (Margolis and Walsh, 2001). For sport clubs, this may mean engaging in activities that promote social well-being in the community, including the long-standing tradition of players visiting sick children and supporters in hospital, as well as hosting training days for schools and community organizations. At another level, and as these processes become more tightly embedded in everyday organizational practice, corporate social responsibility has the potential to result in a redefinition of the organization, so that community engagement activities are not peripheral but are central to organizational practice.

As an example of corporate social responsibility in practice, consider the International Cricket Council's social responsibility initiatives which come under the heading of the 'Spirit of Cricket'. Through this initiative, the ICC has been involved in collaborations with a range of organizations seeking to engage with the global challenge of HIV/AIDS. The ICC claims:

> As part of the ICC's commitment to the Spirit of Cricket, a wide range of activities have been undertaken to raise awareness and reduce stigma around people living with HIV/AIDS. Since 2003, the ICC has been working with UNAIDS to address the issue of HIV/AIDS in cricket-playing countries and in 2006 UNICEF also joined the prominent partnership which supports the 'Unite for Children, Unite Against AIDS' campaign. In 2007 the ICC also began working with the Kaiser Family Foundation and the Global Media AIDS Initiative to deliver messages to a regional and global broadcast audience, working alongside the Caribbean Broadcast Media Partnership on HIV/AIDS and the African Broadcast Media Partnership Against HIV/AIDS. (ICC, 2009a)

In this context, the ICC has worked in collaboration with partner organizations UNAIDS, UNICEF and the Global Media AIDS Initiative (GMAI) to develop a Think Wise initiative. Goals of the initiative include: (1) raising awareness about AIDS, (2) engaging with the stigma and discrimination associated with AIDS and (3) promoting 'informed decision making and help-seeking behaviour' (ICC, 2009b; 2009c).

Such initiatives involve various forms of organizational partnership in which a leading sporting body, in this case the ICC, collaborates with a range of other government, non-government and private sector partners, including UNICEF, UNAIDS and Kaiser. The advantages of such partnerships are that a range of expertizes can be built on so that the social engagement is not dependent on one organization alone. In such partnerships, sports organizations may be well placed to provide financial and infrastructure resources. In addition, and of particular importance, the appeal of sport in the broader community gives such initiatives a prominence and legitimacy that they might not otherwise receive.

Corporate social responsibility initiatives also exist at the level of the individual club. To give one example, the Boston Bruins, an ice hockey club in the NHL, has established a Boston Bruins Foundation, a 'non-profit foundation that assists charitable organisations that demonstrate a commitment to enhancing the quality of life for children throughout New England [the region in which the Bruins are based]' (Boston Bruins, 2010). It does this by providing grants to organizations working in one or more of four areas, namely, athletics, academics, health and community outreach. In some cases, the involvement of the Foundation goes beyond providing grants to being involved in more direct ways, at all times with the goal of improving the quality of life and life chances for disadvantaged children in the region. As Babiak and Wolfe (2009) show, such initiatives have become widespread in US professional sport, with leagues, corporations, teams and athletes undertaking a wide range of community engagement programmes, including fundraising for causes, developing community outreach programmes, charitable donations and engagement with environmental concerns, including programmes to offset carbon emissions and recycling programmes at events (Babiak and Wolfe, 2009, pp. 719–20).

In a similar way, Collingwood Football Club in the Australian Football League has established a number of important community-based initiatives over many years. Indeed, their claim is that:

> Collingwood has a long and proud history of social responsibility and commitment to the community. The club's origins were created from sheer pride as the residents of Collingwood struggled through the depression years and the World Wars.
>
> Collingwood has taken steps to further develop a role of social responsibility and to make a very significant contribution to the community through a series of local, state and national programs.
>
> We are intent on being the biggest philanthropic sporting organisation in Australia. (Collingwood, 2010)

In seeking to achieve this goal, the club is involved in a wide range of community-based initiatives, such as a 'knives scar lives' campaign, a collaboration with the Victorian state government, aimed at raising awareness about the danger of knife violence, through support for various health initiatives including some associated with combating cancer, through to initiatives aimed at promoting multiculturalism and providing support for Indigenous sport clubs and organizations.

At the league level, Netball Australia, the peak organizational body for netball in Australia, has developed a Looking Beyond programme, in collaboration with Beyond Blue, a national depression initiative in Australia. With a particular focus on women and girls, who constitute the majority of netball players in Australia, the Looking Beyond programme seeks 'to help generate awareness about health issues that impact on our netball community, their family and friends and where to go for help' (Netball Australia, 2011).

Finally, we can consider FC Barcelona's (Barcelona Football Club [soccer]) relationship with UNICEF (United Nations Children's Fund) as another instance in which a famous club has used its brand power and reach into the community as a means to promote and engage with social causes. While FC Barcelona has powerful roots in the Catalan region of Spain, its community of influence now is global, meaning that causes it supports and promotes can cross international boundaries. For all of its 111 years of existence, as of 2010, Barcelona has refused to wear any advertising for commercial organizations on its shirts. When it came time to include advertising, Barcelona decided to *pay* UNICEF to feature its name on its shirts. As detailed by UNICEF, as well as wearing the UNICEF name and logo on its shirt, Barcelona agreed in 2006 'to donate at least €1.5 million per year to UNICEF over the next five years to support UNICEF programmes for children all over the world' (UNICEF, 2006). According to UNICEF, 'The first year's donation will support programmes in Swaziland aimed at preventing mother-to-child transmission of HIV, providing treatment of paediatric AIDS, preventing HIV infection among adolescents and protection, and providing care and support for children orphaned and made vulnerable by HIV/AIDS' (UNICEF, 2006). While an initial reaction to such ventures is generally one of suspicion about the motivations involved, there is no doubt this is a significant act by Barcelona. As one of the world's most recognized and well-supported sporting teams, the organization could clearly make many millions in revenue from selling the advertising rights for its shirts to one or more commercial companies. That the club has chosen to support a cause such as UNICEF is an important acknowledgement of the creative ways in which sporting teams can contribute to causes. And, in this instance, of course, it means that the UNICEF logo is not only being seen by supporters at the stadium, but also by viewers on television around the world (UNICEF, 2006; FC Barcelona, 2010).

ETHICAL SPORT GOVERNANCE

In seeking to achieve social justice goals, whether through social inclusion programmes, human rights promotion, or corporate social responsibility initiatives, it is vital that sporting bodies themselves are organized and run to appropriately ethical standards. While we discussed forms of organizational governance in Chapter 8, here we focus on ethical sport governance. There are a number of features that define ethical sport governance (Hoye and Cuskelly, 2007). Hoye and Cuskelly (2007) give the example of one organization, Standards Australia (2003), which has listed seven ethical principles that provide the foundation for ethical governance. These are:

1 **Accountability** – to shareholders and stakeholders
2 **Transparency** – the provision of information to interested parties, excluding that which would infringe the privacy or intellectual property of individuals or is not in the national interest.
3 **Fairness and balance** – in the use of organisational power.
4 **Honesty** – in the provision of information to internal and external stakeholders.
5 **Dignity** – upholding the right to human dignity in all dealings.
6 **Legal** – exhibit full compliance with the law and adhere to conventional codes of behaviour.
7 **Goodwill** – in the conduct of all organisational activities.
                        (Hoye and Cuskelly, 2007, p. 168, numbers in original;
                                        see also Standards Australia, 2003)

While adherence to such a code of ethical behaviour can be argued to be important for all aspects of organizational behaviour, it is certainly of significance for sport organizations engaging in partnerships around promoting social inclusion, human rights and social justice issues. In such contexts, individual clubs or organizations are often taken to be representative of the particular sport, or of all sport, and as such, how the particular organization acts will have an impact on how other organizations outside of the sport world consider that organization and the sport in general. In addition, when sport organizations engage in social justice activities, while there is potential to do a great deal of good, there is also the potential to do harm. This could range from mishandling funds, either deliberately or unintentionally, to raising the hopes of participants in programmes and then not being able to fulfil those hopes and expectations. While there is always a level of uncertainty involved in any social justice initiative, it is critical that, whether they succeed or not, sporting organizations are able to legitimately claim that, in their actions and activities, they were working within an appropriately ethical framework.

CONCLUSION

In this chapter, we have engaged with critical questions around the capacity of sport clubs to promote social justice. In so doing, we have examined a number of ways in which this may be possible, including through:

- The involvement of sporting organizations in social inclusion initiatives.
- The promotion of a human rights agenda in sport.
- The place of corporate social responsibility within sporting organizations.
- The role of ethical governance within sporting organizations.

These examples reveal the potential for sport to promote social justice. At the same time, it is important not to overstate the role of sport alone in these contexts, or to argue that there is a straightforward relationship between sport and achieving social justice goals. There is a critical need to engage with local contexts, and to be aware of both the possible benefits and the limitations associated with sport.

CHAPTER SUMMARY

This chapter has shown that:

- Sport organizations can make a significant contribution to social justice issues.
- They can make these contributions across a range of areas, including social inclusion programmes, promoting human rights, engaging in corporate social responsibility programmes and adopting ethical governance practices.
- We need to be careful not to assume that the introduction of programmes means they will succeed or that they will have their intended outcomes. Further to this, more work needs to be done on evaluating social justice initiatives.
- Despite such challenges, sport is a fruitful site for the promotion of social justice initiatives, and builds on forms of social, political and regulatory practices.

DISCUSSION QUESTIONS

1 Issues of sport and social justice should not be connected. Sport is about entertainment, and it is wrong to see it as a means for promoting social justice. Discuss.

2 The discussion of social inclusion programmes based in sport noted that one challenge is that there has been relatively little evaluation of programmes. If you were going to evaluate whether or not a particular sport-related initiative had been successful in promoting social inclusion, what sorts of questions would you want to ask?

3 A constant challenge for corporate social responsibility programmes is that companies and organizations may discard them when times are tough. Can you think of ways in which it may be possible to make CSR programmes part of the core agenda of sporting organizations, so they are not so easily discarded in tough times?

4 Why should we care about whether or not sporting organizations are governed ethically? Shouldn't our main focus be on whether they are financially profitable, and successful on the field?

FURTHER READING

Coakley, Jay and Pike, Elizabeth (2009) *Sports in Society: Issues and Controversies*, Maidenhead, McGraw-Hill.

Jarvie, Grant (2006) *Sport, Culture and Society: An Introduction*, London, Routledge.

Mann, Jonathan and Tarantola, Daniel (1996) *AIDS in the World II: Global Dimensions, Social Roots and Responses*, New York, Oxford University Press.

Smyth, Paul (2010) 'In or Out? Building an Inclusive Nation', Albert Park and Fitzroy, Victoria, Australian Collaboration and the Brotherhood of St Laurence.

Part IV

The Global Cultures of Sport

Part IV explores the global cultures that provide the context for the first three parts of the book. This part will start from the experience of the individual player and fan, but will analyse these sport actors in terms of their significance as part of the institutions of the broader cultural and political economy of sport. It then discusses the commodification and commercialization of sport, with a particular focus on the media-sport industry. This part of the book explores the processes which connect the cultural dimensions of sport to its political and economic dimensions. Through the analysis in this part it will become evident that to understand sport in contemporary societies it is critical to engage with the global cultures of sport, and to consider the ways in which the cultural dimensions of sport interact with the broader social, political and economic contexts of sport, as it is in these locations that vital power contests occur within the network society.

Chapter 11

The Global Athlete

INTRODUCTION

From Serena Williams to Usain Bolt to David Beckham, the contemporary experience of professional sport for athletes is increasingly organized around factors such as the creation of celebrity, the pursuit of financial reward and movement within and beyond national boundaries, as well as the pursuit of success on the field of play. While there are many aspects of the lives and experiences of professional sports competitors, this chapter focuses on five dimensions:

- Sports Star as a Celebrity.
- Professional Athletes as Role Models.
- Financial Rewards.
- Career Management.
- Migration.

These dimensions of the contemporary experience of professional athletes combine the political and cultural economies of sport with the personal experiences of the individual athlete. As such, a focus on these issues enables us to engage with the main aspects of the life of the professional athlete. While the issues covered in this chapter potentially apply to all athletes, they are particularly pronounced for professional athletes, and therefore it is professional athletes who are the focus here.

THE SPORTS STAR AS CELEBRITY

Over a number of years, sociologists including Ellis Cashmore (2002, 2005) and Steven Jackson and David Andrews (2005) have examined the place of celebrity and celebrity status in contemporary sport. First, they note that sports stars are central to celebrity culture in contemporary societies. Related to the close connection between television and sport, sports stars have also become part of the entertainment industry, taking their place as celebrities alongside film and television stars. Second, while there is a danger that the person of the athlete becomes reduced to a commercialized object in this process of becoming a celebrity, the process of celebrity creation can also benefit the athlete in terms of career progress, social and cultural status, marketability and financial reward.

Two sociological concepts are particularly helpful in engaging with the phenomenon of the celebrity athlete. The first is the concept of 'celebrity' itself, and the second is the concept of 'status'. Celebrities are people who are famous, who are the objects of popular attention through the mass media (Street, 2004). Within sociological literature, the concept of status has a long and important history, with theorists such as Max Weber engaging in debates about the social meaning and significance of status. Status is linked to questions of prestige and power, and is an important source of social inequality (Furze et al., 2008). In particular,

> status groups differ from one another in terms of their lifestyles and the honour in which they are held ... Members of status groups signal their rank by means of material and symbolic culture. They seek to distinguish themselves from others by displays of 'taste' in fashion, food, music, literature, manners, and travel. (Furze et al., 2008, p. 352)

The concepts of celebrity and status take on specific forms in sporting contexts (Horne, 2006). On the one hand, the rise in sport celebrity is connected to a more general shift in society from valuing ascribed status to valuing achieved status. Ascribed status refers to a social position that a person is born with or assumes involuntarily. For example, in monarchies, kings and queens have ascribed status because of the family into which they are born, so their status is based on birth or accident, not on any achievement of the individual involved. By contrast, achieved status refers to a social position that is achieved through the activities and efforts of an individual. Achieved status connects strongly with a culture in which there is an emphasis on rewarding individual effort (Duina, 2011; Horne, 2006). Given its valuing of achievement, as measured through performance in competition, sport is an important site for the attainment of celebrity through achieved status. For example, for much of the 1960s and 1970s boxing was dominated by Muhammad Ali, while in the 1980s, the West Indian Vivian Richards was a world leader in international cricket. Basketball in the 1990s became synonymous with Michael Jordan at a global level. Since the mid-1990s, golf has been dominated by Tiger Woods, who has taken the game to new levels in terms of sustained excellence on the course. Similarly, Serena Williams has performed consistently and outstandingly at the elite level of tennis through the 1990s and 2000s. In each of these high-profile cases, and there are of course many more, it is clear that, as far as is possible to measure, these players were consistently rated as the best of their era or, in some cases, of all time. They attained celebrity status at least in part through their achievements on the field of play. It is also important to note that, while celebrity status is becoming increasingly prominent, it has a long history in sport. The English cricketer William Gilbert 'WG' Grace (1848–1915) and the US baseballer George Herman 'Babe' Ruth (1895–1948) were high-profile sports stars widely revered within their societies.

At the same time, another potentially contradictory dimension of contemporary sport, and societal, culture is that 'celebrities are a product of television and rely "less on doing, more on being noticed"' (Cashmore, quoted in Horne, 2006, p. 83). Indeed, while all of the athletes identified above were the very best in their particular sport, they also became part of a media-based culture, in which they crossed the boundaries from their particular sport to an international sporting, and even non-sporting, audience through being highly visible in the media. These processes have intensified over time so that celebrities in the 2000s are subject to a range and intensity of media exposure that was unimaginable even some 20 years earlier. Nevertheless, the place of performance remains important for sport celebrities:

> Athletes aren't just known for their well-knownness, of course. At least, not initially. The source of their renown is their prowess. Once that's noticed, they can garner recognition by their appearance, their partners, their presence at events, and practically anything that interests their audience … Sports celebrities differ from many others. Their public recognition is contingent on their performance, which means they have to accomplish something that's widely celebrated as having merit. That isn't necessarily the case with other celebs. (Cashmore, 2005, pp. 398–9)

Serena Williams provides a good example of this. She is among the best players of all time in professional tennis. Through constant international television coverage of her career, she has become a global sport celebrity based on the quality of her play and her success in winning major tournaments consistently and over many years. Yet, it is also evident that her status as a celebrity has been enhanced by her highly visible non-sporting activities. In addition to charitable work in a diverse range of areas including education, she has her own fashion line and is involved in many other media-based activities, including celebrity appearances on a range of television programmes (Williams, 2010). Her position in the context of debates around celebrity is nicely captured by her personal website:

> Serena Williams embodies style, power, beauty and courage. Like numerous A-list celebrities, Serena is recognized by the mere mention of her first name. Only 28, Serena has overcome insurmountable odds to win a total of 23 career Grand Slams which include 11 singles titles, 2 mixed doubles and 10 in women's double in order to become one the game's greatest all-time players. Her remarkable tennis skills have skyrocketed her to fame, but only her unique charm and drive could explain her successful endeavours outside of tennis in film, television, fashion and philanthropy. ... Her tennis ability combined with her off-court activity makes her one of the most recognizable names and faces in the world – an icon. (Williams, 2010)

In other words, a combination of tennis skills, successful endeavours off the court and a highly visible mediated profile all contribute to the construction of Williams as a celebrity.

David Beckham, the English footballer (soccer player), is another global sporting celebrity. What adds to the interest around Beckham is that while he has been an exceptional footballer, most people would not claim that he was the best player of all time, or even of his era. Playing at a time when the media was becoming increasingly integral to sport, and playing for Manchester United in the 1990s, perhaps the most famous and well-supported football club in the world, meant that Beckham had a high level of media exposure. As with Williams, Beckham performed in a context where he was associated with highly visible mediated on-field success. Further to this, he became a leading player, and captain, in the English national team. Again as with Williams, however, his celebrity status has become increasingly connected with, and amplified by, his off-field activities. In addition to being involved in a range of charitable activities, and having close connections with the fashion industry, a key moment for Beckham was his marriage to Victoria Adams, solo singer, fashion designer and former member of the successful pop group the Spice Girls, in which she went by the name Posh Spice. In addition to being an important event in his personal life, David Beckham's marriage to Adams, now Victoria Beckham, meant that he was part of a celebrity couple where both partners were part of the global media industry. Over time, both Beckhams have lived a life as high-profile celebrities in which their every move, from the birth of their children to David Beckham's increasingly intricate tattoos and Victoria Beckham's diet regime, has been the subject of intense media interest. Contributing further to this has been a general understanding of David Beckham as being a handsome, media-friendly and high-achieving athlete, but also a man who has remained humble and well grounded with a family (Cashmore, 2002; Moon, 2006; Yu, 2005). Given the international reach of soccer, his appeal has extended well beyond England to all parts of the world. As Yu wrote as early as 2005:

> For sports fans, Beckham's marriage was seen to create the dream couple, combining a successful sport star and an entertainment icon. David and Victoria have been treated as royalty, and are England's undisputed number one celebrity couple ... This combination has achieved a global span of unprecedented magnitude ... In addition, David Beckham was portrayed as a devoted family man ... In contrast to other elite athletes, Beckham also has fashion appeal. He uses fashion to display an inflated degree of cool, confidence and sex appeal ... As a result, news about David Beckham is not only seen in the sports magazines such as Sports Illustrated, but also in the monthly magazines and celebrity magazines and in the major international tabloids. (Yu, 2005, pp. 191–2)

Athletes like Beckham and Williams become celebrities through a combination of sporting excellence and success, followed by engaging in high-profile and media-friendly activities off the field.

In some cases, sporting celebrities become involved in publicly and politically controversial issues. The US boxing superstar Muhammad Ali, for example, was an outspoken opponent of the Vietnam War and an influential voice for the civil rights movement in the United States in the 1960s. His forceful advocacy for these progressive political and social causes resulted in significant personal cost to himself, both in terms of financial consequences related to lost sponsorship opportunities and in being subjected to significant attacks from the political establishment. Through his celebrity status, however, Ali was an important voice for progressive political action and engagement (Zirin, 2008; Boddy, 2008). It should also be noted that, as in other areas of sporting activity, the celebrity domain is not a level playing field. While there are certainly both women and men athletes who become celebrities, over a long period, many more men than women have attained celebrity status and its associated financial rewards and benefits. While the situation is gradually changing, as with other aspects of sport discussed in Chapter 5, this inequality can be attributed to a sporting and societal context in which the achievements of men are prioritized over those of women (Lines, 2001).

ATHLETES AS ROLE MODELS

There is often an expectation that the individual who is outstanding at sport will be a positive role model for others in society, especially for young people. This expectation then raises the question of what constitutes appropriate behaviour for sport stars, and how sport is connected to other spheres of life.

On the one hand, sports stars are understood as representing highly valued 'social ideals' (Lines, 2001, p. 286), such as 'fair play, courage and bravery' (Lines, 2001, p. 291) and 'as embodying values which learnt on the playing fields will readily transfer into everyday life' (Lines, 2001, p. 286). Importantly, such values and behaviours are also highly gendered, so male athletes come to be represented as heroes to a much greater extent than female athletes. At the same time, the move from being a hero and role model to being a villain can occur quickly. Almost on a daily basis, examples of sports stars behaving badly or improperly appear, whether related to relationships within a team or a sport, or in the context of personal relationships and activities outside of the field of play. One of the most significant examples concerns the experience of Tiger Woods, one of the greatest golfers ever.

For many years, Woods' exceptional status as a player was allied with an understanding of him as a loving family man, who managed to balance excellence on the golf course with a happy family. However, in the early part of 2010, this side of Woods' persona cracked in a major and public way when it was revealed that he had been having extra-marital relationships, with numerous women. Aside from the personal ramifications for Woods and his family, in public, he was condemned in much of the media, and many sponsors withdrew their support, meaning that he lost significant endorsements and income. While sporting stars of the status of Woods do continue to play, and do continue to attract supporters and to perform to high standards, the experiences of such players show how rapidly the status of an individual can change (Bissinger, 2010; Gibson, 2010). As Lines has written, when sports stars engage in behaviour that is not seen to coincide with their status as heroes and role models, then 'the social problems of everyday life' (2001, p. 292) begin to emerge:

> These question the idea of individual 'exemplar' and the widely held beliefs about the social and moral benefits of sporting participation. If elite sportsmen can no longer embody this, then the legitimation of such values come under threat. (Lines, 2001, p. 292)

In short, while there is still a belief in the possibility that sports stars can be role models, albeit in a highly gendered form, there is also an increasing recognition that some behaviour undertaken by some athletes means there is a need for extreme caution in making any direct link between sporting excellence and an embodiment of socially admired values.

FINANCIAL REWARDS

A critical dimension of the life of the professional athlete concerns the question of making a living. By definition, professional athletes depend on their job in sport for their livelihood. The question then becomes one of whether they are able to sustain a living from sport. When discussing the financial rewards on offer to professional players, perhaps not surprisingly, the focus tends to be on those at the highest end of the earnings scale. Accounts of leading players in the English Premier League (soccer), the NBA, or the NFL making millions of pounds or dollars a year are staple fare in everyday media coverage, and elite highly paid performers in individual sports such as golf and tennis also receive a great deal of attention in media and other contexts. For example, USA Today reported that, in 2009, median salaries in the NFL (gridiron) ranged from $1,325,000 for members of the San Francisco 49ers through to $488,640 for members of the St Louis Rams. Peyton Manning, the most highly paid player in the NFL in 2010, was reported as being on track to earn US$15.8 million that year (Van Riper, 2010). Meanwhile, in professional tennis, by the middle of 2010, Roger Federer was reported as having earned $56,471,204 over his career, while Rafael Nadal had earned $32,846,702 over his career to that stage. For the year up to 16 August 2010, Nadal and Federer were also the highest-earning male tennis players, having won $5,622,538 and $3,109,135 respectively. By comparison, the highest-earning women were Serena Williams and Venus Williams, who had earned $4,266,011 and $2,223,556 respectively. At that time the Williams sisters were also the highest earners over their careers of currently active players. Serena Williams had earned $32,773,004 and Venus Williams $27,290,546 to that point in their careers. It should also be noted that these figures relate to earnings from competition. Elite and high-profile athletes make money not only from success in competition, but from endorsements, sponsorships and the like (Tennis.com, 2010; Tennis Channel, 2010).

While these are figures for the elite players, even at this level, two important issues emerge. First, at the very elite level, both men and women in some sports are making very large sums of money. Yet, once we go a little down the list, or look at various sports, it is evident that men earn more than women. Even in the world of professional tennis, where elite women such as Serena Williams and Venus Williams are earning in the millions of dollars, the trend through the top money earners is that more men are top earners than women. These trends become even more noticeable in other sports. As one example, a comparison of the NBA with the WNBA reveals stark differences in salaries for players. In the 2009–10 season, the 25 top salaries for individual players in the NBA were $15,000,000 or more, with the top player receiving a salary greater than $23,000,000. By contrast, the maximum salary for a six-year plus player in the WNBA in 2010 was $101,500 (USA Today, 2011; Women's Basketball Online, 2010; Yuille, 2010).

Second, while some men and women are making huge amounts of money, this is by no means the experience for all players, either men or women, in professional sports, many of whom struggle financially (Coakley and Pike, 2009, p. 421). If they are able to secure a sponsor or sponsors, that can help in making ends meet, but sponsors then also make demands on players, not only in terms of the equipment they use, but also in terms of when and where they compete, and under what conditions. Depending on the context in which they are performing, and in particular in individual sports, athletes may also face additional expenses in relation to hiring coaches, accessing medical treatment and securing the services of a player manager or agent and so on (Coakley and Pike, 2009).

Being a professional sports person also requires the capacity to manage financial resources and financial dealings, often involving negotiations with organizations such as clubs and sponsors. In some sports, player associations or unions may be able to help players in their negotiations. However, in many cases, such associations do not exist or do not have the resources to provide the individual attention required by players. In this regard, many professional players will work with player agents, who sometimes themselves have been sports players. Brought into public consciousness with the movie, *Jerry Maguire* (1996), and its catch phrase 'show me the money', agents have a sometimes controversial role in sport. For some, they are seen as critical advocates for players who otherwise would be at the complete mercy of greedy sporting organizations and owners. For others, agents are part of the problem driving the hyper-commercialization of sport. From this perspective, agents not only make unrealistic demands on behalf of their players, but they also seek to make themselves rich on the coattails of the sporting stars that they represent.

In short, while much media and public attention focuses on the high end of the earnings scale, and not without some justification, it is important to remember that many professional athletes struggle to get by on a daily basis, just as do people in a range of other careers.

DISCUSSION POINT

Discussing players' wages in the English Premier League (soccer), in 2007, the Sunday Times newspaper reported that '[t]he average annual salary of a footballer in England's top flight has broken through the £1m ceiling for the first time'. The report went on to note that '[t]he rate of increase [in wages] means that footballers now earn almost as much in a week as the average person is paid in a year' (Gadher and Waite, 2007).

Do football (soccer) players deserve such salaries? How can such salaries for players be justified? What do such salaries suggest about the status of football players in English society? What are the consequences for society, when there is such a gap between what elite sports stars are paid and the average salary in the wider society?

MANAGING THE CAREER

Financial matters and the financial insecurity that many athletes experience mean that career management is a critical issue. While we hear about the long-terms stars, such as Shaquille O'Neal who in 2010 signed a contract with the Boston Celtics in the NBA taking him ever closer to 20 years at the top professional level, for the majority of players, the length of career is much shorter. For example, in the NFL (gridiron), the average playing career is 3.6 years, and 25 per cent of the players rotate out of the league every year

(Carucci, 2010). The reasons for differences in career length vary, ranging from injuries, through to competition for spots, through to level of ability and whether a player 'fits in' to a sport culture.

In an important study of the Australian Football League, Kelly and Hickey (2008, 2010) analysed the ways in which players are managed through their career, including at the recruiting stage. Their research identifies three aspects of the management of players. These are:

1 **The body**: the body of an AFL footballer is an entity 'that can be objectively and scientifically defined, described and developed' (Kelly and Hickey, 2010, p. 31). As we saw in Chapter 7 on the body, the body of an AFL footballer can be worked on, developed and repaired in the same way as a machine.
2 **The mind**: as with the body, the mind can be approached from a scientific framework, and can be considered through 'terms such as coach-ability or teach-ability, or football brain. It can be developed and moulded by concerns for decision making, accountability and discipline-both on and off the field' (Kelly and Hickey, 2008, p. 17).
3 **The soul**: rather than thinking of the soul in spiritual terms, the soul is used to capture concepts such as 'character, attitude, work ethic, courage, and moral judgement' (Kelly and Hickey, 2008, p. 17).

The importance of these dimensions is that they provide a nuanced assessment of factors that contribute to the success, or otherwise, of players in club contexts. Importantly, while the individual player must be able to work across these dimensions, clubs are hiring increasing numbers of professional staff and adopting a variety of organizational practices to seek to develop these dimensions of their players. While this analysis is focused on the AFL, it clearly resonates with trends and experiences in other leagues, and in a variety of sports, both professional and amateur. It shows that the career of a player is not only dependent on pure skill, or on luck with injuries, but is being moulded and judged according to a range of criteria that encompass the mind, the body and the soul.

MIGRATION

For many sports stars in the twenty-first century, a notable feature of their professional life is mobility. Just as a range of sociological research has discussed the growing significance of mobile lives for many people in the global economy, mobility is a component of the lives of many professional sport stars (Elliott, 2009; Maguire, 1999).

For many years, across many professional sports, players that had long careers with the one club were praised for being loyal and dedicated to their team. For example, one of the most revered US baseball players in history is Cal Ripken of the Baltimore Orioles. Remarkably, he played 2,632 consecutive games over 17 seasons, from 30 May 1982 to 20 September 1998 (MLB, 1995/2010). In another incredible record, Tomoaki Kanemoto of the Hanshin Tigers in Japan played 1,492 consecutive games in the Nippon Professional Baseball league, from 21 July 1999 until 18 April 2010, when he was aged 42 (Japan Today, 2010). While these numbers are highly impressive, both in terms of longevity and in terms of loyalty to a club, for many players the current experience of professional sport involves much more movement between clubs within nations and increasingly between nations. In this regard, the mobility of players is also linked to the sport they are playing. While players can be genuinely mobile at a global level in sports such as football (soccer) and basketball (although the NBA and WNBA are clearly the elite basketball leagues), for players performing at the highest level in sports such as American football (gridiron), Gaelic football (in Ireland) and Australian Rules football, one country is so dominant that most of the players in those leagues come from those countries. Nevertheless, even in these sports, there is an increasing awareness of the possibility of recruiting players from other countries, even where those players have competed in different sports. For example, highly regarded Gaelic footballers from Ireland, such as Jim Stynes and Tadhg Kennelly, have been recruited by Australian Rules football clubs, taught how to play the game and have gone on to long and distinguished careers. Similarly, a number of Australian Rules footballers have tried to extend their playing careers by becoming punters in the NFL, based on the high level of kicking skills of Australian Rules footballers.

Within an overall context of increasing mobility, there are different forms and experiences of mobility in contemporary sport. Athletes may move within a nation, continent or across the world (Maguire, 1999). Women are less likely to move for their sport than men (Maguire, 1999). Some forms of mobility are relatively permanent, at least in the context of being a competitive athlete. Other forms of movement are for much more defined periods of time. Cricket provides a good example of this latter model. For example, elite cricket players from Australia may seek to play overseas during the Australian winter for a variety of reasons, including financial ones, gaining the opportunity to experience playing in a different context and creating networks of relations with other players. Over the years, a number of Australian players have represented teams in English county cricket, but not with the intention of staying in England on a permanent basis. Similarly, a number of players from other cricket-playing nations have played in Australia for one or more seasons, often with the same goals. Since its inception in 2008, Indian Premier League cricket has attracted players from all over the world. These players join their IPL team for the particular season, and then move on or return to their home nation immediately after the competition has finished. Such players almost literally become globe trotters, moving around the world depending on the demands of both competition and their teams.

Separate from these forms of movement, other players seek to move, or are sought, on a more permanent basis. In terms of movement within countries, in leagues with a national draft system, this can occur at a relatively young age. In US basketball, for example, a player who excels at the high school level may be recruited by a college or university team in another part of the country. If they then perform to high standards while at college or university, they may be drafted by a professional team in the WNBA or the NBA in yet another part of the country. So by the time a player is just starting their professional career, typically in their early 20s, they may have been based in three different locations in very different parts of the country (high school, college and professional). And, of course, once they start their professional career they may be traded one or more times. Such forms of movement then not only impact on the player's sporting life, but also on their personal life, including in terms of their education, their family life and the relationships they form.

Once we look beyond movement within a country, we must consider the political economy of player movements at the international level. While US-based competitions such as the WNBA and NBA are dominated by US-born players, increasingly clubs in those leagues are recruiting players internationally. Similarly, Major League Baseball (MLB) has significant numbers of players from a range of other countries including, but not limited to, Cuba, Dominican Republic, Venezuela, Canada, Mexico and Japan, while Puerto Rico, 'a self governing commonwealth in association with the United States' (Puerto Rico, 2011), is also well represented. Indeed, Reuters reported in 2008 that 28 per cent of MLB players on the opening day of the season were born outside of the US (Fine, 2008). Even when those countries have leagues of their own, they cannot compete in financial terms with MLB. Football (soccer) emerges here as a truly global sport in terms of players, but also as a sport in which there are global centres of power, in particular in the richer European leagues. While football (soccer) players travel all over the world to pursue their careers, the leagues in countries such as England, Spain, Italy and Germany are highly desirable destinations not only because of the quality of competition, but also because of the possible financial rewards available.

These processes of migration, and the opening up of the possibility of movement, have a number of consequences and challenges. Just as there is concern in many countries about a brain drain, in the context of sport there is an increasing concern about a sporting talent drain. As players from all over the world are attracted either to a single league or to a small number of leagues, in particular those that are able to offer high financial rewards, so there is potential for the leagues in the home nation to be impoverished in talent terms. This was discussed in Chapter 6.

Exploitation of players is also a concern. As clubs look at players of all ages, and in particular as they focus on young players, there is a significant chance that players will be tried out and potentially dumped if they do not make the grade. Taking players from one context at a very young age and not necessarily providing them with adequate infrastructure and support can create significant financial, psychological and other health-related challenges for the athlete. While such issues are challenging enough for athletes in team sports, they may be exacerbated further for athletes in individual sports who may have very little organizational support.

Hostile reception in receiving country is also a potential issue. Just as migrants in other contexts may face discrimination and racism in the receiving country, sports stars may face similar forms of hostile reception. Important here are the resources that clubs and leagues invest, or do not invest, in assisting players to move and settle, and in particular, the extent to which sport organizations facilitate the migration experience beyond the field of play. Over the years, some clubs have begun to provide facilities and resources for young players, and to recognize that they have a duty of care towards such athletes, but this is by no means universal.

Building on these trends, processes of migration in sport are not evenly dispersed but, as with many other patterns of employment-linked migration, are uneven and are dominated by sport organizations at the centre of the global sport industry, in particular, teams in the United States and Western Europe (McGovern, 2000). Powerful transnational commodified sporting organizations are able to dominate global sports because they can afford to pay for talent from all around the world. These sporting organizations (clubs and leagues) benefit from processes of commodification and globalization to consolidate their sporting brands. More peripheral clubs and leagues end up stuck on the margins while the organizations at the core maintain and extend their dominance (McGovern, 2000).

These experiences bring questions of power to the forefront, revealing that while popular discussions of processes of globalization and mobility often appear to assume free flows throughout the global economy, in fact what is developing are structural flows in which countries, leagues and teams at the core dominate, and as they dominate, their domination increases even further. This involves not only flows of players on an individual basis, but also the creation of infrastructure to further these developments. Drawing on the work of Alan Klein around baseball, McGovern (2000) notes that baseball fans in the Dominican Republic have experienced a situation in which most of their top players are signed up by clubs in the US, Canada and Japan. Indeed, as McGovern notes, '[s]ome of these franchises, such as the Toronto Blue Jays and Los Angeles Dodgers, have taken the additional step of establishing academies in the Dominican Republic to locate, sign, and refine talent before sending it to North America for further development' (McGovern, 2000, p. 403). But, as he also notes, the achievements overseas of local players are a source of national pride (McGovern, 2000, p. 415). In other words, the experience of movement may be a contradictory one for elite athletes.

CONCLUSION

There are many privileges associated with being an elite celebrity athlete. These include financial rewards and, sometimes, the renown and associated commercial endorsements that come from celebrity. Most professional sportspeople, however, are not celebrities and in fact many do not make enough money from their sport to cover their competition costs. So sporting celebrities are a small subsection of the community of professional athletes. This chapter has shown that elite athletes are often held up as role models, even though that is at times problematic.

The chapter has also explored how the career trajectories of professional athletes vary depending on the sports played and the locations they are played in. In the global age, athletes are increasingly mobile, and movement is an aspect of a career that needs to be examined in context: some sports (like baseball) have a global market for players, while others (like American football [gridiron]) rely on locally developed players. Nevertheless, even localized competitions can require player mobilities: professional Australian Rules football players often relocate interstate to purse their careers. A key point here is that processes of mobility are not necessarily even. Some sports and leagues are much better resourced than others, so sport in the global age can serve to maintain and even expand inequality, as athletes in more peripheral sporting nations move to more central ones, leaving a dearth of talent behind.

Further to this, the increasing commodification of sport has meant that there is a relationship between commercial sponsors of sport, players and celebrity. So Tiger Woods is not only associated with golf, he is associated with sportswear company Nike, which has long sponsored his golf. When he ran into personal trouble, Nike ran into trouble and the commercial relationship was threatened.

The discussion in this chapter shows that there is a need to consider processes around professional sporting careers including celebrity, role models and career management at a collective and societal level. In other words, and in line with the sociological imagination, these are not only individual experiences, but are defining and more generalized elements of the experience of being an athlete in contemporary society.

CHAPTER SUMMARY

This chapter has shown that:

- While elite athletes have individual experiences, they are connected into a complex set of relations, with other athletes, agents and organizations, among others. In other words, the existence of elite athletes is fundamentally relational.
- Key aspects of being an athlete today involve questions of celebrity, being a role model, financial reward, career management and migration. All of these processes raise challenges for athletes, and carry with them the potential to either empower or to disempower the athlete.
- The increasing commodification of sport has had impacts on the way sport is organized, and the political and economic organization of sport affects the career trajectories of individual athletes by attracting players from disparate locations. The increased global mobility of athletes is not even, with sports in wealthy nations having the power to attract players from less wealthy nations, leading to a variety of consequences in both the sending and receiving countries.

DISCUSSION QUESTIONS

1 What do the disparities in earnings between men and women reveal about sport? Why should sociologists be concerned about such disparities? What can be done to change the situation?

2 We shouldn't hold elite professional athletes up as role models. They are ordinary human beings, just like anyone else. Discuss.

3 The international movement of players from one country to another is a powerful example of both the positive and negative effects of globalization. Discuss.

FURTHER READING

Cashmore, Ellis (2002) *Beckham*, Cambridge, Polity.

Horne, John (2006) *Sport in Consumer Culture*, Basingstoke, Palgrave Macmillan.

Jackson, Steven J. and Andrews, David L. (eds) (2005) *Sport, Culture and Advertising: Identities, Commodities and the Politics of Representation*, New York, Routledge.

Lines, Gill (2001) 'Villains, Fools or Heroes? Sports Stars as Role Models for Young People', *Leisure Studies*, 20, pp. 285–303.

Chapter 12

The Transformation of Fandom

INTRODUCTION

While the people who play the game are critical for the existence of professional sport, so too are the people who support the game, both in person and through the media, as fans or supporters, spectators and members. This chapter explores the place of fans and supporters in sport, describing the range of fans that exist, how fans express their connections to particular sports and some of the challenges of fandom, including in the context of gambling and in becoming actively involved in organizational management in club contexts. The chapter ends by considering possible futures in the experience of being a fan.

The contemporary experience of being a fan can be located within broad societal shifts that indicate that individualism is an organizing principle in many societies around the world (Elliott and Lemert, 2006). Individualism refers to a focus on the individual rather than the collective. In the world of sport and the experience of fandom, the trend towards individualism presents a challenge. On the one hand, there are indications of a movement towards a more individualized and personalized experience of fandom. This includes the introduction of personalized membership and supporter packages available from clubs and leagues, increasingly personalized media subscription options relating to choices available online and through satellite television and mobile phones, and a growing focus on a range of commercial products related to games and teams that can be purchased and consumed by the individual. On the other hand, one of the most basic and enduring elements of being a supporter is the capacity to engage in a shared experience with sometimes tens of thousands of other supporters at a stadium watching a major sporting event. Even in an increasingly online world, there are opportunities to interact with geographically dispersed supporters through blogs, interactive chat rooms and other electronically mediated forums. So, while being a supporter carries with it significant collective elements, supporters are also engaging in an individualized world. This chapter explores the contemporary meaning of being a supporter, influenced by these societal trends.

SPORTING SUPPORTERS: IDENTITY AND BELONGING

Sport is a significant factor in the lives of millions of people around the world. For some, it becomes an all-encompassing aspect of their everyday lives, while for others it is more peripheral. Beyond the basic point that people engage with sport by attending games, consuming sport through various types of media, and discussing sport as part of their everyday interactions, there are differences between supporters related to the level of their commitment to the game, their enjoyment of the game and how much of a role sport plays in their everyday lives. So there is a diversity of forms of support and of supporters. Morrow suggests that:

> At one extreme we have the traditional representation of the supporter, where the club is a complex and living symbol of his or her public identity and where the supporter has emotional ties to the club's ground and to its community significance. At the other extreme consumer spectators have a more market-centered relationship centering on consumption of club products. (Morrow, 2003, pp. 50–1)

In between these two extremes we have a range of types of fan engagement and connection to the clubs they support. We can also distinguish between 'a fan's personal connection with a sport team, and a fan's connection with other fans as a group' (Reysen and Branscombe, 2010, p. 177). A fan might enjoy sport and support a team but really participate for the connection they feel to their supporter group. Another fan might love the sport regardless of their connection with other fans. Some fans would have both a personal affinity for a team and a connection with other supporters.

Fan engagement with sport also comes from rituals associated with attending games. In some instances, rituals will be associated with actions like sitting or standing in the same place at every home game; wearing a lucky scarf or some other item of clothing; or going to the game with the same group of friends or family each week. Some rituals will also be associated with activities undertaken either before or after the game. These may include following a particular set of practices, such as going to a particular restaurant or pub before or after the game. These rituals also contribute to the formation of particular identities around sport.

An interesting example of ritualistic behaviour in sport is found in research undertaken by Drenten and her colleagues (2009) on game day tailgating parties held by supporters of the American football (gridiron) team of a large US university. Across the US, tailgate parties occur prior to sport games, when supporters gather together in the car park, or parking lot, and share more or less elaborate meals, typically some form of barbeque along with various drinks, with supplies brought and stored in the back of the car.

Based on interviews with seasoned tailgate party participants, Drenten and her colleagues (2009, p. 96) argue that people participate in these rituals for reasons including: the social interaction, the involvement in preparing and participating, and for the contribution to the participants' identities. These motivations are important to an understanding of supporter practices for a number of reasons. Among these are the finding that tailgating is not just a spontaneous event that occurs on a few weekends each year. The planning and preparation involved means that it becomes a year-round event. Further to this, tailgating is not just about having a meal and is not just an individual activity. Tailgate parties involve the development and maintenance of relations over time with other supporters, and the creation of a sense of community in which participants come to understand themselves as members of a collectivity. At the same time, forms of individualism also exist, as tailgaters compete with each other to put on the best party (Drenten *et al.*, 2009).

While being a supporter is a collective experience involving attendance at games and being part of a community of supporters, it is also important to reflect on the more personal and individual aspects of being a fan. As supporters move around in their daily lives, they carry with them images and understandings of their place in the world connected to their personal sense of engagement with the teams they support. Keen fans often have a deep, personal engagement with their team. This engagement can exist without attending or watching the team play, and it can feel like a very personal connection. The following section presents stories from fans who have written about their own experiences. These stories highlight the importance of personal reflection in understanding supporters and their experiences. (For a breakthrough book in this genre, see Hornby, 1992.)

Long-distance fans

A Liverpool Football Club (soccer) fan born and living in South Africa for many years, Grant Farred (2002) has written about his experiences of being a long-distance fan, or what he refers to as his long-distance love for Liverpool, in the following terms:

> What is distinct about my fantasy is not even the geographical origin of this love affair ... The salience of my dream is, rather, that most of my Liverpool recollections, all my memories, my entire narrative about this English FC, was born and nourished without the benefit of ever having seen my team play. (Farred, 2002, p. 8)

He goes on to suggest that:

> LDL [long-distance love] is about the depth, the intensity, and the enduring passion of that imagined other, far off (but not so far off) space. Geographic remove cannot undermine how real, tangible and consequential Liverpool is, or can be made to be. (Farred, 2002, p. 9)

Farred is clearly passionate about Liverpool. Despite being physically isolated from the city of Liverpool, and in fact never seeing the team play, Farred still imagines himself as part of a community of supporters. His experience of being a fan is likely quite different from those who go to every game. Comments such as these give an indication of the way in which fans gain a sense of identity through imagining that they are members of a particular community.

Conflicted fans

Unlike Farred, committed supporter of English football (soccer) team Chelsea Sut Jhally does attend games. He writes:

> Chelsea is part of my being and has been since 1965, when I was 9 and went to my first game at Stamford Bridge stadium (lost 1–0 to Liverpool).

> I was an immigrant kid (born in Kenya of Indian parents), 3 years in a country where Asian faces were still rare, desperately trying to belong, to connect, with a society that had no role models for people like me ... [O]nce I had connected with Chelsea (and by extension England) it become part of my identity and I can no more discard that part of me than I can my ethnicity. (Jhally, 1998, p. 224)

This type of deep connection can also raise challenges at particular moments. For example, Jhally (1998) recollects a period in the 1990s when Chelsea was sponsored by the US beer manufacturer Coors. For Jhally, Coors was a highly problematic sponsor as it was a 'company well known in the United States as a leading force of the radical right and the frightening politics of intolerance and racial bigotry that it represents' (Jhally, 1998, p. 224). What was even more disconcerting for Jhally was that this sponsorship occurred at the same time as the club had appointed its first black manager, the famous Dutch footballer Ruud Gullit. For Jhally, this contradiction was hard to reconcile. But at the same time, he admits that he was not able to give up supporting the team, despite his strong opposition to Coors. For Jhally, being a fan is an intrinsic part of who he is. Even when he disapproved of decisions the club made, his connection to the team did not diminish. The type of connection fans like Jhally feel is an enduring and personally meaningful one.

Connected fans

Finally, in their analysis of Australian rules football supporters living in Melbourne, Australia, John Cash and Joy Damousi (2004) found that supporting particular football teams provided a means of creating connections and relations with significant others. One of their participants, Christine commented about her understanding of being a supporter:

> It was a way of reconnecting with cousins. We don't have much in common. So football is now a means of reconnecting. When you see them you can talk about football and you can tease each other about your teams. Before that we had very little to say, now we have something to say to one another ... [And] I think it's broken the gender segregation [where] the men will sit in a corner and talk about things and the women will sit in another corner and talk about various other things ... The football has really broken that because we all sit mixed together and talk about football. And it's great, it's

a lot of fun ... it allows us to cross these traditional boundaries. (Cash and Damousi, 2004, p. 223)

Another participant in their research, Helen, commented on how football was important in her life in enabling her to connect with a friend at a time of difficult family circumstances:

[I]t was a very important friendship for me at that stage, because we could talk about other intimate things because we had this bond and every weekend I would become part of her family and we would truck off to the football together and that was great fun doing that. (Cash and Damousi, 2004, p. 224)

What these excerpts reveal is that sport can be an immensely powerful presence in the lives of supporters. Sport is also a means through which supporters, such as those discussed here, seek to make sense of issues in their lives that go beyond the field of play, whether that be related to a sense of belonging, race and racism, or other factors. In short, sport is more than competition; it is a meaningful presence and factor in the lives of many people.

CLUB ORGANIZATION AND THE SUPPORTER EXPERIENCE

The experience of being a supporter who attends games is also influenced by the organization of the club, particularly the stadiums that host games. In particular, in professional sport, an important trend is the emergence of corporatized and commercialized stadiums (van Uden, 2005). While sports stadiums still serve the purpose of being venues for sporting events, many now set themselves up to be much more than that. In addition to the luxury corporate boxes, which companies can hire to entertain clients with full service dinners, surround-sound television and internet access, all the while in sound-proofed comfort, many stadiums also have conference rooms, dining rooms that operate throughout the week and megastores selling all forms of merchandise associated with the club. In addition, major stadiums around the world have moved away from having standing room areas to being seating-only venues, and increasing numbers of stadiums for outdoor sports also have retractable roofs. While there is no doubt that such developments increase the comfort of fans on game day, they also signal a change in the role of the stadiums. In particular, hosting matches becomes just one of the functions of a stadium.

Along with the more general corporatization of the game, it has become increasingly hard for people on low incomes to access professional games. Increasing numbers of seats are sold as season tickets, and for match-day sales, prices have increased in many sports and are now out of the reach of a person on low income, in particular if they wish to take their family. The availability of merchandise at grounds, at club shops and at department and general sports stores, is another feature of these trends. While fans of clubs have long worn team clothing and accessories, such as scarves and team badges, as a sign of allegiance, this practice has become hyper-commercialized. Club shops are now megastores, selling products ranging from the traditional scarves and team shirts through to art, homewares and gifts such as jewellery and watches. Many club shirts are now sold with the names of the club sponsors on them. This has at least two effects. First, it means that when fans wear a team shirt, not only are they wearing their club colours, they are also actively promoting a separate corporate entity. In addition, when clubs change sponsors, they also change their shirts. This means that, for a fan to remain up to date, there is constant pressure to buy the latest shirt with the latest sponsor. Through processes such as this, supporters are drawn into a spiral of purchasing and repurchasing new material to show their support for their club (Redhead, 1997; van Uden, 2005).

Another factor influencing the level of engagement of fans relates to how clubs position and present themselves. While for many years it was accepted that the major purpose of clubs was to compete against other clubs, in more recent years, clubs in many different sports have been repositioning themselves as part of a broader entertainment industry. In his analysis of the Dutch professional football club (soccer) Vitesse, for example, Jacco van Uden (2005) argues that, over a number of years, the club has proposed that it transform itself from being merely a football club to becoming a 'total experience entertainment company' (2005, p. 184). The logic behind this strategy is embodied in the business model at the club which captures the notion of 'finding new ways to make a profit from football and at the same time ... leaving the company less vulnerable to (poor) performance by the Vitesse squad' (2005, p. 189). Overall, such a reinvention of core activities of the club signifies an attempt to become part of 'the potentially very lucrative *experience economy*' (2005, p. 197, italics in original). This in turn has significant organizational implications. As van Uden's analysis shows, becoming a total experience entertainment company is not just a matter of adding a few extra elements to the existing club. Rather it requires wholesale structural changes, including reimagining the central purpose of the organization. As this process of reinvention occurs, it raises significant questions for supporters about whether they wish to continue to support clubs that are reinventing themselves in this way. For supporters, such sentiments are related to whether or not they continue to feel a sense of connection with the club.

An important development in fandom has been the emergence of supporters groups and networks concerned with the increasing commercialization and commodification of sports. While these movements often contain a sense of nostalgia for a past, either real or imagined, that has been lost, there is also a significant dimension of such movements engaged with bringing power relations that often remain hidden to the surface. In an earlier chapter, we discussed the case of BSkyB and its attempt to buy Manchester United. As we saw in that case study, the Independent Manchester United Supporters' Association played an important role in preventing the takeover. Around the world, many similar movements exist, sometimes embodied in particular organizations or in individuals. For example, in the United States, people such as the journalist Dave Zirin and the rap artist Chuck D have been outspoken about ownership and related organizational and political issues in the context of professional sports in the United States. Both have spoken out against controversial anti-immigration legislation in the state of Arizona, and have argued that players, clubs, supporters and leagues should boycott games in Arizona and games involving teams from Arizona as a means of protesting against the legislation (Zirin, 2008; Zirin, 2010).

Meanwhile, in Spain, the supporters group L'Elefant Blau was instrumental in bringing problems with the membership system at FC Barcelona in the 1990s and into the 2000s to the surface. In particular, the organization was established to counter what a group of supporters saw as the attempt by the then administration to turn the club from a member-based organization into a public liability company – that is, a company organized around shareholders. The movement made an important argument that while the organization of the club appeared democratic in its formal official documents, in practice it was anything but democratic, with power being taken and controlled by a small group of people. The group appealed to the broader sense of Spanish democracy in making its argument, claiming that while the position of Catalonians in Spanish society had improved since the time of the Franco dictatorship, the position of members of Barcelona had declined (L'Elefant Blau, 1999).

These examples give an indication of some of the ways in which supporters have sought to become more actively involved in the sports they are passionate about. This indicates that sport is not only a form of entertainment or an activity which supporters consume passively. Depending on the particular context and the issues at stake, there is scope for supporters to become actively involved and to seek to create social and political change, both in and through sport.

DISCUSSION POINT

Consider the following argument. These days, it is not enough for sporting clubs to provide a venue for a competition between two teams. Today's supporters want a much more developed spectator experience, involving comfortable surroundings and sophisticated pre-game and post-game entertainment opportunities. Indeed, for the contemporary fan, the game itself is just one part of an overall entertainment experience.

What do make of this argument? Do you agree with it? What evidence is your opinion based on?

VIOLENT BEHAVIOUR AT SPORTING EVENTS

One issue that has been a long-time source of concern has been fan behaviour at sporting events, particularly violent behaviour. Over a number of years, a range of sociological approaches have been developed that have attempted to explain why particular groups engage in violence at sporting events, often called hooliganism. Sociological approaches to violent fan behaviour provide insights into the social dimensions of such behaviour. Whereas much media and policy discussion of violent behaviour takes an individualistic and law-and-order approach to fan violence, these sociological approaches suggest the need to examine the social, political and economic contexts within which such behaviour takes place. These contexts are important for the development of effective measures to reduce or prevent violent behaviour. In particular, sociological approaches indicate that, while there is clearly a need for regulation of violence, such regulation needs to be aware of a broad range of social factors that may influence behaviour.

One set of approaches to understanding hooliganism, based in micro-level participant research, emphasizes the ritualistic and gendered dimensions of violent behaviour and argues that men engage in this type of behaviour as a symbol of masculinity (Coakley and Pike, 2009). Second, for researchers working from conflict perspectives, violence is linked to notions of alienation among the working class in a class-based society. Here, violence becomes a means through which dispossessed people seek to express their outrage and sense of disconnection from society (Coakley and Pike, 2009).

A third set of approaches, connected with the Centre for Contemporary Cultural Studies at the University of Birmingham, a foundational site for the emergence of cultural studies, argues that there is a need to analyse violence as part of a set of cultural practices connected to broad processes of cultural and societal transformation (Coakley and Pike, 2009). Next, a figurational approach, closely linked with researchers at the University of Leicester and drawing on the work of Norbert Elias, argues that violence at games is a manifestation of historical processes and change (Coakley and Pike, 2009). From this view, when social transformation impacts negatively on certain groups, such as working-class men, by increasing their relative deprivation, '[f]ootball then becomes a site for these men to defend and/or assert community and identity through violence directed at the new status quo' (Coakley and Pike, 2009, p. 256; see also, Giulianotti, 1999; King, 2000; Spaaij, 2006, 2008). Finally, in their analysis of violence among spectators, Coakley and Pike (2009, p. 257) identify three factors underlying crowd violence:

- Violence on the field in the context of the sports event.
- 'Crowd dynamics' (2009, p. 257) and the context in which fans watch the game.
- Broad societal context in which the sporting event occurs.

Coakley and Pike suggest that effective management or control of crowd violence needs to engage with these three dimensions. It is not enough to focus on a pure law and order approach, in which perpetrators of violence are expelled from games, fined, barred from attending in the future, or even jailed (2009, p. 261). Rather, there is a need to engage with the broader context surrounding spectator violence. Of course, this is difficult, time consuming and expensive, so is not an easy set of arguments to sell in public or policy debate. Nevertheless, a focus on such factors is an example of how a sociological approach can enrich understandings of complex social processes, while also providing suggestions for action to engage with social challenges.

GAMBLING AND FANS

Another issue that has been a source of concern has been gambling. A striking trend in sport is the ever closer and more open connection between sport and gambling, which in turn is having an influence on how fans interact with the game (Forrest and Simmons, 2003). It is now common-place at sporting events for betting odds to be announced and progressively updated during a game through scoreboard updates and mobile media announcements. Supporters can bet in an increasing number of ways, from the traditional way of going to a bookmaker or betting shop through to betting online or through a mobile phone while at the game. With the inter-net, and in the absence of restrictive legislation, there are few limits to what events a person can bet on. Someone living in Australia can bet on events occurring in India, Japan, the United States and Germany all at the same time, while also attending and betting on a game in Australia. There are also increasing numbers of aspects of sport that can be bet on, ranging from the outcome of a game through to who will score the first goal, make the most runs, or shoot the most baskets in a single game or over a season. The connection between sport and gambling is being normalized through commercial processes that see betting organizations sponsoring teams. For example, betting company Intralot has sponsored Melbourne Victory in the A-League, the elite professional football (soccer) competition in Australia, while betting organizations also sponsor tournaments, with Betfair, for example, having sponsored the Australian Open Tennis tournament (Rossingh and Baynes, 2010).

In considering the connection between betting on sports and fandom, Ellis Cashmore (2005) sets out three reasons why people like to bet. These are:

- 'It adds to the thrill' (Cashmore, 2005, p. 346).
- 'Competition lends itself to gambling' (Cashmore 2005, p. 346). While much gambling is grounded entirely in chance, in sport, there is an opportunity for people to use their expert knowledge in making deci-sions – for example, about which team is likely to win, or which player will hit the lowest round in a golf event.
- 'Historically, sport and gambling have been intertwined' (Cashmore, 2005, p. 346). It is important not to think of the connection between gambling and sport as new. Indeed, certain sports such as horse racing have existed over time in large part because of betting. At the same time, however, trends associated with the emergence of the network society, such as the reduced significance of time and space, give betting on sport in the twenty-first century a new dimension.

For some, including those working in the gambling industry, betting is an important dimension of sport, and one that should be encouraged because it adds to the enjoyment of following sport. And, indeed, it would appear to be the case that an occasional bet, or partaking in an office tipping competition or sweep stakes, can add a level of enjoyment and community-building. At the same time, however, gambling raises many challenges in the context of sport. For some, gambling on sport can become an addiction, with negative health and financial consequences both for the individual and for those around them, including family members. Significant challenges also emerge for sport if gambling raises doubts about the integrity of the game and of the competition. Sport is grounded in a basic trust that all the participants are genuine in their competitiveness. Once this is challenged, then one of the foundations of sport is removed, and the basis for sport itself is challenged.

Over the years, many sports have been the subject of gambling and betting concerns and scandals. For example, tennis players have been suspected of throwing games, or tanking (Ford, 2007), while a scandal arose in European football (soccer) in 2009 when it was revealed that players, referees, coaches and others were involved in betting-related activities linked to organized crime (Gibson, 2009). In the early 2000s, cases of betting involving leading international players rocked the world of cricket. Two of the leading Australian cricketers at the time, Shane Warne and Mark Waugh, were fined for providing a bookmaker with information about pitch conditions and the weather. In 2000, the South African cricket captain, Hansie Cronje, admitted that he had accepted bribes from bookmakers to provide information and to fix results, resulting in his receiving a life-long ban from the sport. While Cronje's case was one of the most high profile, his actions were symptomatic of a much wider problem with betting and corruption in world cricket at the time. Following such cases, the International Cricket Council established an Anti Corruption and Security Unit to pursue three objectives of investigation, education and prevention, in relation to betting and other activities (Bose, 2001; ICC, 2009a).

This discussion of the relationship between gambling and sport raises critical issues for understandings of the place of the fan in sport. While betting can be a source of pleasure for supporters, it can also very quickly become a source of financial difficulty. Further to this, once gambling becomes linked to players or to other people involved in the sport industry, the integrity of the sport may be compromised. In such contexts, the very meaning of being a supporter or a fan also becomes compromised, as the essential element of genuine competition is removed from the sport.

THE FUTURE OF FANDOM

As with the other issues discussed through this book, the state of being a fan is not unchanging. Smith and Westerbeek, in their analysis of *The Sport Business Future* (2004), argue that the place of the fan, and of the sport consumer, will undergo important and fundamental transformations in the years ahead. Mirroring transformations in other areas of social life, and most particularly the media, they suggest that, in the near future, rather than just watching games, fans will actively participate in them (Smith and Westerbeek, 2004). Writing in 2004, they identified the emergence of cyber-sport as a new form of spectator involvement in sport (Smith and Westerbeek, 2004). In cyber-sport, participants engage in digital competitions, perhaps online through avatars, or in person through games consoles like the Nintendo Wii (Smith and Westerbeek, 2010). Although this type of fan involvement has not yet caught on at a mass level, it is clear that the role of the fan will be transformed through technological innovations.

In considering the future, we need to think further about the role of technology in our experiences of sport. In the network society we have myriad ways of interacting with sport that involve neither attending games nor watching them on a television screen. For example, fans are able to watch their favourite teams and players from anywhere in the world, often in real time, on mobile phones. This takes the focus of sport out of its geographic space and places it into virtual spaces that can be accessed anywhere (Smith and Westerbeek, 2004). We can also create our own virtual 'fantasy' teams where we select the players that we consider the best from teams in our actual leagues to imagine a better team. Fantasy leagues use the on-field performance statistics of real players to determine how the imaginary teams perform in their imaginary competition against other similarly imagined teams. As individuals we can participate in fantasy sport leagues anywhere in the world. This type of fandom requires knowledge of teams and players that is enhanced by digital communication technologies.

Ultimately, the result of these processes will be a situation in which the new type of fan has more control and more choice. In this view, information and communication technologies provide a foundation for a revolution in the experience of what it means to be a fan. The fans of the future will take a variety of forms, but competitive fact-to-face sport will remain the basis of fandom for the foreseeable future. Even much fantasy sport is based around actual players, and while cyber-sports might eventually be considered genuine sport, the corporate and other interests behind sport suggest it will be difficult to dislodge establish sports as the centres of sport.

CONCLUSION

Fans engage with sport in a variety of ways, including through their individual feelings of identifying with a club and their emotional attachments to it (Morrow, 2003; Reysen and Branscome, 2010), and through their feelings of connection with other fans of their team (Reysen and Branscome, 2010). In experiencing being a fan, people may participate in individual or group practices that relate to their feelings about supporting their team and that enhance their identity as fans (Drenten *et al.*, 2009). From a sociological perspective, the main point to take is that both individual and group-based experiences of being a fan are socially shaped. Even when an individual dons a lucky scarf, the act of doing so is something that others also do, and emerges out of social processes and practices around sport.

This chapter has discussed a variety of experiences of being a fan, including the ambivalence some people feel towards the team they love. The chapter has also discussed particularly challenging practices such as the increasing corporatization of sport, fan violence and sport-related gambling, arguing that they all shape and are shaped by the social contexts surrounding the fan experience.

This chapter has engaged with aspects of being a supporter, ranging from definitional issues through to challenges around violence and gambling and onto questions about supporter activism and the future of fandom. This analysis shows the significant contribution that sociology has made to understandings of supporters, in particular identifying the need to engage with the social, political, cultural and economic contexts within which supporters live, and which shape their experiences of being supporters.

CHAPTER SUMMARY

This chapter has shown that:

■ Fans are central to the practice of professional sport. Without supporters, professional sport would not exist in the form we understand it today.

- Fans can be distinguished along a number of axes, including in terms of their personal attachment to a game or a team, and in terms of their connection to a collective, either real or imagined.
- When we consider violence among spectators, sociology reminds us that we cannot look for explanations for such behaviour, or for possible solutions to such behaviour, by focusing on individuals or even groups of individuals in isolation. We need to consider the broader social, political and economic contexts within which violence occurs.
- An important means of gaining insight into what sport means for people is to listen to what they say in their narratives.
- Technological change has already contributed to transformations in the experience of being a fan, and even in the question of what it is to be a fan. As technology continues to develop, even more challenges and changes in fandom will occur.
- Fans are not powerless in the face of sporting changes that they do not agree with. As examples such as independent supporters' movements show, supporters are able to mobilize with important effect and influence.

DISCUSSION QUESTIONS

1   Interview a member of your class about their interest in sport as a fan. What sport(s) do they consume? Do they go to games and/or consume games through the media? What sense of attachment do they have to particular games or teams? Where do they think this sense of attachment comes from?

2   Do you think it is possible to be as strongly attached to a team as a supporter if you only support them through the media? Does a real fan need to attend games in person? Why or why not?

3   Fans shouldn't get involved in the political and organizational aspects of sport. It is best to leave those sorts of issues to the experts who run the clubs. Discuss.

4   Why are some people so passionate about sport? And why are some people so indifferent to sport? Where do these differences in attitude to sport come from?

FURTHER READING

Coakley, Jay and Pike, Elizabeth (2009) *Sports in Society: Issues and Controversies*, Maidenhead, McGraw-Hill.

Giulianotti, Richard (2002) 'Supporters, Followers, Fans, and Flaneurs', *Journal of Sport and Social Issues*, 26(1), pp. 25–46.

Hornby, Nick (1992) *Fever Pitch*, London, Indigo.

Morrow, Stephen (2003) *The People's Game? Football, Finance and Society*, Basingstoke, Palgrave Macmillan.

Reysen, Stephen and Branscombe, Nyla R. (2010) 'Fanship and Fandom: Comparisons between Sport Fans and Non-Sport Fans', *Journal of Sport Behavior*, 33, pp. 176–93.

Chapter 13

The Media and Consumption of Sport

INTRODUCTION

An important feature of sociological research over an extended period of time has related to questions of commercialization and commodification, and their links to the importance of consumption (Schor, 2004). Commercialization refers to the production of a good for profit. Commodification refers to the process through which something, sport in this context, that is not normally regarded as a product comes to be bought and sold, primarily with the aim of making a financial profit (Moor, 2007; Schor, 2004). Commodification captures the process through which activities such as sport are transformed from having one set of meanings – for example, around entertainment and enjoyment for participants – to become objects that can be bought and sold. Players, teams, stadiums and so on become the same as any other good in the market system, whether it be a fridge or a computer or a bottle of milk. They are objects to which a monetary value can be attached and which can be subject to financial transactions in the marketplace. To the extent that commodification and commercialization become dominant within sport, they pose a challenge to the broader public goods often claimed to be associated with sport. In other words, commercialization and commodification in the context of sport refer to processes that link sport to economic activities in a capitalist society.

To make this discussion of commercialization and commodification more precise, this chapter focuses on the relationship between media and sport. First, the place of media in society in general is discussed, and used as a means of presenting ownership patterns that have emerged in the media-sport industry over a number of years. Second, critical dimensions of the media process in the context of sport are analysed, focusing on issues that have emerged around ownership, production, content and audience engagement with the media. Next, the world of sports journalism and its audiences is explored. Finally, the chapter discusses the emergence of e-gaming, which has been described as 'sport as media' (Hutchins, 2006, p. 4). Through considering these varying dimensions of the media–sport relationship, called the 'match made in heaven' (Cashmore, 2005, p. 319), the chapter provides insights into the significance of media, commercialization and commodification in contemporary sport (see also Moor, 2007).

MEDIA IN SOCIETY

When considering how contemporary societies are organized, it is critical to analyse the media. Such has been the expansion of the media into all aspects of life that it is now almost impossible to imagine how life would be without it. Whether reading newspapers, looking at billboards, listening to the radio or an mp3 player, watching television, going online with a computer or mobile phone, the media is part of the fabric of everyday life (Deuze, 2007). This is the case whether we are talking about politics, business, entertainment, or sport. And, in turn, these areas of human life would not be the same without the media. In the context of sport, for example: what would our own experience of sport be like if we didn't have access to the media? Apart from questions such as how we would find out when and where our favourite team or competitor was playing at any particular moment, much of our connection with sport between games or competitions would be greatly diminished. We can also ask: what would sport be like without the media? In the context of professional sport, in particular, sport would be completely different. The media not only provides a means for promoting sport, through showing and reporting on games, and attracting advertisers, but it also provides major financial support to sports, through television rights deals, sponsorship and, in some cases, the ownership of teams.

The importance of the media in the global network society is linked to a number of critical factors. First, when analysing sites of power and influence within the global economy, it is important to consider the industries that produce and disseminate knowledge and information, which are themselves becoming increasingly significant as commodities (Castells, 2009). While organizations such as universities, schools and governments produce information, at the global level, the amount they put forward pales in comparison to the information and knowledge produced by major media corporations, regardless of arguments about the quality of such material (Balnaves *et al.*, 2001, p. 60).

Second, the media provides a lens through which to view and experience the world, whether that is in terms of news and current affairs, or entertainment such as sport. While people can contest the messages that are delivered through various media, everyday discussions and knowledge are often framed by those messages.

Third, the media is central in a networked society. Many members of society are connected to the media, either directly through working in the media or indirectly through working in industries that themselves are connected to the media, such as sport. As Castells has written, 'new information technologies [including media and communications technologies] are transforming the way we produce, consume, manage, live and die' (Castells, 1989, p. 15). Given the significance of the media at a societal level, it is not surprising that it has had a profound influence on sport.

Within this overall context, the media can be conceptualized in terms of a media process. Specifically, the media process is constituted by production of media, media content and reception of media by audiences. The precise ways in which this process unfolds are in turn influenced by patterns of media ownership and the political and economic context within which the media is situated (Marjoribanks, 2011).

OWNING THE MEDIA-SPORT INDUSTRY

Around the world, media corporations, and individuals associated with the media, have become owners and stakeholders within the sport industry, sometimes at the level of the team or club, sometimes at a league level, and in some instances in relation to other dimensions of the sport industry such as stadium and player sponsorship. When people consider the business of sport today, as well as thinking of leading teams and leagues, quick to come to the surface are the names of leading media entrepreneurs including Rupert Murdoch, Ted Turner and Silvio Berlusconi, and major global and national media corporations such as News Corporation, Time Warner and Fininvest. Indeed, such is the closeness of the business relationship between professional sport and media organizations that some suggest that there is a need to do away with the conceptual distinctions between media and sport, and talk instead of a single industry, the mediasport industry. Lawrence Wenner, for example, has used the phrase 'media-sport' (Wenner, 1998), while Law *et al.* have discussed the 'global sport mass media oligopoly' (2002, p. 279) and Joseph Maguire analyses what he refers to as 'the global media-sport complex' (1999, 2005), constituted by the interaction of sports teams, marketing companies and transnational corporations.

These concepts highlight the importance of the emergence of new networks of relations between sport and media organizations. These networks operate at a global level and influence not only which sports and teams are broadcast, but how people are able to view sport on television and through the internet, often having a profound impact on the economics of sport. The media individuals and organizations involved also often have very close direct or indirect links with political leaders, or, as in the case of Silvio Berlusconi in Italy, are political leaders themselves. The media-sport relationship therefore raises significant political questions, and provides an important example of sport having an independent influence on the political process. The relationship also points to sport as a site of power, not only in reflecting power relations in the broader society, but in its own right.

The following two case studies of media-sport owners Silvio Berlusconi and Rupert Murdoch explore ownership, economics and politics in media-sport further.

TWO CASE STUDIES OF MEDIA-SPORT

Case study: Silvio Berlusconi

Silvio Berlusconi is one of the most influential individuals in the world, filling a range of high-profile positions within Italian politics, media and sport. In addition to being Prime Minister of Italy on a number of occasions, he is the owner of a wide range of media interests in Italy through the financial holding company Fininvest, which he founded and in which his family has a significant interest (Fininvest, 2010). He is also the owner of AC Milan, one of the most powerful teams in Italian and world football (soccer). In 2010, Forbes magazine ranked AC Milan as the seventh richest football club in the world, and the richest in Italy (Schwartz *et al.*, 2010).

While Berlusconi denies this, his critics argue that he has an unhealthy and problematic role in Italian society. His positions as both a politician and a media owner have led to charges that he has a conflict of interest. Added to this is his ownership of a club in a sport that is very important in the social and political life of Italy. In many ways, Berlusconi is the embodiment of the media-sport relationship, with the added dimension of being an influential politician. Given the global popularity both of football as a sport and of AC Milan as the self-styled 'best team in football' (AC Milan, 2010a), ownership of the club gives Berlusconi a presence beyond the borders of Italy and of Europe that he otherwise would not have. As one indicator of this, in addition to the club website being available in Italian, Spanish, Portuguese and English, it is also available in Japanese and Chinese, thereby ensuring that fans around the world have access to information about the club. The club is also sponsored by a range of global corporations, including the airline Emirates, the sports company Adidas, the beauty product company Nivea, the car company Audi and many others (AC Milan, 2010b).

Through his ownership of AC Milan, Berlusconi exercises both direct and indirect forms of power and influence. Direct forms of power exist in that he is able to use his wealth to purchase such a club, which then becomes connected to his presence in Italy across a range of public arenas. This is the case even in relation to the on-field performances of AC Milan, and on a number of occasions he has been critical of team selection and strategy processes. At the same time, ownership of a club also results in indirect forms of power. For example, when the club succeeds both at the national and the international level, Berlusconi becomes identified with a successful product. The global nature of the AC Milan brand also becomes a vehicle Berlusconi can use to present himself to an international audience through television, the internet and other media forms.

Case study: Rupert Murdoch

Over many years, Rupert Murdoch and his global media organization News Corporation have been at the forefront of revolutionary changes in the relationship between media and sport. Murdoch has at times owned various sport teams and other sport entities, such as the US Major League Baseball team the LA Dodgers. He has also been involved in the creation of a league, the Super League in Australian Rugby League. His more significant long-term interventions in sport, however, have come about through his approach to television coverage of sport (Law *et al.*, 2002). Perhaps better than anyone else, even his great rival Ted Turner, Murdoch has seen the potential benefits for his company of being involved in televized sport coverage and has been able to act on that insight. Today, after shaky beginnings, both Fox and Sky are central to News Corporation and are major broadcasters of sport around the world.

Securing the rights to broadcast sport has been central to the global strategy of News Corporation. Murdoch has been reported to the effect, for example, that sport has been a 'battering ram' that increases pay television subscriptions overall for his organization (Milliken, 1996). When people around the world pay for subscriptions to popular sports channels they are also enticed to subscribe to other channels. At the same time, News Corporation, in particular through Fox and Sky, has been a crucial player in transforming the quality of televized coverage of sport, including angles of vision, numbers of cameras and so on. Through struggles over securing broadcasting rights, News Corporation has had the opportunity to influence government policy around what sports should be shown on free to air television and what sports should be available only through subscription-based television (BSkyB, 2010a; Rowe 1999, 2003).

As a result of activities such as this, while Murdoch has not been involved as a formal political actor in the same way as Berlusconi, he has had an important political influence in sport. In terms of indirect power, even when rival organizations seek to articulate a position that is different to that taken by News Corporation, such is the presence of News Corporation that they are forced to respond to an agenda and context created by Murdoch and his organization. This was evident in the case of News Corporation's failed bid to purchase Manchester United, discussed earlier, where new policies were set in place by the British government around sporting team ownership in response to News Corporation's strategies, which other media organizations have also had to comply with (Brown, 2000).

DISCUSSION POINT

Through their ownership of media and sports organizations, and additionally in Berlosconi's case, his position as a politician, both Rupert Murdoch and Silvio Berlusconi have shaped government policy around sport broadcasting. Some might argue that the intermingling of media and sport by Murdoch and Berlusconi has been good for sport, whereas others would argue the opposite. On balance, which side of the debate do you find more persuasive, and why?

Within the ownership context discussed above, it is possible to identify a number of dimensions of the media-sport process. These are (Marjoribanks, 2011):

- Production processes.
- Media content.
- Audience and consumer engagement.

While each of these elements of the media process can be separated out for analytic purposes, it is also important to recognize that they intersect with each other over time. In other words, media-sport can be considered as a relational process.

PRODUCTION PROCESSES

Taking a historical view of the relationship between sport and media, it has been a relationship which has both benefited and at times frustrated media and sport organizations respectively (Rowe, 1999). From an early stage, print media such as newspapers and magazines reported on sport and, later on, radio and television both reported and broadcast sporting contests. For sport, reporting was valuable as a means of promoting interest in the particular game, both among existing supporters and among potential new supporters. For media organizations, reporting on and covering sport was an important means of boosting circulation (audience numbers) and attracting advertising: the popular interest in sport could be translated into money.

Even in its early stages, there were tensions in the relationship between sport and media that, particularly in the context of television, continue today (Boyle and Haynes, 2000; Horne, 2006; Rowe, 1999). Sporting administrators were concerned about live free to air television broadcasts, especially in the city or region in which the game was being played. Clubs gain revenue from fans attending live matches, and their concern was that fans would stay at home to watch a game on television if it was shown live rather than attending the game in person. Even today, many sport organizations do not allow live television broadcasts of their games, preferring a delayed broadcast where, for example, the game is shown on television 30 minutes or one hour after the game has started. It is interesting to note that this same concern has not extended to radio, which has long played a central role in delivering live broadcasts of games (Boyle and Haynes, 2000; Rowe, 1999; Wenner, 1998).

For media organizations, sport also is a major source of revenue (Horne, 2006). Many newspapers have significant numbers of staff writing for their sports pages based on a recognition that many people start reading their newspapers from the back, the traditional location of sports news (Rowe,

1992). Sport coverage is also typically featured prominently in online news-papers (Lange *et al.*, 2007). For television stations, sport is powerful because it attracts both viewers and advertisers (Horne, 2006). Companies will pay substantial fees to have their products advertised during sporting events on television, and advertising fees reach stratospheric amounts during major sport events such as the National Football League Super Bowl, and global sporting events such as the FIFA World Cup (Boyle *et al.*, 2002; Boyle and Haynes, 2000; Rowe 1992, 1999).

Moving beyond long-established media forms, the emergence of new information and communications technologies, and of online content, provides a series of confronting challenges, but also possible opportunities, for both the media and sport industries (Hutchins and Rowe, 2009, p. 357). As Hutchins and Rowe (2009) argue, we are in the midst of a shift from broadcast scarcity to a situation of digital plenitude, or, as John Keane has argued, we are experiencing a shift from communicative scarcity to communicative abundance (Keane, 2009). Whereas the media has historically been dominated by notions of scarcity – for example, in terms of limited airwaves and in the costs associated with printing presses – the digital revolution has potentially opened up access to the media in ways that were until recently almost unimaginable.

There are now numerous production possibilities available for delivery of sporting content, including combining text, visual and audio content through the internet (Hutchins and Rowe, 2009; Smith and Westerbeek, 2004, 2010). Similarly, digital television provides more opportunities for a range of delivery formats than was possible with broadcast television. At the same time, these trends also have the potential to challenge the capacity of global media organizations to control media access and ownership. To give one example, increasing numbers of teams and clubs are now setting up their own internet-based media as a means of providing fans with information, either on a free or paid basis. The advantage for clubs is that they can directly control the information that is sent out to the public, and can avoid the perceived risk of being misrepresented by the mainstream media. Fans can tune in knowing they will only get information about the team they are interested in. The other side of this development is that critical analysis tends to be missing from in-house coverage (Hutchins, 2008; Hutchins and Rowe, 2009).

Developments in media and communication technologies are also creating new possibilities in the production context around interactivity (Ruddock *et al.*, 2010). Whereas previously production of sport for media was the domain of powerful media organizations, spectators can now also participate in production. One example of this is the use of mobile phones to record moments of games which are then uploaded on to a website such as YouTube for all to see. Such an example, while a small instance in itself, represents potentially larger transformations in the media production process. These trends suggest that, as technology workable by individuals becomes even more powerful, supporters at games will have greater opportunities to record and to present coverage of sport in ways that may rival what is done by major media organizations. In other words, the previously clear demarcations between producers and consumers are being challenged (Hutchins and Rowe, 2009; Ruddock *et al.*, 2010).

MEDIA REPRESENTATIONS OF SPORT

As discussed in Part II, media representations of sport operate both to produce and reproduce dominant power relations in societal contexts. Significant sociological research has been conducted on a range of dimensions relating to how media represents sport, including around race, ethnicity, gender, sexuality, disability, nation and class. While such research indicates that, over time, there are examples where the media has provided a means for rethinking dominant understandings of social relations, by and large, media representations tend to reproduce dominant understandings. This concern remains, even in an emerging context of communicative abundance, where the possibility for a multiplicity of voices and perspectives exists. As Keane (2009) warns, a multiplicity of voices does not necessarily constitute an opening up of debate and contestation. There may be a multiplicity of voices all presenting the same perspective, or operating within a narrow range of views. Alternatively, even where a genuine multiplicity of perspectives exists, there may be some perspectives that are in a more powerful position than others. For example, the resources available to major media organizations are much greater than the resources available to an individual blogger. This does not mean that an individual blogger cannot have an effect, but it does mean that there is a need to be careful in making any claims that communicative abundance in itself leads to some form of level playing field. In short, a multiplicity of voices does not necessarily mean a diversity of influences, or an equalizing of influences.

The work of Messner *et al.* (2000) on the 'televised sports manhood formula' provides an important example of how media represents sport. Messner and his colleagues (2000) analysed a range of televized sport in the US that had been identified by the Amateur Athletic Foundation as the sports most watched by boys aged eight to 17 in the US. Based on a textual analysis of 23 hours of sport programming, they found that men dominated the coverage. In particular, white men were portrayed as authority figures and were a dominant presence in both commentary and advertising. In contrast, non-white people were virtually invisible. Further, women were portrayed as sexy props or as prizes for men's successful sports performances. In terms of sport itself, the coverage portrayed aggression and violence positively, mobilizing images of war and bodily sacrifice (Messner *et al.*, 2000). When these themes are combined, they constitute a mediatized 'message about what it means to be a man' (Messner *et al.*, 2000, p. 390). In particular, 'A Real Man is strong, tough, aggressive, and above all, a winner in what is still a Man's World' (Messner *et al.*, 2000, p. 390). Such representations are not only important in themselves, but because they connect to the industries that come together in the media-sport context (Messner *et al.*, 2000). Such representations indicate that, in addition to considering the relationships between sport and media, there is a need to consider the 'huge network of multi-billion-dollar automobile, snack food, alcohol, entertainment, and other corporate entities that sponsor sports events and broadcasts' (Messner *et al.*, 2000, p. 391). In the context of the representations that occur in the media-sport world, in other words, it is important not only to consider the actual representations of sport that occur, but also the related coverage that occurs in advertising.

This example reveals that representations of sport are not neutral, but are constructed in particular ways that reflect particular power relations. While it is important not to assume that all people who watch the programming agree or engage with the representations being produced and transmitted, these representations form an important context surrounding the sport that is being consumed by television viewers. There may, however, also be a case for testing these findings further. The results discussed here were published in 2000, and based on research undertaken in the United States in 1999. Before simply accepting that this is still the current state of affairs, it would be appropriate to (1) conduct a similar analysis of television coverage of sport today; and (2) consider television coverage in countries other than the United States. It would be interesting in conducting such a study to see which of the findings still hold, and which seem to have been challenged. While it is to hoped that the findings from the original study had been superseded by more progressive and socially inclusive media coverage, even an anecdotal watching of a single televized sporting event suggests that many of the original findings are still relevant in the context of contemporary sports coverage, and in a range of countries.

When considering the debates around media-sport representations, it is also important to look at the work of sports journalists (Boyle and Haynes, 2000). For many consumers of sport, knowledge of games comes not only from attending games and discussing sports with family, friends and colleagues, but also from reading or listening to sports journalists. Importantly, sports journalists do not only report on matches or events. They also report on the lives and lifestyles of players, on the financial dimensions of sport, and on the sport industry as a whole. Across these areas of coverage, sports journalists adopt varying reportage strategies, including so-called objective news reporting, opinion-based reporting, and more critical and politicized engagements with sport (Rowe, 1992, 1999; Boyle *et al.*, 2002).

An excellent example of critically engaged journalism is the work of Dave Zirin, a US sports journalist who runs a blog entitled the 'Edge of Sport'. Among the many tasks to which this site contributes is making explicit the political dimensions of sport, and arguing that sport and politics cannot be separated. In being interviewed about his style of journalism and what he seeks to do, Zirin said:

I'm a sports writer by trade and I try to write in the language and style of sports writing, which has its own vernacular, to be sure. My beat is that messy, jagged place where sports and politics smash together. Sometimes this happens covertly, as in the way patriotism intertwines with big sporting events, and sometimes it happens with a megaton explosion, like the ongoing drama of the Beijing Olympics. But however you slice and dice it, politics are an enduring, constant, and historic presence in sports. The goal is to try to get the mainstream sports media, athletes and fans, to acknowledge this, and if they happen to be unhappy with the politics of sport, challenge it to change. (Zirin, interview, in King, 2008, p. 335)

Zirin closes the interview with some relevant words of advice for everyone who is interested in the sociology of sport. He argues:

I find so much of sports sociology remarkable in its breadth and power to, as Dr Ben Carrington says, 'debunk' accepted truths. But it's too ghettoized and too coded in academic language presented for other academics. I'm not saying there isn't a place for academic writing, but every sports sociologists [sic] department should also ... have a sports and society column in their college paper. Every sports and sociology student should try to intern in their athletics departments. Let's get the ideas out there in the oxygen. There are way too many brilliant trees falling quietly in the forest. (Zirin interview, in King, 2008, p. 342)

Underlying Zirin's words is an argument that, to make a difference, there is a need for people to stand up for issues they believe in, and to speak out in the face of social injustice. In this regard, the claims of Zirin connect closely with the arguments around sport and social justice discussed in Chapter 10, while also showing that sports journalists (and sociologists) can do much more than simply report on the outcomes of sporting events.

Finally, in this discussion of issues confronting sports journalism, it is important to note that, as in other areas of the media, sports journalism is being affected by the emergence of internet-based media. In their analysis of online sports journalists in Australia, Lange *et al.* (2007) found that there was a critical emphasis on the need for both immediacy and interactivity. For the sports journalists interviewed, these demands were both a source of advantage and a source of constraint or concern. The immediacy of the internet meant that online journalists were constantly providing more up-to-date content than was possible in newspapers, with their more fixed and relatively slow deadlines. On the other hand, however, many of the online journalists interviewed in the study felt that they had less opportunity to do original reporting. Instead, many of them perceived that what they were doing was cutting and pasting from other sources and that they were, in effect, tied to their desk and computer. From the perspective of these journalists, there was a divide between internet and print journalists, with the internet journalists believing that they were positioned lower in the hierarchy.

AUDIENCES, FANS AND CONSUMERS

Central to the media process are the consumers of media content: the readers, viewers or listeners that make up the media audience. As much media research has shown, it is important to recognize that the ways in which an audience receives and interprets messages sent from the media is contested (Horne, 2006). While media producers may have a specific intended effect with their programming and with the messages contained within that programming, members of the audience may react to that message in ways that are at odds with the intentions of the producers. As Stuart Hall (1973) has argued, there are a wide variety of responses that a reader or viewer may have in the context of media messages. For example, they may accept the message from the media, they may accept it with some reservations or questions, or they may reject the message.

The position of the audience in the context of sport is perhaps even further heightened because of the great passion that many millions of people have for sport, both professional and amateur. Even a cursory listen to a sport talk-back radio show, or a scan of sport blogs, will reveal how passionate, and also how well informed, many people are about sport. Sport is an area where many people feel empowered to put their own views and perspectives forward, and in many cases may also feel empowered to challenge media representations and analyses. At the same time, questions arise about how deeply such questioning goes. How particular individuals or groups respond to media messages is an empirical question, requiring investigations of audiences in particular social situations.

In addition to the issue of media effects, the mediatization of sport can influence the processes through which fans consume sport. For many fans, as discussed in the previous chapter, rituals emerge around watching games or competitions on television, just as when going to a game in person. In some contexts, such rituals may occur in isolation. An individual may wear their lucky clothing or sit in a lucky seat when watching a game. With the increasing presence of the internet, an individual may watch a game and, at the same time, follow online discussion groups and play-by-play expert commentary, while also sending text messages to friends or following tweets. Or, rather than watching in isolation, the fan may watch with friends or family, either at home or at a local pub or restaurant showing the game live. In these ways, just as with supporters who attend live games, rituals can emerge around watching sport on television and through the internet that can be powerful and meaningful for the people involved.

In considering the relationship between the sport fan, media representations of sport, and consumption of sport through the media, potentially contradictory processes involving individualization and community-building become apparent (Elliott and Lemert, 2006). Individualization occurs when fans watch games by themselves in their own houses. While being able to observe what occurs among the fans on the televized representation of the game, the viewer is not a physical part of the game. But, at the same time, the individual fan may be part of a bigger collective, or of an imagined community (Anderson, 1991). And, with the emergence of online technologies, there is now the possibility for people to interact with each other, even when sitting in physical isolation (Smith and Westerbeek, 2004). Following and contributing to real-time blogs as games progress, joining sporting communities on Facebook and using other social networking forms such as Twitter, mean that people can be engaged and interactive with others across time and space in ways that may be just as meaningful as if they were interacting in person. In these ways some of the collective experiences fans get from attending games can be achieved at home.

E-GAMING

In e-gaming, the very idea of what it is to be an athlete is being challenged by the increasingly close relationship between media and sport. Indeed, in e-gaming, sport is media, and media is sport, and this raises questions about the status and identity of those who compete in e-games (Hutchins, 2008). Are they athletes or something else? In e-gaming the media has become the actual site of the competition. E-games are competitions where competitors play digital games – for example, Counter-Strike or Guitar Hero – and compete for prize money. E-gamers are the competitors involved (Hutchins, 2006).

From 2000 onwards, the World Cyber Games (WCGs) have taken place, representing a convergence of gaming, computing, media and sport in the one location (World Cyber Games, 2010). For example, the 2005 games, which were held in Singapore, involved 800 participants from 70 countries, and 55,000 spectators. Prior to the actual games themselves, over 1 million participants entered the preliminary rounds of the games. As in the Olympic Games, the World Cyber Games has medal tables, national teams, fair play awards and so on. The competitors, or cyber-athletes, develop skills through rigorous training, just as in on field sports, and also seek to attract endorsements and to win prize money. It is also important to note that the WCGs also function as a trade event for multinational ICT and gaming corporations, with the games operating as a form of business conference (Hutchins, 2006).

The picture of an e-athlete

One of the first e-athletes to reach prominence at the international level was Jonathan Wendel, born in 1981 and known as Fatal1ty (Fatal1ty, 2010). As a professional e-sport player, he has secured winnings in excess of US$500,000, and has competed in the Cyberathlete Professional League. In addition to being a leading competitor, he also has secured significant endorsements and became a media celebrity, a global spokesperson, and an e-sport commentator. By the late 2000s, he had won five world championship titles, based on a regime of practising at least eight hours every day. Through all of these activities, he also built a Fatal1ty brand, using it as an opportunity to promote particular products (Fatal1ty, 2010; Hutchins, 2008).

While e-gaming certainly is a long way removed from many of the sports discussed in this book, its prominence and popularity, and the level of organization and competition it involves, indicate that it could be considered as a sport, meaning also that those competing can be considered as athletes. To this end, while all sports involve an interaction between humans and various forms of technology, e-gaming takes this to a new level, in particular in the context of the relations between sport and media. As Hutchins writes about e-gaming:

> This is sport *as* media. Intense competition occurs in digitally constructed environments, and matches between players and teams are indivisible from the computing networks that provide the platform for competition. The WCG bears witness to a significant historical moment in the development of media content, sport and networked information and communications technologies (ICTs): the seamless interpenetration of previously distinct spheres. (Hutchins, 2006, p. 4)

Given these trends, e-gaming is an important example of sport as a social construction. As societal and technological circumstances transform over time, so contemporary understandings and views on what constitutes sport and what constitutes an athlete change (Smith and Westerbeek, 2004). While many would still dispute the status of e-gaming as a sport, many others argue that it is clearly a sport – indeed, in line with the definition of sport used in this book. And, with the increasing importance of computer-based technologies in all aspects of our lives, it seems clear that, over time, e-gaming will be accepted completely as a sport with the same legitimacy and status as other longer-standing sports. The consequence of this will be that those competing in e-games also come to have the same status as athletes in non-gaming contexts. In other words, as sport transforms over time, so too do the practices of those who are athletes. In the case of e-gaming, digital media are essential to these processes.

CONCLUSION

The trends discussed in this chapter are underpinned by the claim that sport and the media are now inseparable, in particular at the level of elite professional sport, and that professional sport and media are increasingly connected to a broader set of economic relations organized around commodification and commercialization. This relationship is evident across a number of dimensions, including, most notably, (1) the financial resources that media brings to sport; (2) the ways in which sport is represented through the media; and (3) the importance of sport for media organizations and vice versa. Given that much discussion of the relationship between media and sport tends to focus on how media is taking over increasing areas of sporting activity, this final point is of particular importance. It suggests that the relationship between media and sport is not just one of domination of one set of actors over another set of actors, but is a relationship that is constituted by a contested power relationship, and which is of benefit to both parties. In the context of the overall argument of this book, this claim is important in showing that there is a need to consider the dynamic nature of the relationship between media and sport. In particular, analysing the connections between media and sport provides a greater understanding of the ways in which sport is connected to broader economic, political and social processes, including trends towards greater commercialization and commodification.

CHAPTER SUMMARY

This chapter has shown that:

- An engagement with the relationship between sport and media is critical to understanding contemporary sport. Media not only presents and reports on sport, but is fundamentally involved in the organization of sport in societies around the world.
- In considering the relationship between media and sport, there is a need to analyse ownership relations, as located in broader economic, political and social relations. It is also important to analyse the media process, involving production, representations and consumption.
- Current developments in media technologies challenge the role of sports journalists, with online journalists working under different constraints than television and print journalists, and with the emergence of interactive media technologies raising critical questions around the boundaries between producers and consumers of media.
- The emergence of e-gaming provides a challenge, to understandings both of what constitutes sport and of who is an athlete. Given contemporary societal, media and technological trends, it appears that more cases of

this sort will emerge, providing further evidence for the importance of considering what it means to be an athlete as a social construction.

■ The relationship between media and sport is a contested one. While both industries benefit from their relationship, concerns also emerge over issues such as who controls sport, and for what purposes.

DISCUSSION QUESTIONS

1 Why is the relationship between sport and media so important? Who do you think benefits most from the relationship, sport or media?
2 What do you understand by commodification? Do you think it is necessarily a bad thing for sport to be commodified? Why, or why not?
3 Have a look at a television schedule for a week, including both free to air and pay television. What sports figure in the schedule? Do some feature more frequently than others? Why do you think this is the case? Are there some sports that should feature that don't?
4 What types of ads are shown during sport? Analyse the ads that play during a sporting contest for how race, gender and class are portrayed. What do you notice?

FURTHER READING

Deuze, Mark (2007) *Media Work*, Cambridge, Polity.

Hutchins, Brett (2008) 'Signs of Meta-change in Second Modernity: The Growth of e-Sport and the World Cyber Games', *New Media and Society*, 10(6), pp. 851–69.

Hutchins, Brett and Rowe, David (2009) 'From Broadcast Scarcity to Digital Plenitude: The Changing Dynamics of the Media Sport Content Economy', *Television and New Media*, 10(4), pp. 354–70.

Messner, Michael A., Dunbar, Michele and Hunt, Darnell (2000) 'The Televised Sports Manhood Formula', *Journal of Sport and Social Issues*, 24(4), pp. 380–94.

Rowe, David (1999) *Sport, Culture and the Media: The Unruly Trinity*, Buckingham, Open University Press.

Part V

Conclusion

Chapter 14

Conclusion: Sport, Society and Sociology

REVISITING THE CENTRAL ARGUMENT

Mobilizing the sociological imagination, the central argument of this book has been that sport and society are in a constant and ongoing process of interaction, where the practices and organization of both are shaped by their connections and relations in specific social, political and economic contexts. As shown through the examples presented in the book, while sport is certainly influenced by its societal context, sport also has an impact on that context. For instance, sport has been important in a range of nation-building processes, and also has significant potential in relation to policy initiatives towards social inclusion. At the same time, inequalities in society around gender, race, disability, sexuality and other social relations are often reproduced in sporting contexts.

Sport has been defined in this book as a set of activities that are organized or institutionalized; involve physical activity and skill; involve competition and reward; are inextricably linked to their social, political and economic context and will both be influenced by that context and will influence that context; and are the outcome of social processes, such that they can be transformed over time and will vary by location. While it is often relatively straightforward to recognize whether or not an activity constitutes a sport, in some contexts it can be more challenging. The example of e-gaming poses important questions in this regard. Should an activity that does not involve much physical activity, at least as usually understood in sporting contexts, and which is so dependent on technology be defined as a sport? Working

215

from the perspective that sport is a social construction – that is, the outcome of human activity in specific social contexts – and is constantly taking different and new forms depending on factors such as the social and technological context, it is appropriate to consider e-gaming as a sport. Similarly, while football (soccer) is today recognized the world over as a sport, at previous moments in history its status as a sport was questioned by those in positions of authority. These examples illustrate that sport is the outcome of social processes and therefore may vary over time and by location; this is an important dimension of sociological approaches to sport.

The analysis developed through the book has shown that a sociological engagement with sport requires consideration of sport's societal context; the relationships that constitute sport; the power dynamics that underpin sport; and the processes that unfold over time within sport. An engagement with these issues in turn requires consideration of the relations between conflict and consensus, and between structure and agency, as well as social relations, in particular societal contexts (Elliott, 2009, pp. 11–15).

In developing an analysis across these varying dimensions, three themes have provided the focus in this book. Part 2 engaged with central issues around sport and societal processes. An analysis of the interaction of sport with social relations such as gender, sexuality, race and the nation illustrated ways in which sport often reinforces dominant power relations around these social relations. At the same time, examples do exist where sport provides a means for social change.

Part 3 explored critical questions around the regulation of sport. The focus here was on regulation and governance across a number of levels, ranging from the club and league level through to the state at the national level, and to global forms of regulation. This discussion revealed that forms of regulation are highly contested, with the approaches and perspectives of organizations and individuals being influenced by their societal location. The evidence presented indicated ways in which sport is a site for the exercise of power in society, with outcomes that have the potential for a broader impact than only on the world of sport. For example, the possible contribution that sport can make to social justice issues within society was considered, exploring debates around social policy and social inclusion, human rights, corporate social responsibility and ethical governance. An outcome of this analysis was that while sport certainly has the potential to contribute to social justice issues, it is not possible to assume that there is a direct causal relationship between sport and progressive social justice outcomes.

Part 4 engaged with issues around the global cultures of sport, including the place of fans, players and the emerging global media-sport industry. These chapters brought to the surface the increasingly significant role of the media in contemporary sport, while also emphasizing the need to under-stand the relations between media, players and fans. This section of the book also argued that although fans and players are individuals, a significant dimension of their role in sport occurs at a collective level.

Underpinning these three themes was recognition of the importance of both theory and research to developing sociological insights into sport. In particular, the combination of theory and methods provides sociologists with the tools to go beyond everyday description to developing analytically sound and empirically robust engagements with the world of sport. In this book, a social constructionist approach has been adopted, which has enabled a critical engagement with sport. This framework has provided a means for questioning what is often taken for granted in everyday sporting contexts, and to reveal the power relations influencing such contexts. In particular, the framework has brought to the surface forms of inequality and conflict in sport.

FUTURE DEVELOPMENTS IN THE SOCIOLOGY OF SPORT

While the primary focus of sociology is on engaging with and seeking to explain contemporary events, often informed by engaging with history as well, it is also important to consider possible future developments in sport and the challenges that such developments may raise, both for sport and for sociological analysis of sport. While sociologists are not able to see into the future, it is possible, based on knowledge of the present and past, to consider issues that may arise in the future. How these issues play out specifically will be an empirical matter requiring sociological investigation.

A matter that has emerged throughout the book concerns the sometimes controversial relationship between sport and technology (Longman, 2007). Current trends around the relationship between the human body and tech-nology, as captured in the concept of the cyborg, are likely to become further heightened into the future (Butryn and Masucci, 2003). For example, as computer technologies become even more sophisticated into the future, ques-tions will arise around the implantation of such technologies in the human body, and the impacts they may have on performance in sport. Such tech-nologies may contribute not only to physical performance, but to the think-ing and decision-making capacity of athletes. As noted with emerging trends in this area already, questions will arise around whether such technologies should be prohibited altogether, or whether they are acceptable as long as all competitors have access to them. Such developments go to the question of what it means to be a human, and to the question of who should be allowed to compete in particular sports and under what conditions (Haraway, 1991).

It also seems likely that, in particular at the professional level, the relations between media and sport will become ever more entwined and interconnected in the future (Hutchins and Rowe, 2009). As seen in examples such as the Indian Premier League cricket competition, the rapidly increasing role of media in sport is providing fundamental challenges to traditional ideas of sporting teams as being located in particular physical places. This has an impact not only on competitors, but also on supporters who traditionally support teams associated with particular locations. Such developments will increasingly challenge competitor–supporter relations. These developments also very much highlight processes of commodification in sport (Jackson and Andrews, 2005). Not only are supporters being offered more packages and more goods to purchase as part of their consumption of sport, so too are players becoming more and more commodified, being bought and sold, and sent around the world, by teams, owners and leagues. Important questions arise here around how far such processes can go before the focus on commodification and related money-making processes supersedes competition among athletes as the primary focus of sport (Moor, 2007; Smith and Westerbeek, 2004).

A third set of crucial emerging issues relates to the role, actual or potential, of sport in social justice processes (Duina, 2010; Tacon, 2007). While examples discussed in this book indicate that sport can play a crucial role in promoting social justice – for example, through social inclusion initiatives – as sport becomes increasingly commercialized, its continued capacity to do so is challenged. On the one hand, commercialization and commodification provide important financial and other resources that can potentially be applied by sporting organizations to social justice issues. On the other hand, the drive for profit maximization that underpins many of these processes may put pressure on social justice processes that could be seen to run counter to the financial concerns of sporting organizations and clubs. The ways in which these competing imperatives are managed in sporting contexts will be a critical challenge for individual sport organizations, and for more general understandings of the place of sport in society (Spaaij, 2010; Smyth, 2010).

Central to all of these emerging developments is the question of power, which has been a key concept in this book (Lukes, 2005; Smith, 1990). As issues such as those discussed here begin to emerge, power relations will be critical in terms of how they unfold. For example, the relative power of media organizations, sporting organizations, athletes and supporters will play an important role in terms of how these issues move forward. There is a vital role here for sociologists in bringing such issues to the surface, so that they do not just develop in an unnoticed fashion before becoming accepted as the new common sense.

The analysis and discussion through the book has shown the crucial contribution that a mobilization of the sociological imagination can make to our understanding of and engagement with sport. By connecting individual experiences with broader social, economic and political processes, it is possible to gain important insights into, and understandings of, the contested social relations and power issues that are central to sport. In this way, sociology also provides an understanding of practices associated with sport that goes beyond the everyday or the anecdotal, and instead emphasizes issues such as the importance of relationships, power and process, and how those factors operate within and across specific societal contexts.

In conclusion, one of the most exciting aspects of the sociology of sport is that, even as sociological frameworks provide a means of understanding historical and contemporary sporting practices, relations and organization, so new forms of sporting practice and organization emerge which require renewed questioning of what we are observing in the context of sport. The theoretical frameworks and research tools set out in this book provide one means for developing a critical understanding of, and engagement with, sport in contemporary and historical societal contexts. To the extent that they do this, they also have the potential to be beneficial in developing descriptions, understandings and explanations of new forms of sport in new societal contexts in the future that have not yet even begun to emerge.

Glossary

ACRONYMS

AFL   Australian Football League
BBC   British Broadcasting Corporation
BSkyB   British Sky Broadcasting Group
cAIS   complete Androgen Insensitivity Syndrome
CEO   Chief Executive Officer
CSR   Corporate Social Responsibility
DGFT   Director General of Fair Trading
FARE   Football Against Racism in Europe
FIFA   Fédération Internationale de Football Association
GMAI   Global Media AIDS Initiative
IAAF   International Association of Athletics Federations
ICC   International Cricket Council
ICT   Information and Communications Technologies
IOC   International Olympic Committee
ITV   Independent Television
MLB   Major League Baseball
MMC   Monopolies and Mergers Commission
NBA   National Basketball Association
NCAA   National Collegiate Athletic Association
NFL   National Football League
NHL   National Hockey League
NOPES   New Opportunities for PE [Physical Education] and Sport
NRL   National Rugby League
OECD   Organisation for Economic Co-operation and Development
OFT   Office of Fair Trading
pAIS   partial Androgen Insensitivity Syndrome
RPC   Restrictive Practices Court
TRA   Temporary Relocation Area

UDHR	Universal Declaration of Human Rights
UN	United Nations
UNAIDS	Joint United Nations Programme on HIV/AIDS
UNICEF	United Nations Children's Fund
WADA	World Anti-Doping Agency
WCG	World Cyber Games
WNBA	Women's National Basketball Association

DEFINITIONS OF SPORT

While sport is increasingly global, a number of sports are played only in one or a few countries. Brief definitions are provided here of sports discussed in the book that may not be equally well known in all countries.

Australian Rules Football: Officially called Australian Football, but popularly known as Australian Rules Football, this ball sport involves two teams of 18 players on an oval shaped grass field of play, with an oval shaped ball. The object of the game is for one team to score more points, constituted by goals worth six points and behinds worth one point, than the other team. The ball is moved by kicking and handpassing.

Baseball: A sport constituted by two teams of nine players each. Games involve a bat and ball, four bases in a diamond shaped in-field in a larger, outdoor ground. Each team takes turns in batting and fielding, over nine innings. The object is for one team to score more runs than the other team.

Basketball: A ball sport involving two teams of five players, played on a rectangular court. Teams move the round ball by bouncing, or dribbling, and passing. The aim is to score by throwing the ball through a raised basket located at the end of the court. The team which has scored most points at the end of the game wins.

Cricket: A sport involving two teams of eleven players each. It is a bat and ball game, involving a batting and fielding side. In the traditional version of the game, each team has two innings to bat and two innings to field. A rectangular pitch is located in the middle of a larger oval shaped ground. The batting team tries to score as many runs as possible, while the fielding team seeks to dismiss the batting team for as few runs as possible. The team that scores the most runs at the end of the game is the winner, although games can also be drawn if all batters are not dismissed.

Field Hockey: A stick and ball sport involving two teams of eleven players. The game is played on a rectangular pitch, and players move the ball by hitting it with their sticks. Whichever team scores more goals at the end of the game is the winner.

Football/Soccer: A sport involving two teams of eleven players each. Played on a rectangular pitch, the ball is moved by foot and head. Each team tries to score more goals than the other by kicking or heading the ball into the opposition goal. The team with the most goals at end of the game is the winner.

Gaelic Football: A ball game involving two teams of 15 players each, played on a rectangular field. The ball is moved by running, kicking, and hand-passing, with the object being for one team to score more points than the other, by scoring goals worth three points, and points.

Gridiron Football/American Football: A sport played on a rectangular field by two teams of eleven people. The object is for one team to score more points than the other. The ball is moved by throwing and running, with each team having four turns or downs to move the ball a particular distance or else lose possession. Points are scored by touchdowns, extra points and field goals.

Ice Hockey: A sport played on an ice rink. Each team is made up of six players, who move the puck by hitting it with a stick. The object is to score goals by hitting the puck into a net located at the end of the rink. The team that scores the most goals by the end of the game wins.

Netball: A ball sport played by two teams of seven players on a rectangular court, with a raised net at each end. The round ball is moved by players passing the ball to each other with their hands. Players are not allowed to run with the ball. The team that scores the most goals, which are scored by throwing the ball through the net, wins.

Pickup Sport e.g., pick up basketball: a casual game, often played among friends or people living in the same area. Participants usually go to the court/field and play with whoever is present.

Rugby League: A ball sport, played on a rectangular, grass, outdoor pitch. Two teams of 13 players each move an oval shaped ball by running and passing, and kicking. Teams score tries, conversions, penalties and drop goals. The team with the most points at the end of the game is the winner.

Rugby Union: A ball sport, played on a rectangular, grass, outdoor pitch. Two teams of 15 players each move an oval shaped ball by running and passing, and kicking. Teams score tries, conversions, penalties and drop goals. The team with the most points at the end of the game is the winner.

Softball: A bat and ball sport, played by two teams of nine players, over seven innings. Games involve four bases in a diamond shaped in-field in a larger ground. Each team takes turns in batting and fielding. The object is for one team to score more runs than the other team.

FURTHER INFORMATION

The following websites provide information about sports discussed in the book, including more detailed definitions of the sport, rules of the sport, information about the history of the sport and current issues in relation to the sport.

American Football (Gridiron)
http://www.nfl.com (National Football League)

Association Football (Soccer)
http://www.fifa.com (Federation Internationale de Football Association)

Athletics
http://www.iaaf.org (International Association of Athletics Federations)
http://www.olympic.org (International Olympic Committee)

Australian Rules Football
http://www.afl.com.au (Australian Football League)

Baseball
http://mlb.mlb.com (Major League Baseball)

Basketball
http://www.wnba.com (Women's National Basketball Association)
http://www.nba.com (National Basketball Association)

Bicycle Racing (Tour de France)
http://www.letour.fr/indexus.html (Tour de France)

Cricket
http://icc-cricket.yahoo.net (International Cricket Council)

(Field) Hockey
http://www.fih.ch/en/sport/rules (International Hockey Federation)

Gaelic Football
http://www.gaa.ie (Gaelic Athletic Association)

Ice Hockey
http://www.iihf.com (International Ice Hockey Association)
http://www.nhl.com (National Hockey League)

Motor Car Racing (Formula 1)
http://www.formula1.com (Formula 1)

Netball
http://www.netball.asn.au (Netball Australia)
http://www.netball.org (International Federation of Netball Associations)

Rowing/Crew
http://www.worldrowing.com (World Rowing)

Rugby League
http://www.rlif.com/index.php (Rugby League International Federation)

Rugby Union
http://www.irb.com (International Rugby Board)

Softball
http://www.softball.org.au (Softball Australia)

Tennis
http://www.wtatennis.com (WTA)
http://www.atpworldtour.com (ATP)

References

(Unless otherwise stated, website links last accessed in August 2010.)

ABS (Australian Bureau of Statistics) (2007a), 'Article: Participation in Sports and Physical Recreation', Australian Social Trends, Catalogue No.4102.0, Canberra, Australian Bureau of Statistics.

ABS (Australian Bureau of Statistics) (2007b), 'Participation in Sport and Physical Recreation, Australia 2005–06', Catalogue No. 4177.0, Australian Bureau of Statistics.

AC Milan (2010a) AC Milan homepage, http://www.acmilan.com/

AC Milan (2010b) 'Main Sponsors', AC Milan website, <http://www.acmilan.com/InfoPage.aspx?id=15739>.

AFL (Australian Football League) (2010) 'Indigenous Programs', *AFL homepage*, <http://www.afl.com.au/indigenous%20programs/tabid/14340/default.aspx>.

Agassi, Andre (2009) *Open: An Autobiography*, New York, Knopf.

Akermanis, Jason (2010) 'Stay in the Closet, Jason Akermanis tells Homosexuals', *Herald Sun*, Sports Section, 20 May, <http://www.heraldsun.com.au/sport/afl/stay-in-the-closet-jason-akermanis-tells-homosexuals/story-e6frf9ix-1225868871934>.

Allison, Lincoln (1998) 'Sport and Civil Society', *Political Studies*, XLVI, pp. 709–26.

Allison, Lincoln (ed) (2005) *The Global Politics of Sport: The Role of Global Institutions in Sport,* London, Routledge.

Althusser, Louis (1969) *For Marx*, London, Allen Lane.

Amis, John and Cornwell, T. Bettina (eds) (2005) *Global Sport Sponsorship*, Oxford, Berg.

Anderson, Benedict (1991) *Imagined Communities: Reflections on the Origin and Spread of Nationalism*, London, Verso.

Anthias, Floya and Yuval-Davis, Nira (1992) *Racialised Boundaries: Race, and Nation, Gender, Colour and Class and the Anti-Racist Struggle*, London, Routledge.

ASH (Action on Smoking and Health) (2010) 'Victory for Health as Tobacco Sponsorship of Major Tennis Tournament is Axed', ASH, 11 August, <http://www.

ash.org.uk/media-room/press-releases/:victory-for-health-as-tobacco-sponsorship-of-major-tennis-tournament-is-axed>.

Associated Press (2008a) 'NBA has Highest Percentage of Minority Presidents in Men's Pro Sports History', downloaded 26 August 2010 from ESPN.com: <http://sports.espn.go.com/nba/news/story?id=3417300>.

Associated Press (2008b) 'MLB gets Best Grade for Diversity in Hiring: Number of Blacks on Field Drops', downloaded 26 August 2010 from ESPN.com: <http://sports.espn.go.com/mlb/news/story?id=3347739>.

Associated Press (2008c) 'Diversity Study: Number of Black Coaches in FBS Falls to Four', downloaded 26 August 2010 from ESPN.com: <http://sports.espn.go.com/ncf/news/story?id=3686028>.

Australian Sports Commission (2010) 'ASC Recognition', <http://www.ausport.gov.au/supporting/nso/asc_recognition>.

Australian Story (2005) 'Interview with Ian Roberts', *ABC*, 26 September, <http://www.abc.net.au/austory/content/2005/s1468762.htm>.

AWM (Australian War Memorial) (2010) 'The ANZAC Day tradition'. http://www.awm.gov.au/commemoration/anzac/anzac_tradition.asp

Azzarito, Laura and Harrison, Lewis Jr (2008) ' "White Men Can't Jump": Race, Gender and Natural Athleticism', *International Review for the Sociology of Sport*, 43, pp. 347–64.

Babiak, Kathy and Wolfe, Richard (2009) 'Determinants of Corporate Social Responsibility in Professional Sport: Internal and External Factors', *Journal of Sport Management*, 23(6), pp. 717–42.

Bairner, Alan (1996) 'Sportive Nationalism and Nationalist Politics: A Comparative Analysis of Scotland, the Republic of Ireland, and Sweden', *Journal of Sport and Social Issues*, 20(3), pp. 314–34.

Bairner, Alan and Hwang, Dong-Jhy (2010) 'Representing Taiwan: International Sport, Ethnicity and National Identity in the Republic of China', *International Review for the Sociology of Sport*, published online 12 August 2010, pp. 1–18.

Balnaves, Mark, Donald, James and Donald, Stephanie Hemelryk (2001) *The Global Media Atlas*, London, BFI.

Bamshad, M. J., Wooding, S., Watkins, W. S., Ostler, C. T., Batzer, M. A. and Jorde, L. B. (2003) 'Human Population Genetic Structure and Inference of Group Membership', *American Journal of Human Genetics*, 72(3), pp. 578–89.

Barmy Army (2010) Barmy Army homepage, <http://www.barmyarmy.com/home.php>.

Bauman, Zygmunt and May, Tim (2001) *Thinking Sociologically*, 2nd edn, Malden, MA, Blackwell.

BBC Sport (2003) 'Beckham Ties Up Real Move', *BBC Sport*, 2 July, <http://news.bbc.co.uk/sport2/hi/football/3026196.stm>.

BBC Sport (2007) 'Wimbledon Pays Equal Prize Money', *BBC Sport*, 22 February, <http://news.bbc.co.uk/sport2/hi/tennis/6385295.stm>.

BBC Sport (2010) 'Ex-Olympic Chief Juan Antonio Samaranch Dies', *BBC Sport*, 22 April, <http://news.bbc.co.uk/sport2/hi/olympic_games/8633190.stm>.

BBC Sport (2011) 'Steven Davies Backed After Confirming He is Gay', *BBC Sport*, 28 February, <http://news.bbc.co.uk/sport2/hi/cricket/9409211.stm>.

Beckham, David (2010) David Beckham personal webpage, <http://www.davidbeckham.com/>.

Benedict, Jeffrey (2010) 'An Alarming Number of College Athletes Charged with Serious Crime', *Sports International Online*, posted 8 September 2010. Available at: <http://sportsillustrated.cnn.com/2010/writers/jeff_benedict/09/08/athletes.crime/index.html#ixzz0yx8IPtqi>.

Benedict, Jeffrey and Klein, Alan (1997) 'Arrest and Conviction Rates for Athletes Accused of Sexual Assault', *Sociology of Sport Journal*, 14(1), pp. 86–94.

Berri, David J. and Simmons, Rob (2009) 'Race and the Evaluation of Signal Callers in the National Football League', *Journal of Sports Economics*, 10(1), pp. 23–43.

Bilton, Tony, Bonnett, Kevin, Jones, Pip, Lawson, Tony, Skinner, David, Stanworth, Michelle and Webster, Andrew (2002) *Introductory Sociology*, 4th edn, Basingstoke, Palgrave Macmillan.

Bissinger, Buzz (2010) 'Tiger in the Rough', *Vanity Fair*, February, <http://www.vanityfair.com/culture/features/2010/02/tiger-woods-201002>.

Boddy, Kasia (2008) *Boxing: A Cultural History*, London, Reaktion.

Booth, Douglas and Tatz, Colin (2000) *One-Eyed: A View of Australian Sport*, St Leonards, NSW, Allen & Unwin.

Bose, M. (2001) 'A Game in Shame', *Wisden*, <http://www.espncricinfo.com/wisdenalmanack/content/story/154143.html>.

Boston Bruins (2010) 'Boston Bruins Foundation homepage', <http://bruins.nhl.com/club/page.htm?id=38862>.

Bourdieu, Pierre (1990) 'Program for a Sociology of Sport', in Pierre Bourdieu, *In Other Words: Essays Towards a Reflexive Sociology*, translated by Matthew Adamson, Stanford, CA, Stanford University Press, pp. 156–67.

Boyle, Raymond, Dinan, William and Morrow, Stephen (2002) 'Doing the Business? Newspaper Reporting of the Business of Football', *Journalism*, 3(2), pp. 161–81.

Boyle, Raymond and Haynes, Richard (2000) *Power Play: Sport, the Media, and Popular Culture*, New York, Longman.

Branston, Rob, Cowling, Keith and Brown, Nestor Duch (1999). 'Strategic Decisions and the Public Interest: Modern Corporations and the Case of Soccer'. Paper prepared for the Corporate Governance of Professional Football Conference, Clore Management Centre, Birkbeck College, University of London, 3 February.

Brookes, Rod (2002) *Representing Sport*, London, Arnold.

Brown, Adam (1998) *Fanatics! Power, Identity and Fandom in Football*, London, Routledge.

Brown, Adam (2000) 'Sneaking in Through the Back Door? Media Company Interests and Dual Ownership of Clubs', in Sean Hamil, Jonathan Michie,

Christine Oughton and Steven Warby (eds), *Football in the Digital Age. Whose Game is it Anyway?*, Edinburgh, Mainstream, pp. 81–92.

Bruce, Toni (2004) 'Marking the Boundaries of the "Normal" in Televised Sports: The Play-by-play of Race', *Media, Culture and Society*, 26(6), pp. 861–79.

Bryman, Alan (2004) *Social Research Methods*, 2nd edn, New York, Oxford University Press.

BSkyB (British Sky Broadcasting) (1999) *Annual Report and Accounts*, <www.sky.com/home/GeneralIndex.html>.

BSkyB (British Sky Broadcasting) (2000) 'Chelsea Village plc and BskyB Announce Strategic Alliance', *BSkyB Press Release*, 3 March.

BSkyB (British Sky Broadcasting) (2010a) Mission Statement, <http://corporate.sky.com/about_sky/what_we_do/our_mission.htm>.

BSkyB (British Sky Broadcasting) (2010b) Key Facts and Figures, <http://corporate.sky.com/about_sky/key_facts_and_figures.htm>.

BSkyB (British Sky Broadcasting) (2010c) Our Content, <http://corporate.sky.com/about_sky/what_we_do/our_content.htm>.

BSkyB (British Sky Broadcasting) (2010d) Sky Timeline, <http://corporate.sky.com/about_sky/timeline.htm>.

Burawoy, Michael (2005) '2004 American Sociological Association Presidential Address: For Public Sociology', *British Journal of Sociology*, 56 (2), pp. 260–90.

Butryn, Ted M. and Masucci, Matthew A. (2003) 'It's Not About the Book. A Cyborg Counternarrative of Lance Armstrong', *Journal of Sport and Social Issues*, 27(2), pp. 124–44.

Byrne, Clare (2010) 'Speedy Justice in World Cup Courts', *Mail and Guardian Online*, 16 June, <http://www.mg.co.za/article/2010-06-16-speedy-justice-in-world-cup-courts>.

Cahn, Susan K. (1994) *Coming on Strong: Gender and Sexuality in 20th-Century Women's Sport*, Cambridge, Harvard University Press.

Campbell, Rook (2011) 'Staging Globalization for National Projects: Global Sport Markets and Elite Athletic Transnational Labor in Qatar', *International Review for the Sociology of Sport*, 46(1), pp. 45–60.

Canseco, Jose (2005) *Juiced: Wild Times, Rampant 'Roids, Smash Hits, and How Baseball Got Big*, New York, William Morrow.

Capling, Ann and Marjoribanks, Tim (2004) 'Connecting Commerce and Culture in Third Sector Organisations: The Case of Australian Football League Clubs', *Third Sector Review*, 10(1), pp. 61–76.

Capling, Ann and Marjoribanks, Tim (2008) 'Between Commerce and Culture: Australian Football League Clubs', in Jo Barraket (ed.), *Strategic Issues in the Not for Profit Sector*, Sydney, University of New South Wales Press, pp. 143–62.

Carrington, Ben (1988) 'Sport, Masculinity and Black Cultural Resistance', *Journal of Sport and Social Issues*, 22(3), pp. 275–98.

Carrington, Ben and McDonald, Ian (2001) 'Introduction: 'Race', Sport and British Society', in Ben Carrington and Ian McDonald (eds), *'Race', Sport and British Society*, London, Routledge, pp. 1–26.

Carrington, Ben and McDonald, Ian (2002) 'Sport, Racism and Inequality', *Sociology*, 36(1), pp. 8–13.

Carucci, Vic (2010) 'NFLPA Head Smith Briefs Rookies on Labor Deal, Money Management', *NFL.com*, 27 June, <http://www.nfl.com/news/story/09000d5d818de12e/article/nflpa-head-smith-briefs-rookies-on-labor-deal-money-management>.

Cash, John and Joy Damousi (2004) 'Inside Footy Mania', *Meanjin*, 63(4), pp. 218–25.

Cashmore, Ellis (2002) *Beckham*, Cambridge, Polity.

Cashmore, Ellis (2005) *Making Sense of Sports*, 4th edn, Abingdon, Routledge.

Castells, Manuel (1989) *The Informational City: Information Technology, Economic Restructuring and the Urban-Regional Process*, Oxford, Blackwell.

Castells, Manuel (2000) 'Materials for an Exploratory Theory of the Network Society', *British Journal of Sociology*, 51(1), pp. 5–24.

Castells, Manuel (2009) *Communication Power*, Oxford, Oxford University Press.

Chadwick, S. and Parker, G. (1997) 'Philanthropy or Profit? Football, Entrepreneurs and Premier League Success', *Teaching Business and Economics*, 1(1), pp. 3–6.

Chandler, Helen (2010) 'Merlene Ottey Hopes Age will be No Barrier in the Long Run', *Guardian*, 31 July, <http://www.guardian.co.uk/sport/2010/jul/31/merlene-ottey-oldest-competitor>.

Coad, David (2008) *The Metrosexual: Gender, Sexuality, and Sport*, Albany, State University of New York Press.

Coakley, Jay and Dunning, Eric (eds) (2000) *Handbook of Sports Studies*, London, Sage.

Coakley, Jay and Pike, Elizabeth (2009) *Sports in Society: Issues and Controversies*, Maidenhead, McGraw-Hill.

Coalter, Fred (2007) *A Wider Social Role for Sport: Who's Keeping the Score?* London, Routledge.

Cockerill, Michael (2003) 'Australian gets Job as Beckham's Amigo', *The Age*, 23 July, <http://www.theage.com.au/articles/2003/07/22/1058853069566.html>.

Collingwood Football Club (2010) Community Programs, <http://www.collingwoodfc.com.au/community/tabid/6851/default.aspx>.

Collins, Patricia Hill (2000) *Black Feminist Thought: Knowledge, Consciousness, and the Politics of Empowerment*, New York, Routledge.

Competition Commission (1999) *Annual Review and Accounts 1998/99*, London, Competition Commission.

Connell, Raewyn (1995) *Masculinities*, Cambridge, Polity.

Cottle, Simon (ed.) (2003) *Media Organization and Production*, London, Sage.

Cowie, C. and Williams, M. (1997) 'The Economics of Sports Rights', *Telecommunications Policy*, 21, pp. 619–34.

Daly, Mary (2003) 'Governance and Social Policy', *Journal of Social Policy*, 32(1), pp. 113–28.

Department of Sport and Recreation (2005) 'Participation Patterns in Sport and Recreation Activities in South Africa: 2005 Survey', Pretoria, Republic of South Africa Department of Sport and Recreation.

DePauw, Karen P. and Gavron, Susan J. (2005) *Disability Sport*, 2nd edn, Champaign, IL, Human Kinetics.

Deuze, Mark (2007) *Media Work*, Cambridge, Polity.

Doern, G. Bruce and Wilks, Stephen (1996) *Comparative Public Policy: National Institutions in a Global Market*, Oxford, Clarendon.

Dreger, Alice (2010) 'Sex Typing for Sport', *Hastings Center Report*, 40(2), pp. 22–4.

Drenten, Jenna, Peters, Cara Okleshen, Leigh, Thomas and Hollenbeck, Candice R (2009) 'Not Just a Party in the Parking Lot: An Exploratory Investigation of the Motives Underlying the Ritual Commitment of Football Tailgaters', *Sport Marketing Quarterly*, 18, pp. 92–106.

Duina, Francesco (2011) *Winning. Reflections on an American Obsession*, Princeton, Princeton University Press.

Durkheim, Emile (1984) *Division of Labour in Society*, New York City, Free Press.

Edwards, Allan, Gilbert, Keith and Skinner, James (2002) *Extending the Boundaries: Theoretical Frameworks for Research in Sport Management*, Altona, VicCommon Ground.

Elling, Agnes and Janssens, Jan (2009) 'Sexuality as a Structuring Principle in Sport Participation: Negotiating Sports Spaces', *International Review for the Sociology of Sport*, 44(1), pp. 71–86.

Elliott, Anthony (2009) *Contemporary Social Theory: An Introduction*, London, Routledge.

Elliott, Anthony and Lemert, Charles (2006) *The New Individualism: The Emotional Costs of Globalization*, London, Routledge.

Elliott, Richard and Weedon, Gavin (2011) 'Foreign Players in the English Premier Academy League: "Feet-drain" or "Feet-exchange"?', *International Review for the Sociology of Sport*, 46(1), pp. 61–75.

Essed, Philomena (1991) *Understanding Everyday Racism*, Newbury Park, Sage.

Ezzy, Douglas (2006) 'The Research Process', in Maggie Walter (ed.), *Social Research Methods: An Australian Perspective*, South Melbourne, Oxford University Press, pp. 29–51.

Farquharson, Karen and Marjoribanks, Tim (2003) 'Transforming the Springboks: Re-imagining the South African Nation Through Sport', *Social Dynamics*, 29(1), pp. 27–48.

Farquharson, Karen and Marjoribanks, Tim (2006) 'Representing Australia: Race, the Media and Cricket', *Journal of Sociology*, 42(1), pp. 25–41.

Farred, Grant (2002) 'Long Distance Love: Growing Up a Liverpool Football Club Fan', *Journal of Sport and Social Issues*, 26(1), pp. 6–24.

Fatal1ty (2010) Fatal1ty.com, <http://www.fatal1ty.com/fatal1ty/bio>.

FC Barcelona (2010) 'More than a Club' FC Barcelona website, <http://www. fcbarcelona.com/web/english/club/club_avui/mes_que_un_club/mesqueunclub. html>.

FIFA (Fédération Internationale de Football Association) (2010) 'Mission', <http://www.fifa.com/aboutfifa/federation/mission.html>.

Fifield, Dominic (2010) 'World Cup 2010: Fabio Capello condemns John Terry's "Big Mistake"', *Guardian*, 22 June, <http://www.guardian.co.uk/football/2010/ jun/22/world-cup-2010-fabio-capello-john-terry>.

Findlay, Jeanette, Holahan, William L. and Oughton, Christine (1999) 'Revenue Sharing from Broadcasting Football: The Need for League Balance', in Sean Hamil, Jonathan Michie and Christine Oughton (eds), *The Business of Football: A Game of Two Halves?*, Edinburgh, Mainstream, pp. 124–38.

Fine, Larry (2008) 'International Players Comprise 28 pct of MLB Rosters', *Reuters*, 1 April, <http://www.reuters.com/article/idUSSP8408520080402>.

Fininvest (2010) Fininvest homepage, <http://www.fininvest.com/>.

Ford, Bonnie (2007) 'Tours Trying to be Proactive with Gambling Issue', *ESPN.com*, 25 October, <http://sports.espn.go.com/sports/tennis/news/story?id=3050009>.

Forrest, David and Simmons, Robert (2003) 'Sport and Gambling', *Oxford Review of Economic Policy*, 19(4), pp. 598–611.

Fort, Rodney, Lee, Young Hoon and Berri, David (2008), 'Race, Technical Efficiency, and Retention: The Case of NBA Coaches', *International Journal of Sport Finance*, 3(2), pp. 84–97.

Foucault, Michel (1995) *Discipline and Punish: The Birth of the Prison*, trans. from the French by Alan Sheridan, New York, Vintage.

Furze, Brian, Savy, Pauline, Brym, Robert J. and Lie, John (2008) *Sociology in Today's World*, South Melbourne, Cengage.

Gadher, Dipesh and Waite, Roger (2007) 'Mr Average of Football Nets £1m' *The Sunday Times*, 18 November, <http://www.timesonline.co.uk/tol/sport/football/ article2890953.ece>.

Gardiner, Greg (2003) ' "Black" Bodies – "White" Codes: Indigenous Footballers, Racism and the Australian Football League's Racial and Religious Vilification Code', in John Bale and Mike Cronin (eds), *Sport and PostColonialism*, Oxford, Berg.

Germov, John (2005) 'Imagining Health Problems as Social Issues', in John Germov (ed.), *Second Opinion: An Introduction to Health Sociology*, 3rd edn, South Melbourne, Oxford University Press, pp. 3–27.

Germov, John and Poole, Marilyn (eds) (2011a) *Public Sociology: An Introduction to Australian Society*, 2nd edn, Crows Nest, NSW, Allen & Unwin.

Germov, John and Poole, Marilyn (2011b) 'The Sociological Gaze: Linking Private Lives to Public Issues', in John Germov and Marilyn Poole (eds), *Public Sociology: An Introduction to Australian Society*, 2nd edn, Crows Nest, NSW, Allen & Unwin, pp. 2–18.

Gibson, Owen (2009) 'Europe Hit by "Biggest-ever" Match-fixing Scandal', *Guardian*, 20 November, <http://www.guardian.co.uk/sport/2009/nov/20/uefa-match-fixing-germany>.

Gibson, Owen (2010) 'Tiger Woods Begs Forgiveness for "Selfish and Foolish" Behaviour', *Guardian*, 19 February, <http://www.guardian.co.uk/world/2010/feb/19/tiger-woods-begs-for-forgiveness>.

Giddens, Anthony (1984) *The Constitution of Society: Outline of the Theory of Structuration*, Cambridge, Polity.

Giddens, Anthony (1999) 'Runaway World: Lecture One – Globalization – London', BBC Reith Lectures 1999, downloaded on 8 September 2010 from: <http://news.bbc.co.uk/hi/english/static/events/reith_99/week1/week1.htm>.

Gilroy, Paul (1992) *There Ain't No Black in the Union Jack: The Cultural Politics of Race and Nation*, London, Routledge.

Giulianotti, Richard (1999) *Football: A Sociology of the Global Game*, Cambridge, Polity.

Giulianotti, Richard (2002) 'Supporters, Followers, Fans, and Flaneurs', *Journal of Sport and Social Issues*, 26(1), pp. 25–46.

Giulianotti, Richard (ed.) (2004) *Sport and Modern Social Theorists*, Basingstoke, Palgrave Macmillan.

Giulianotti, Richard (2005) *Sport: A Critical Sociology*, Cambridge, Polity.

Goffman, Erving (1966) *Behavior in Public Places: Notes on the Social Organization of Gatherings*, New York, Free Press.

Goldblatt, David (2006) *The Ball is Round: A Global History of Football*, London, Viking.

Good, Byron J. (1994) *Medicine, Rationality, and Experience: An Anthropological Perspective*, Cambridge, Cambridge University Press.

Gramsci, Antonio (1971) *Selections from the Prison Notebooks of Antonio Gramsci*, ed. and trans. by Quintin Hoare and Geoffrey Nowell Smith, London, Lawrence & Wishart.

Gratton, Chris and Jones, Ian (2004) *Research Methods for Sport Studies*, London, Routledge.

Guardian (2000) 'BSkyB's Grip on Premiership Tightens', *Guardian*, 3 March.

Hagon, Toby (2010) 'Webber in Cigarette Controversy', *The Age*, 20 May, <http://brisbanetimes.drive.com.au/motor-news/webber-in-cigarette-controversy-20100520-vg89.html>.

Hall, Irene and Hall, David (2004) *Evaluation and Social Research: Introducing Small-scale Practice*, New York, Palgrave Macmillan.

Hall, Stuart (1973) *Encoding and Decoding in the Television Discourse*, Birmingham, Centre for Contemporary Cultural Studies, University of Birmingham.

Hallinan, Chris and Judd, Barry (2009) 'Race Relations, Indigenous Australia and the Social Impact of Professional Football', *Sport in Society*, 12(9), pp. 1220–35.

Hamil, Sean (1999) 'Football Clubs as Social or Financial Institutions'. Paper prepared for the Corporate Governance of Professional Football Conference, Clore Management Centre, Birkbeck College, University of London, 3 February.

Hamil, Sean, Michie, Jonathan and Oughton, Christine (eds) (1999) *The Business of Football: A Game of Two Halves?*, Edinburgh, Mainstream.

Hamil, Sean, Michie, Jonathan, Oughton, Christine and Warby, Steven (eds) (2000) *Football in the Digital Age: Whose Game is it Anyway?*, Edinburgh, Mainstream.

Hamil, Sean, Michie, Jonathan, Oughton, Christine and Warby, Steven (eds) (2001) *The Changing Face of the Football Business: Supporters Direct*, London, Frank Cass.

Hamil, Sean, Holt, Matthew, Michie, Jonathan, Oughton, Christine and Shailer, Lee (2004) 'The Corporate Governance of Professional Football Clubs', *Corporate Governance*, 4(2), pp. 44–51.

Haraway, Donna (1991) 'A Cyborg Manifesto: Science, Technology, and Socialist-Feminism in the Late Twentieth Century', in Donna Haraway, *Simians, Cyborgs and Women: The Reinvention of Nature*, New York, Routledge, pp. 149–81.

Hardin, Marie, Dodd, Julie E. and Walsdorf, Kristie (2004) 'Sporting Images in Black and White: Race and the Newspaper Coverage of the 2000 Olympic Games', *The Howard Journal of Communications*, 15, pp. 211–27.

Harding, Sandra (ed.) (2003) *The Feminist Standpoint Theory Reader: Intellectual and Political Controversies*, New York, Routledge.

Hargreaves, Jennifer (1994) *Sporting Females: Critical Issues in the History and Sociology of Women's Sport*, London, Routledge.

Harrington, Austin (2005a) 'Introduction: What is Social Theory?', in Austin G. Harrington (ed.), *Modern Social Theory: An Introduction*, Oxford, Oxford University Press, pp. 1–15.

Harrington, Austin (ed.) (2005b) *Modern Social Theory: An Introduction*, Oxford, Oxford University Press.

Harris, N. (2000). 'Chelsea Takes £40m As Sky Expands Empire', *The Independent*, 4 March.

Hartmann, Douglas (2003) 'What Can We Learn from Sport if We Take Sport Seriously as a Racial Force? Lessons from C. L. R. James's *Beyond A Boundary*', *Ethnic and Racial Studies*, 26(3), pp. 451–83.

Hartmann, Douglas (2007) 'Rush Limbaugh, Donovan McNabb, and "A Little Social Concern": Reflections on the Problems of Whiteness in Contemporary American Sport', *Journal of Sport and Social Issues*, 31(1), pp. 45–60.

Hawkins, Mary (2006) *Global Structures, Local Cultures*, South Melbourne, Oxford University Press.

Henslin, James (2008) *Essentials of Sociology: A Down to Earth Approach*, 8th edn, Boston, Allyn & Bacon.

Hill, Jeffrey (2003) 'Introduction: Sport and Politics', *Journal of Contemporary History*, 38(3), pp. 355–61.

Hogan, Jackie (2003) 'Staging the Nation: Gendered and Ethnicized Discourses of National Identity in Olympic Opening Ceremonies', *Journal of Sport and Social Issues*, 27 (2), pp. 100–23.

Hong, Fan (2005) 'Epilogue: Nationalism, Orientalism and Globalization: The Future of the Asian Games', *Sport in Society*, 8(3), pp. 515–51.

Hoop Dreams (1994) Dir. Steve James, film, Kartemquin Films.

Hornby, Nick (1992) *Fever Pitch*, London, Indigo.

Horne, John (2006) *Sport in Consumer Culture*, Basingstoke, Palgrave Macmillan.

Horne, John and Manzenreiter, Wolfram (2006a) 'An Introduction to the Sociology of Sports Mega-events', *The Sociological Review*, 54, pp. 1–24.

Horne, John and Manzenreiter, Wolfram (eds) (2006b) *Sports Mega-Events: Social Scientific Analyses of a Global Phenomenon*, Malden, MA, Blackwell.

Houlihan, Barrie (1997) 'Sport, National Identity and Public Policy', *Nations and Nationalism*, 3 (1), pp. 113–37.

Houlihan, Barrie (2000) 'Politics and Sport', in Jay Coakley and Eric Dunning (eds), *Handbook of Sports Studies*, London, Sage, pp. 213–27.

Houlihan, Barrie (2005) 'Public Sector Sport Policy: Developing a Framework for Analysis', *International Review for the Sociology of Sport*, 40(2), pp. 163–85.

Howe, P. David (2001) 'An Ethnography of Pain and Injury in Professional Rugby Union: The Case of Pontypridd RFC', *International Review for the Sociology of Sport*, 36(3), pp. 289–303.

Hoye, Russell (2004) 'Leader–Member Exchanges and Board Performance of Voluntary Sport Organizations', *Nonprofit Management and Leadership*, 15(1), pp. 55–70.

Hoye, Russell and Cuskelly, Graham (2007) *Sport Governance*, Amsterdam, Elsevier.

Hoye, Russell, Smith, Aaron, Westerbeek, Hans, Stewart, Bob and Nicholson, Matthew (2006) *Sport Management: Principles and Applications*, Oxford, Elsevier.

Hughes, Rob (2010) 'Swift and Severe Justice at World Cup Courts', *New York Times*, 20 June, <http://www.nytimes.com/2010/06/21/sports/soccer/21iht-wcsoccer.html?pagewanted=1&_r=1>.

Hutchins, Brett (2002) *Don Bradman: Challenging the Myth*, Melbourne, Cambridge University Press.

Hutchins, Brett (2006) 'Computer Gaming, Media and E-sport', Refereed conference proceedings, *The Australian Sociological Association (TASA) 2006 Annual Conference*, University of Western Australia and Murdoch University.

Hutchins, Brett (2008) 'Signs of Meta-change in Second Modernity: The Growth of e-Sport and the World Cyber Games', *New Media and Society*, 10(6), pp. 851–69.

Hutchins, Brett and Rowe, David (2009) 'From Broadcast Scarcity to Digital Plenitude: The Changing Dynamics of the Media Sport Content Economy', *Television and New Media*, 10(4), pp. 354–70.

Hyde, Marina (2010) 'World Cup 2010: Fans, Robbers and a Marketing Stunt Face Justice, Fifa Style', *Guardian*, 20 June, <http://www.guardian.co.uk/football/2010/jun/20/world-cup-2010-fans-marketing-justice-fifa>.

Hylton, Kevin (2009) *Race and Sport*, London, Routledge.

ICC (International Cricket Council) (2009a) 'Anti-Corruption Overview', *ICC*, <http://icc-cricket.yahoo.net/anti_corruption/overview.php>.

ICC (International Cricket Council) (2009b) 'Social Responsibility', *ICC*, <http://icc-cricket.yahoo.net/the-icc/social_responsibility/overview.php>.

ICC (International Cricket Council) (2009c) 'Think Wise', *ICC*, <http://icc-cricket.yahoo.net/the-icc/social_responsibility/think_wise/index.php>.

Institute for Diversity and Ethics in Sport (2008) 'The Buck Stops Here: Assessing Diversity Among Campus and Conference Leaders for Football Bowl Subdivision (FBS) Schools in the 2008–09 Academic Year', a report from the Institute for Diversity and Ethics in Sports, University of Central Florida, College of Business Administration, Orlando, Florida, downloaded 30 August 2010 from: <http://www.tidesport.org>.

Invictus (2009) Dir. Clint Eastwood, film, Spyglass Entertainment, Revelations Entertainment and Malpaso Productions.

IOC (International Olympic Committee) (2009) 'IOC: The Organization', *IOC*, <http://www.olympic.org/en/content/The-IOC/The-IOC-Institution1>.

Jackson, Steven J. and Andrews, David L. (eds) (2005) *Sport, Culture and Advertising: Identities, Commodities and the Politics of Representation*, New York, Routledge.

Jackson, Steven J. and Hokowhitu, Brendan (2002) 'Sport, Tribes, And Technology: The New Zealand All Blacks *Haka* and the Politics of Identity', *Journal of Sport and Social Issues*, 26 (2), pp. 125–39.

James, C. L. R. (1993) *Beyond A Boundary*, Durham, Duke University Press.

Japan Today (2010) 'Kanemoto's "Iron Man" Streak Ends at 1,492 Games', *Japan Today*, 18 April, <http://www.japantoday.com/category/sports/view/kanemotos-iron-man-streak-ends-at-1492-games>.

Jarvie, Grant (2006) *Sport, Culture and Society: An Introduction*, London, Routledge.

Jarvie, Grant and Walker, Graham (eds) (1994) *Scottish Sport in the Making of the Nation: Ninety Minute Patriots?*, Leicester, Leicester University Press.

Jeffery, Nicole (2009) 'Ian Thorpe Says He's Not Gay, Again', *The Australian*, 30 January, <http://www.theaustralian.com.au/news/thorpe-says-hes-not-gay-again/story-e6frg7mo-1111118705833>.

Jerry Maguire (1996) Dir. Cameron Crowe, film, TriStar Pictures, Gracie Films.

Jessop, Bob (1990) *State Theory: Putting the Capitalist State in its Place*, Cambridge, Polity.

Jhally, Sut (1998) 'Free at Last: Fanship, Fascism and Sponsorship', *Journal of Sport and Social Issues*, 22(2), pp. 224–6.

John, Emma (2009) 'Into the Light', *The Observer*, 31 May, <http://www.guardian.co.uk/sport/2009/may/31/interview-jelena-dokic>.

Johnston, Lloyd D., Delva, Jorge and O'Malley, Patrick (2007), 'Sports Participation and Physical Education in American Secondary Schools: Current Levels and Racial/Ethnic and Socioeconomic Disparities', *American Journal of Preventive Medicine*, 33 (4S), pp. S195–S208.

Jones, Carwyn and Wilson, Cassie (2009) 'Defining Advantage and Athletic Performance: The Case of Oscar Pistorius', *European Journal of Sport Science*, 9(2), pp. 125–31.

Kahn, Lawrence M. (2006) 'Race, Performance, Pay And Retention Among National Basketball Association Head Coaches', *Journal of Sports Economics*, 7(2), pp. 119–49.

Kahn, Lawrence M. and Shah, Malav (2005) 'Race, Compensation and Contract Length in the NBA: 2001–2', *Industrial Relations*, 44(3), pp. 444–62.

Keane, John (2009) *The Life and Death of Democracy*, New York, W. W. Norton.

Kelly, Peter and Hickey, Christopher (2008) *The Struggle for the Body, Mind and Soul of AFL Footballers*, North Melbourne, Vic., Australian Scholarly.

Kelly, Peter and Hickey, Christopher (2010) 'Professional Identity in the Global Sports Entertainment Industry: Regulating the Body, Mind and Soul of Australian Football League Footballers', *Journal of Sociology*, 46(1), pp. 27–44.

Kerin, Paul (2010) 'How to be a Good Sport', *The Age*, 14 May, <http://www.theage.com.au/business/how-to-be-a-good-sport-20100513-v1tp.html>.

Kick It Out (2010a) *Kick It Out Homepage*, <http://www.kickitout.org/>.

Kick It Out (2010b) *Kick It Out Equality Standard*, <http://www.kickitout.org/829.php>.

Kidd, Bruce and Donnelly, Peter (2000) 'Human Rights in Sport', *International Review for the Sociology of Sport*, 35(2), pp. 131–48.

Ki-moon, Ban (2010) 'Secretary-General's Message: World Day of Social Justice', *United Nations website*, 20 February, <http://www.un.org/en/events/socialjusticeday/sgmessage.shtml>.

King, Anthony (1998) *The End of the Terraces: The Transformation of English Football in the 1990s*, London, Leicester University Press.

King, Anthony (2000) 'Football Fandom and Post-National Identity in the New Europe', *British Journal of Sociology*, 51(3), pp. 419–42.

King, C. Richard (2008) 'Toward a Radical Sport Journalism: An Interview with Dave Zirin', *Journal of Sport and Social Issues*, 32(4), pp. 333–44.

Klein, Alan (2008) 'Progressive Ethnocentrism: Ideology and Understanding in Dominican Baseball', *Journal of Sport and Social Issues*, 32(2), pp. 121–38.

Knox, Malcolm (2003) 'Lehmann Reveals the Unwitting Racism that Infuses Australia', *The Age*, 27 January, accessed online 14 March 2011 from: <http://www.theage.com.au/articles/2003/01/26/1043533952023.htm>.

Lange, Kirsten M., Nicholson, Matthew and Hess, Rob (2007) 'A New Breed Apart? Work Practices of Australian Internet Sport Journalists', *Sport in Society,* 10(4), pp. 662–79.

Law, Alan, Harvey, Jean and Kemp, Stuart (2002) 'The Global Sport Mass Media Oligopoly: The Three Usual Suspects and More', *International Review for the Sociology of Sport,* 37(3–4), pp. 279–302.

Lee, Jung Woo and Maguire, Joseph (2009) 'Global Festivals through a National Prism', *International Review for the Sociology of Sport,* 44(1), pp. 5–24.

Lee, Simon (1999). 'Bringing the Game into Disrepute? The BSkyB Bid for Manchester United PLC'. Paper prepared for the Corporate Governance of Professional Football Conference, Clore Management Centre, Birkbeck College, University of London, 3 February.

L'Elefant Blau (1999) 'The Struggle for Democracy at Barcelona FC', in Sean Hamil, Jonathan Michie and Christine Oughton (eds), *The Business of Football: A Game of Two Halves?,* Mainstream, Edinburgh, pp. 202–8.

Levy, A. (2009) 'Either/Or: Sports, Sex, and the Case of Caster Semenya', *The New Yorker,* November 30, <http://www.newyorker.com/reporting/2009/11/30/091130fa_fact_levy>.

Lewis, Michael (2004) *Moneyball: The Art of Winning an Unfair Game* (with a new afterword), New York, W. W. Norton.

Lines, Gill (2001) 'Villains, Fools or Heroes? Sports Stars as Role Models for Young People', *Leisure Studies,* 20, pp. 285–303.

Ling, Pamela M., Haber, Lawrence A. and Wedl, Stefani (2010) 'Branding the Rodeo: A Case Study of Tobacco Sports Sponsorship', *American Journal of Public Health,* 100(1), pp. 32–41.

Lloyd, Matthew (2010) 'Tough Men Content to Play Through Injury', *The Age,* 23 May, <http://www.theage.com.au/afl/afl-news/tough-men-content-to-play-through-injury-20100522-w321.html>.

Long, Jonathan (2000) 'No Racism Here? A Preliminary Examination of Sporting Innocence', *Managing Leisure,* 5, pp. 121–33.

Long, Jonathan and Hylton, Kevin (2002) 'Shades of White: An Examination of Whiteness in Sport', *Leisure Studies,* 21, pp. 87–103.

Longman, Jere (2007) 'An Amputee Sprinter: Is He Disabled or Too-abled?' *New York Times,* 15 May, <http://www.nytimes.com/2007/05/15/sports/othersports/15runner.html>.

Loy, John W. and Elvogue, Joseph F. (1970) 'Racial Segregation in American Sport', *International Review for the Sociology of Sport,* 5(5), pp. 5–24.

Lukes, Steven (2005) *Power: A Radical View,* 2nd edn, Basingstoke, Palgrave Macmillan.

Lupton, Deborah (2005) 'The Body, Medicine and Society', in John Germov (ed.), *Second Opinion: An Introduction to Health Sociology,* 3rd edn, South Melbourne, Oxford University Press, pp. 195–207.

Lusted, Jim (2009) 'Playing Games with "Race": Understanding Resistance to "Race" Equality Initiatives in English Local Football Governance', *Soccer and Society*, 10(6), pp. 722–39.

Macionis, John J. and Plummer, Ken (2008) *Sociology: A Global Introduction*, 4th edn, Harlow, Pearson.

Madden, Janice Fanning (2004), 'Differences in the Success of NFL Coaches by Race, 1990–2002: Evidence of Last Hire, First Fire', *Journal of Sports Economics*, 5(1), pp. 6–19.

Magdalinski, Tara (2009) *Sport, Technology and the Body: The Nature of Performance*, London, Routledge.

Magee, Jonathan and Sugden, John (2002) ' "The World at their Feet": Professional Football and International Labor Migration', *Journal of Sport and Social Issues*, 26(4), pp. 421–37.

Maguire, Joseph (1999) *Global Sport: Identities, Societies, Civilizations*, Cambridge, Polity.

Maguire, Joseph (2005) *Power and Global Sport: Zones of Prestige, Emulation and Resistance*, London, Routledge.

Maguire, Joseph, Poulton, Emma and Possamai, Catherine (1999) 'Weltkrieg III? Media Coverage of England versus Germany in Euro 96', *Journal of Sport and Social Issues*, 23(4), pp. 439–54.

Mann, Jonathan and Tarantola, Daniel (1996) *AIDS in the World II: Global Dimensions, Social Roots and Responses*, New York, Oxford University Press.

Margolis, Joshua D. and Walsh, James P. (2001) *People and Profits? The Search for a Link between a Company's Social and Financial Performance*, Mahwah, NJ, Lawrence Erlbaum Associates.

Marjoribanks, Timothy (2011) 'Media and Popular Culture', in John Germov and Marilyn Poole (eds.), *Public Sociology*, 2nd edn, Crows Nest, NSW, Allen & Unwin, pp. 421–36.

Martin, Emily (1987) *The Woman in the Body: A Cultural Analysis of Reproduction*, Boston, Beacon.

Marx, Anthony W. (2003) *Faith in Nation: Exclusionary Origins of Nationalism*, Oxford, Oxford University Press.

Marx, Karl (1976) *Capital, Vol. 1, A Critique of Political Economy*, Harmondsworth, Penguin.

Mason, Daniel S. (2002) ' "Get the Puck Outta Here!" Media Transnationalism and Canadian Identity', *Journal of Sport and Social Issues*, 26(2), pp. 140–67.

Massao, Prisca Bruno and Fasting, Kari (2010) 'Race and Racism: Experiences of Black Norwegian Athletes', *International Review for the Sociology of Sport*, 45(2), pp. 147–62.

McCarthy, David and Jones, Robyn L. (1997) 'Speed, Aggression, Strength, and Tactical Naïveté: The Portrayal of the Black Soccer Player on Television', *Journal of Sport and Social Issues*, 21(4), pp. 348–62.

McCormick, Robert E. and Tollison, Robert D. (2001) 'Why Do Black Basketball Players Work More for Less Money?', *Journal of Economic Behavior and Organization*, 44, pp. 201–19.

McGee, Tara Renae (2007) 'Sociological Investigations: Doing Sociological Research', in John Germov and Marilyn Poole (eds), *Public Sociology: An Introduction to Australian Society*, Crows Nest, NSW, Allen & Unwin, pp. 67–87.

McGovern, Patrick (2000) 'The Irish Brawn Drain: English League Clubs and Irish Footballers, 1946–1995', *British Journal of Sociology*, 51(3), pp. 401–18.

McHugh, Josh (2007) 'Blade Runner', *Wired*, 15.03, March, <http://www.wired.com/wired/archive/15.03/blade.html>.

McIlveen, Luke (2008) 'Lauren Jackson Suffering Ankle Injury at Beijing Olympics', *The Telegraph*, 20 August, <http://www.dailytelegraph.com.au/news/jackson-injured-ahead-of-clash/story-eb/reyp0-1111117248550>.

Merritt, Stephanie (2001) 'Rafter Uncovered in Bermuda Shorts,' *The Observer*, 24 June, <http://www.guardian.co.uk/sport/2001/jun/24/tennis.stephaniemerritt>.

Messner, Michael A. (2002) *Taking the Field: Women, Men, and Sports*, Minneapolis, University of Minnesota Press.

Messner, Michael A., Dunbar, Michele and Hunt, Darnell (2000) 'The Televised Sports Manhood Formula', *Journal of Sport and Social Issues*, 24(4), pp. 380–94.

Mewett, Peter (2007), 'Sporting Life', in John Germov and Marilyn Poole (eds), *Public Sociology: An Introduction to Australian Society*, Crows Nest, NSW, Allen & Unwin, pp. 173–91.

Michie, Jonathan (2000) 'The Governance and Regulation of Professional Football', *The Political Quarterly*, 71(2), pp. 184–91.

Michie, Jonathan and Walsh, Andy (1999) 'Ownership and Governance Options for Football Clubs'. Paper prepared for the Corporate Governance of Professional Football Conference, Clore Management Centre, Birkbeck College, University of London, 3 February.

Miller, David (2003) *The Official History of the Olympic Games and the IOC: Athens to Beijing, 1894–2008*, Edinburgh, Mainstream.

Milliken, Robert (1996) 'Sport is Murdoch's "Battering Ram" for Pay TV', *The Independent on Sunday*, 16 October, <http://www.independent.co.uk/sport/sport-is-murdochs-battering-ram-for-pay-tv-1358686.html>.

Mills, C. Wright (1959) *The Sociological Imagination*, London, Oxford University Press.

Mills, James and Dimeo, Paul (2003) ' "When Gold is Fired it Shines": Sport, the Imagination and the Body in Colonial and Postcolonial India', in James Bale and Mike Cronin (eds), *Sport and Postcolonialism*, New York, Berg, pp. 107–22.

MLB (Major League Baseball) (1995/2010) 'Iron Man: Cal Ripken breaks Lou Gehrig's Consecutive Game Streak', *MLB.com*, <http://mlb.mlb.com/mlb/baseballs_best/mlb_bb_gamepage.jsp?story_page=bb_95reg_090695_calbal>.

MMC (Monopolies and Mergers Commission) (1999) *British Sky Broadcasting Group plc and Manchester United PLC: A Report on the Proposed Merger*, London, Stationery Office.

Moon, Simon (2006) 'Beckham the Worldwide Brand', *This Is Money*, accessed 8 June 2010, <http://thisismoney.co.uk>.

Moor, Liz (2007) 'Sport and Commodification: A Reflection on Key Concepts', *Journal of Sport and Social Issues*, 31(2), pp. 128–42.

Morrow, Stephen (2003) *The People's Game? Football, Finance and Society*, Basingstoke, Palgrave Macmillan.

Muller, Tiffany K. (2007) 'The Contested Terrain of the Women's National Basketball Association Arena', in Cara Aitchison and Sheila Scraton (eds), *Sport and Gender Identities: Masculinities, Femininities, and Sexualities*, London, Routledge, pp. 37–52.

Netball Australia (2011) 'Looking Beyond', downloaded 1 February 2011 from netball.asn.au: <http://www.netball.asn.au/extra.asp?id=4738&OrgID=1&menu=10650>.

Newman, Paul (2009) 'Dokic Rebuilds her Career in the Green and Gold', *The Independent on Sunday*, 7 January, <http://www.independent.co.uk/sport/tennis/dokic-rebuilds-her-career-in-the-green-and-gold-1229821.html>.

Nixon, Howard L. II and Frey, James H. (1996) *A Sociology of Sport*, Belmont, CA, Wadsworth.

NRL (National Rugby League) (2010) 'Melbourne Storm Breach NRL Salary Cap', *National Rugby League home page*, 22 April, <http://www.nrl.com/news/news/newsarticle/tabid/10874/newsid/58359/melbourne-storm-breach-nrl-salary-cap/default.aspx>.

OFT (Office of Fair Trading) (1996) *The Director General's Review of BSkyB's Position in the Wholesale Pay TV Market*, December.

Omi, Michael and Winant, Howard (1994) *Racial Formation in the United States: From the 1960s to the 1990s*, New York, Routledge.

ONS (Office of National Statistics) (2001) Census, April http://www.statistics.gov.uk/cci/nugget.asp?id=273 accessed on 24 August 2010.

Parsons, Talcott (1970) *The Social System*, London, Routledge & Kegan Paul.

Perera, Suvendrini (2000) ' "Cricket, with a Plot": Nationalism, Cricket and Diasporic Identities', *Journal of Australian Studies,* June, pp. 14–26.

Poli, Raffaele (2007) 'The Denationalization of Sport: De-ethnicization of the Nation and Identity Deterritorinalization', *Sport in Society*, 10(4), pp. 646–61.

Puerto Rico (2011) 'Welcome to Puerto Rico', <http://welcome.topuertorico.org/government.shtml>.

Quirk, James and Rodney Fort (1999) *Hard Ball: The Abuse of Power In Pro Team Sports*, Princeton, NJ, Princeton University Press.

QUIT (2010) 'Tobacco Advertising and Promotion', *QUIT*, <http://www.quit.org.au/article.asp?ContentID=7161>.

Raghavan, Sudarsan (2010) 'In Preparation for World Cup, the Poor in Cape Town are being Relocated', *The Washington Post*, 11 June, <http://www.washington-post.com/wp-dyn/content/article/2010/06/10/AR2010061002060.html?nav=emailpage>.

Ragin, Charles C. and Amoroso, Lisa M. (2011) *Constructing Social Research: The Unity and Diversity of Method*, 2nd edn, Thousand Oaks, CA, Sage.

Rasmussen, Ricky, Esgate, Anthony and Turner, David (2005) 'On Your Marks, Get Stereotyped, Go! Novice Coaches and Black Stereotypes in Sprinting', *Journal of Sport and Social Issues*, 29(4), pp. 426–36.

Redhead, Steve (1997) *Post-fandom and the Millenial Blues: The Transformation of Soccer Culture*, London, Routledge.

Rees, C. Roger (1996), 'Race and Sport in Global Perspective: Lessons from Post-apartheid South Africa', *Journal of Sport and Social Issues*, 20 (1), pp. 22–32.

Reysen, Stephen and Branscombe, Nyla R. (2010) 'Fanship and Fandom: Comparisons between Sport Fans and Non-Sport Fans', *Journal of Sport Behavior*, 33, pp. 176–93.

Rhoden, William C (2006) *Forty Million Dollar Slaves: The Rise, Fall and Redemption of the Black Athlete*, New York City, Crown.

Rhoden, William C. (2009) 'Paying a Price for Playing in the Moment', *New York Times*, 14 November, <http://www.nytimes.com/2009/11/15/sports/football/15rhoden.html?_r=2&fta=y>.

Robinson, Joshua (2008) 'Amputee Sprinter's Beijing Quest is Over', New York Times, 19 July,<http://www.nytimes.com/2008/07/19/sports/olympics/19track.html?_r=1>.

Roche, Maurice (2000) *Mega-events and Modernity: Olympics and Expos in the Growth of Global Culture*, London, Routledge.

Roebuck, Peter (2010) 'ICC Arena No Place for this Inexpert Right-arm Slow', *Sydney Morning Herald*, 23 January, <http://www.smh.com.au/sport/cricket/icc-arena-no-place-for-this-inexpert-rightarm-slow-20100121-mob3.html>.

Rossingh, Danielle and Baynes, Dan (2010) 'Bets on Federer Pay Australian Open as Tennis Embraces Gambling', *Bloomberg*, 13 January, <http://www.bloomberg.com/apps/news?pid=newsarchive&sid=aX8e6Nv_wmk4>.

Rowe, David (1992) 'Modes of Sports Writing', in Peter Dahlgren and Colin Sparks (eds), *Journalism and Popular Culture*, London, Sage, pp. 96–112.

Rowe, David (1999) *Sport, Culture and the Media: The Unruly Trinity*, Buckingham, Open University Press.

Rowe, David (2003) 'Sport and the Repudiation of the Global', *International Review for the Sociology of Sport*, 38(3), pp. 281–94.

Rowe, David, McKay, Jim and Miller, Toby (1998) 'Come Together: Sport, Nationalism, and the Media Image', in Lawrence A. Wenner (ed.), *MediaSport*, London, Routledge, pp. 119–33.

RPC (Restrictive Practices Court) (1996) In the matter of the Restrictive Trade Practices Act 1976 and in the matter of an agreement between the Football Association Premier League Limited and the Football Association Limited and the Football League Limited and their respective member clubs and in the matter of an agreement relating to the supply of services facilitating the broadcasting on television of Premier League football matches and the supply of services consisting in the broadcasting on television of such matches.

Ruddock, Andy, Hutchins, Brett, and Rowe, David (2010) 'Contradictions in Media Sport Culture: The Reinscription of Football Supporter Traditions Through Online Media', *European Journal of Cultural Studies*, 13(3), pp. 323–39.

Russell, Kate (2007), '"Queers, Even in Netball?' Interpretations of the Lesbian Label Among Sportswomen', in Cara Aitchison and Sheila Scraton (eds), *Sport and Gender Identities: Masculinities, Femininities, and Sexualities*, London, Routledge, pp. 106–21.

Sailes, Gary A. (1991) 'The Myth of Black Sports Supremacy', *Journal of Black Studies*, 21(4), pp. 480–7.

Saundry, Richard (1998) 'The Limits of Flexibility: The Case of UK Television', *British Journal of Management*, 9, pp. 151–62.

Scalmer, Sean (2007) 'Cricket, Imperialism and Class Domination', *WorkingUSA: The Journal of Labor and Society*, 10, December, pp. 431–42.

Scherer, Jay (2001) 'Globalization and the Construction of Local Particularities: A Case Study of the Winnipeg Jets', *Sociology of Sport Journal*, 18, pp. 205–30.

Schor, Juliet (2004) *Born to Buy: The Commercialised Child and The New Consumer Culture*, New York, Scribner.

Schwartz, Peter J., Maidment, Paul and Ozanian, Michael K. (2010) 'The Business of Soccer', *Forbes.com*, 21 April, <http://www.forbes.com/2010/04/21/soccer-value-teams-business-sports-soccer-10-intro.html>.

Schwarz, Alan (2009) 'Dementia Risk Seen in Players in NFL Study', *New York Times*, 29 September, <http://www.nytimes.com/2009/09/30/sports/football/30dementia.html>.

Seidman, Steven (2008) *Contested Knowledge: Social Theory Today*, 4th edn, Malden, MA, Blackwell.

Shaw, Sally (2007) 'Gender in Sport Management: A Contemporary Picture and Alternate Futures', in Cara Aitchison and Sheila Scraton (eds), *Sport and Gender Identities: Masculinities, Femininities, and Sexualities*, London, Routledge, pp. 74–90.

Shilbury, David, Deane, John and Kellett, Pamm (2006) *Sport Management in Australia: An Organizational Overview*, 3rd edn, East Bentleigh, Vic, Strategic Sport Management.

Silk, Michael and Andrews, David L. (2001) 'Beyond the Boundary? Sports, Transnational Advertising, and the Reimagining of National Culture', *Journal of Sport and Social Issues*, 25(2), pp. 180–201.

Sjoqvist, Folke, Garle, Mats and Rane, Anders (2008) 'The Use of Doping Agents, Particularly Anabolic Steroids, in Sports and Society', *The Lancet*, 371, 31 May, pp. 1872–82.

Skocpol, Theda (1992) *Protecting Soldiers and Mothers: The Political Origins of Social Policy in the United States*, Cambridge, MA, Belknap Press of Harvard University Press.

Slack, Trevor (2004) *The Commercialization of Sport*, London, Routledge.

Slot, Owen (2009) 'Lord Coe seeks Rule Changes after Caster Semanya Case' *The Times*, 17 September, <http://www.timesonline.co.uk/tol/sport/more_sport/athletics/article6837646.ece>.

Smith, Aaron and Stewart, Bob (1999) *Sports Management: A Guide to Professional Practice*, Crows Nest, NSW, Allen & Unwin.

Smith, Aaron and Westerbeek, Hans (2004) *The Sport Business Future*, Basingstoke, Palgrave Macmillan.

Smith, Aaron and Westerbeek, Hans (2010) ' "From Enhancement to Engagement": Reflections on the future of Sport Consumption', *Sport in Society*, 13(2), pp. 344–53.

Smith, David (2010) 'Life in "Tin Can Town" for the South Africans Evicted Ahead of World Cup', *Guardian*, 1 April, <http://www.guardian.co.uk/world/2010/apr/01/south-africa-world-cup-blikkiesdorp>.

Smith, Dorothy E. (1990) *The Conceptual Practices of Power: A Feminist Sociology of Knowledge*, Boston, Northeastern University Press.

Smyth, Paul (2010) 'In or Out? Building an Inclusive Nation', Albert Park and Fitzroy, Victoria, Australian Collaboration and the Brotherhood of St Laurence.

Spaaij, Ramon (2006) *Understanding Football Hooliganism: A Comparison of Six Western European Football Clubs*, Amsterdam, Amsterdam University Press.

Spaaij, Ramon (2008) 'Men Like Us, Boys Like Them: Violence, Masculinity, and Collective Identity in Football Hooliganism', *Journal of Sport and Social Issues*, 32(4), pp. 369–92.

Spaaij, Ramon (2010) 'Using Recreational Sport for Social Mobility of Urban Youth: Practices, Challenges and Dilemmas', *Sociétés et Jeunesses en Difficulté*, 9, 26pp, <http://sejed.revues.org/index6641.html>.

Sparkes, Andrew C. (2004) 'Bodies, Narratives, Selves, and Autobiography: The Example of Lance Armstrong', *Journal of Sport and Social Issues*, 28(4), pp. 397–428.

Sport Development (2010) *Report of the Policy Action Team 10: The contribution of Sport and the Arts*, <http://www.sportdevelopment.info/index.php?option=com_content&view=article&id=67:report-of-the-policy-action-team-10-the-contribution-of-sport-and-the-arts&catid=48:policy&Itemid=65>.

Sport England (2005) 'Participation in Sport in England: Sports Equity Index 2002', London, Sport England.

Sport England (2009) 'Active People Survey 2007/08', <http://www.sportengland.org/research>.

St Louis, Brett (2004) 'Sport and Common-Sense Racial Science', *Leisure Studies*, 23(1), pp. 31–46.

St Louis, Brett (2005) 'Brilliant Bodies, Fragile Minds: Race, Sport and the Mind/Body Split', in Claire Alexander and Caroline Knowles (eds), *Making Race Matter: Bodies, Space and Identity*, Basingstoke, Palgrave Macmillan, pp. 113–31.

Standards Australia (2003) Australian Standard AS 8000-2003 Good Governance Principles, Sydney, Standards Australia.

Stewart, Bob and Smith, Aaron (2000) 'Australian Sport in a Postmodern Age', *International Journal of the History of Sport*, 17(2 and 3), pp. 278–304.

Stewart, Bob and Smith, Aaron C. T. (2008) 'Drug Use in Sport: Implications for Public Policy', *Journal of Sport and Social Issues*, 32(3), pp. 278–98.

Street, John (2004) 'Celebrity Politicians: Popular Culture and Political Representation', *British Journal of Politics and International Relations*, 6(4), pp. 435–52.

Tacon, Richard (2007) 'Football and Social Inclusion: Evaluating Social Policy', *Managing Leisure*, 12(1), pp. 1–23.

Taylor Report (1990) 'The Hillsborough Tragedy'. Final Report of an Inquiry by the Rt Hon. Lord Justice Taylor, January, Cm 962.

Teather, David and Brodkin, Jon (2000) 'Murdoch's £40m Stake in Chelsea Takes Football Club Collection to Five', *Guardian*, 4 March, <http://www.guardian.co.uk/football/2000/mar/04/newsstory.sport11/print>.

Tennis Channel (2010) Scores and rankings, <http://www.tennischannel.com/scores/rankings.aspx?page=1&tour0=tour2&tab=0>.

Tennis.com (2010) Money Leaders, <http://www.tennis.com/rankings/money_women.aspx>.

Tomlinson, Alan (2005) 'Olympic Survivals', in Lincoln Allison (ed.), *The Global Politics of Sport. The role of global institutions in sport*, London, Routledge, pp. 46–62.

Traganou, Jilly (2010) 'National Narratives in the Opening and Closing Ceremonies of the Athens 2004 Olympic Games', *Journal of Sport and Social Issues*, 34(2), pp. 236–51.

Turner, Bryan S. (2008) *The Body and Society: Explorations in Social Theory*, London, Sage.

UNICEF (United Nations Children's Fund) (2006) 'Futbol Club Barcelona, UNICEF Team Up for Children in Global Partnership', UNICEF, 7 September, <http://www.unicef.org/media/media_35642.html>.

USA Today (2011) 'Salaries Databases: NBA', http://content.usatoday.com/sportsdata/basketball/nba/salaries/player/top-25

Van Riper, Tom (2010) 'The NFL's Highest-paid Players', Forbes.com, 12 August 2010, <http://www.forbes.com/2010/08/12/manning-mcnab-asomugha-business-sports-nfl-highest-paid.html>.

Van Uden, Jacob (2005) 'Transforming a Football Club into a "Total Experience" Entertainment Company: Implications for Management', *Managing Leisure*, 10, pp. 184–98.

VicHealth (2002) 'Media Release: Tobacco Free Sports – How Sport Finally Gave Up the Tobacco Habit in Victoria', VicHealth, 31 May, <http://www.vichealth.vic.gov.au/en/Search.aspx?q=tobacco%20sport>.

Waddington, Ivan (2000) 'Sport and Health: A Sociological Perspective', in Jay Coakley and Eric Dunning (eds), *Handbook of Sports Studies*, London, Sage, pp. 408–21.

Walby, Catherine (1990) *Theorising Patriarchy*, Oxford, Blackwell.

Walter, Maggie (2006a) 'The Nature of Social Research', in Maggie Walter (ed.), *Social Research Methods: An Australian Perspective*, South Melbourne, Oxford University Press, pp. 1–28.

Walter, Maggie (ed.) (2006b) *Social Research Methods: An Australian Perspective*, South Melbourne, Oxford University Press.

Waring, Amanda and Mason, Carolynne (2010) 'Opening Doors: Promoting Social Inclusion Through Increased Sports Opportunities', *Sport in Society*, 13(3), pp. 517–29.

Washington, Robert E. and Karen, David (2001) 'Sport and Society', *Annual Review of Sociology*, 27, pp. 187–212.

Wedgwood, Nikki (2008) 'For the Love of Football: Australian Rules Football and Heterosexual Desire', *Journal of Sport and Social Issues*, 32(3), pp. 311–17.

Wellman, Barry (2002) 'Little Boxes, Glocalization, and Networked Individualism', in M. Tanabe, P. van den Besselaar and T. Ishida (eds), *Digital Cities*, Berlin, Springer-Verlag, pp. 10–25.

Wenner, Lawrence A. (ed.) (1998) *MediaSport*, London, Routledge.

Westerbeek, Hans (2010) 'Rules of Engagement', *The Age*, 20 May, <http://www.theage.com.au/business/rules-of-engagement-20100519-vfar.html>.

White, Kevin (2004) 'The Social Origins of Illness and the Development of the Sociology of Health', in Carol Grbich (ed.), *Health in Australia*, 3rd edn, Frenchs Forest, NSW, Pearson, pp. 28–45.

Wilks, Stephen (1999a) *In the Public Interest: Competition Policy and the Monopolies and Mergers Commission*, New York, Manchester University Press.

Wilks, Stephen (1999b). 'The MMC in Retrospect: A History of the Monopolies and Mergers Commission', in Competition Commission, *Annual Review and Accounts 1998/99*, London, Competition Commission, pp. 14–16.

Williams, Jack (2001) *Cricket and Race*, Oxford, Berg.

Williams, Jack (2003) '"Paki Cheats!" Postcolonial Tensions in England–Pakistan Cricket', in John Bale and Mike Cronin (eds), *Sport and Postcolonialism*, Oxford, Berg, pp. 91–105.

Williams, John (1994) 'The Local and the Global in English Soccer and the Rise of Satellite Television', *Sociology of Sport Journal*, 11, pp. 376–97.

Williams, Serena (2010) Serena Williams personal webpage, <http://www.serenawilliams.com/bio.php>.

Willis, Evan (2004) *The Sociological Quest: An Introduction to the Study of Social Life*, 4th edn, Sydney, Allen & Unwin.

Women's Basketball Online (2010) WNBA Salary Scale, <http://womensbasketballonline.com/wnba/rosters/salary.html>.

World Cyber Games (2010) World Cyber Games Official Site, <www.worldcybergames.com>.

Yu, Chia-Chen (2005) 'Athlete Endorsement in the International Sports Industry: A Case Study of David Beckham', *International Journal of Sports Marketing and Sponsorship*, April, pp. 189–99.

Yuille, Brigitte (2010) 'Top WNBA Salaries: How Do They Stack Up?', *Financial Edge*, <http://financialedge.investopedia.com/financial-edge/0410/Top-WNBA-Salaries.aspx>.

Zirin, Dave (2008) *A People's History of Sports in the United States: 250 Years of Politics, Protest, People and Play*, New York, New Press.

Zirin, Dave (2010) ' "This is Beyond Sports" Chuck D on the Fight in Arizona', *Edge of Sports*, 11 May, <http://www.edgeofsports.com/2010-05-11-531/index.html>.

Index